Book of Show Jumping

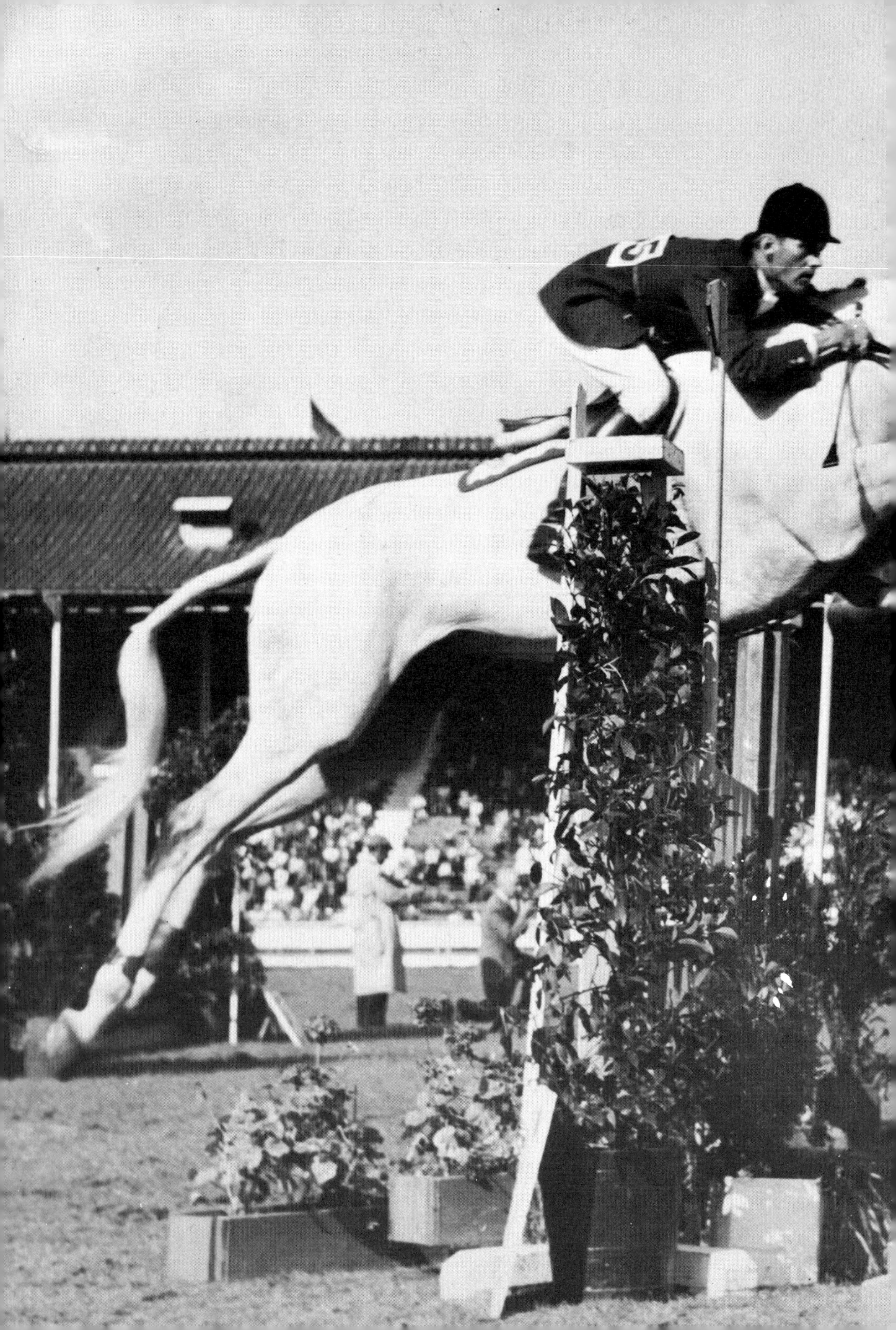

Bill Steinkraus and Ksar d'Esprit

INTERNATIONAL
Book of Show Jumping

Alan Smith

Collins London and Glasgow

General Editor: G. V. Rainey
First published 1970

ISBN 0 00 434535 5
© The Daily Telegraph 1970
Printed in Great Britain by Collins Clear-Type Press

Contents

1 Story of the Sport, *9*

2 People in the Sport, *80*

3 Competitions, Rules and Records, *124*

4 Courses and Training, *138*

5 Appendix – Results of Major Competitions, *152*

Glossary, *159*

Acknowledgements

Barratt's Photo Press Ltd.
Jean Bridel
Oscar Cornaz
Findlay Davidson
Werner Ernst
Fox Photos Ltd.
E. D. Lacey
L'Actualité Hippique
Leslie Lane A.I.I.P.
Roger Levalleur
Pierre Manciet
A. Mengendon
Monty
Pony/Light Horse
The Press Association Ltd.
Col. Paul Rodzianko
The Sport and Central Press Agency Ltd.
United Press
Elizabeth Weilland

Introduction

Although the history of show jumping can be traced back for nearly a century, it is only since the last war that it has become a major sport in this country. In many countries it ranks second only to football; this particularly so in Germany.

This Guide gives the history of the sport from the early days, pictures of many of those people who have and still are playing an important part in its development and gives an insight into the training of horses and the many details that go into making show jumping the desperately exciting sport it now is, not only for the rider but also the spectator.

The pictures, many of then rare indeed, and the results section, the most detailed ever published, provide a most valuable contribution to show jumping literature.

I am delighted to have been asked to write this brief introduction and not only do I congratulate the author but at the same time thank him, as I feel confident that those who read this book will gain even greater pleasure from a sport of which I am very fond.

COL. SIR MICHAEL ANSELL C.B.E., D.S.O.
Chairman, British Show Jumping Association.

Foreword

The internationally popular sport of show jumping, with all its glamour and drama, has come a long way since the first "leaping" competitions of the 19th century.

This book is an attempt to portray the origins and development of the sport on a world-wide basis; to give brief pen-portraits of some of the riders who have been most significantly involved; and, with sections on the component parts, to give a clearer picture of the sport as a whole.

Inasmuch as this attempt has succeeded, I am indebted to many friends and colleauges for their help: to Max Ammann in New York; to Roger-Louis Thomas in France; to Helmut Wagner in Germany; to François-Achill Roch in Switzerland; to Bernard Gale of the South African National Equestrian Federation; to Reg Brown of the B.H.S.; to John Gross, the B.S.J.A.'s senior course-builder; to the photographers who have helped to illustrate the book; and many others. And, most of all, to my wife.

ALAN SMITH

Capt. R. d'Inzeo and Bowjack

1 Story of the Sport

Origins of show jumping

Men have been riding horses for more than 3,000 years. First as a means of transport, and then as an effective means of waging war. But, almost invariably, this was work 'on the flat'. Only in the latter half of the 18th century did the idea of leaving the ground begin to gain general favour.

Cavalry schools only became interested in jumping at a stage in the development of transport when their own demise was imminent: the French Cavalry Manual mentioned it first in 1788.

In Britain jumping became an integral part of hunting with the increased use of hedges and fences to enclose fields, a practice begun after the time of the first Queen Elizabeth which reached its culmination in the Enclosure Acts of the 18th century.

Horses were used for sport thousands of years ago. Chariot racing was introduced in the 25th Olympiad in 680 BC; it was followed 32 years later by mounted horse racing. Yet the first record of competitive jumping was a steeplechase in Ireland in 1752, a match between two hunting men. Show jumping comparable to that which we know today came into being about a century later.

It would be difficult to identify the region in which jumping began as a sport, for, despite a long delayed start, within two or three decades it was being practised in various parts of Europe.

Certainly the Irish were again in the forefront, befitting a country which for so long has relied upon the horse as one of its prime sources of national income. Competitions for 'wide' and 'high' leaps were recorded at the Royal Dublin Society's show in 1865. The Russians were probably organising competitions at about this time, and there was one in Paris in 1866. In this, however, the competitors, after being paraded before the public in the ring, were sent off into the country to do their jumping over predominantly natural fences.

Perhaps the most significant event at this time was the birth of Federico Caprilli in 1868 in Leghorn, Italy. He lived only 39 years, but in that time evolved and propagated theories about riding, and especially about riding over fences, which had, and still have, an indisputable effect upon almost all concerned with the training of horse and rider. There will be more of Caprilli and his teachings in the section devoted to training.

The officers of the French Cavalry school at Saumur included in their 1875 display of Haute Ecole, an exhibition of jumping without stirrups. In England, too, attention was turning to this new sport. The agricultural shows often included a 'leaping' contest; but they bore no relation to the contests witnessed today. Judges were at liberty to decide how they would reach their decisions, whether it was based on the size of the fences or purely on style.

At the five-day show in 1876 at the Agricultural Hall, Islington, London, horses entered in the show classes were able to enter the leaping classes, without extra charge. The four competitions, judged by Masters of Foxhounds, gave a great deal of latitude to riders and were, it appears, decided solely on style.

Nor were these developments confined to Europe, for in 1883 the National Horse Show was begun at Madison Square Garden, New York. The 'Garden' has moved twice since then (the second move as recently as 1968), but the Show is still going strong.

Yet even then recognition of show jumping as an equestrian sport was by no means universal. It was not even mentioned in *Principles of Dressage and Equitation* (1890) by James Fillis, an Englishman who traversed Europe in pursuit of equestrian knowledge, and who was one of the most influential writers at the turn of the century. Progress had been made, however, and it was not to be thwarted. It took a major step forward when Baron Pierre de Coubertin founded the International Olympic Committee in 1894, which, a bare two years later, initiated the first Modern Olympic Games at Athens.

By the dawn of the 20th century show jumping had been firmly established on the sporting scene. Germany, which was to become one of the strongest nations, had shows in towns throughout the country; in France, glittering affairs backed by an aura of social significance were being staged at the Grand Palais in Paris.

Indeed, at the 1900 Olympic Games in Paris there were three jumping competitions, held in conjunction with the World Fair. Not much is

Capt. Federico Caprilli

known about either the competitions or the competitors, but in the 'Show Jumping' event there were seventeen riders from four countries. It was won by Haegeman of Belgium, with Van der Poele from the same country second and de Champsavin of France third. The 'High Jump' with eighteen riders from four countries, was won by Gardère of France at a height of 6 ft $1\frac{3}{16}$ in, with Italy's G. Trissino second. Trissino was also second to Van Vangendonck of Belgium, who jumped 20 ft $\frac{3}{16}$ in, in the 'Long Jump'. Gold medals were awarded to the winners.

The first horse show at which there was international jumping was probably that held in Turin in 1901, when German Army officers were invited to pit their skill against their Italian counterparts.

In 1906 the Swedish Count Clarence von Rosen proposed to the I.O.C. Congress in Athens that equestrian events should be officially included in the Olympic Games. This was a suggestion received without too much enthusiasm: it was thought to be too expensive, and likely to attract insufficient support to be worthwhile. But the far-sighted de Coubertin, President of the Congress, suggested that von Rosen should present details of the proposed events at the following year's meeting. Von Rosen returned to Sweden, formed a committee, and, twelve months later, presented his proposals. They were for three events: dressage, an equestrian pentathlon and for a game called Jeu de Rose—a sort of 'tag' on horseback.

The 1908 Olympic Games were due to be held in London, and the British members of the I.O.C. Congress agreed to the inclusion of the equestrian events. Von Rosen travelled to London, and it was arranged that the committee of the International Horse Show would hold the Olympic events provided that there was a minimum of 24 entries from 6 different countries. Perhaps it was the breadth of the response (there were 88 entries from 8 countries) that overwhelmed the London committee, for at the eleventh hour they dropped the idea of holding them and the equestrian events had to be abandoned. No doubt the London committee felt they had enough on their plate, for 1907 was the first year of the International Horse Show at Olympia.

Of all the great names in the British horse show calendar only Richmond Royal, which, regrettably, closed in 1967 after years of financial struggle, was then in existence. However, the International was conceived with such bold extravagance and showmanship that it deserved to succeed: indeed it did so immediately.

From an idea arising out of a meeting of several English horsemen in the Hague in 1905 the show opened on 7th June, 1907, under the presidency of the Earl of Lonsdale. For 26 years the 'Yellow Earl' directed the show with such energy, meticulous attention to detail and imagination that it became a model for all others.

The international aspect of the show was ensured by the presence, both on the board of directors and in the judges' box, of men from North America and Europe, and the eleven jumping competitions were advertised as being 'open to the world'. 'High jumps' and 'wide jumps' were on the programme and the prize money included first prizes of up to £120. The Dutch and Belgians dominated that inaugural show, but Tommy Glencross, who was to be such a significant figure on the British scene for many years, won a high jump competition. Two years later the first Lucerne International was held, with Italians, Germans, French and Belgians coming to oppose the Swiss.

In the same year international jumping began at the National Horse Show in New York. Alfred G. Vanderbilt, who was then president of the New York show, decided to ask overseas riders to compete at the 1909 show: in response, there came five British Army officers, led by Major J. G. Beresford. The highest fence was 4 ft 3 in, and the British contingent delighted their hosts by providing the winner of the second competition. Four years later there was a Military Team competition at the show, which, like so many other sporting ventures, was suspended during the First World War.

At Olympia, France had won the inaugural King Edward VII Cup (for teams) in 1909 and again in 1911 and Belgium in 1910 before the Russians, in a final blaze of Imperial glory, swept the board with three wins in succession. The Russian Captain d'Exe had won one of the main competitions at the 1911 International, but without doubt the principal architect of Russia's hat-trick was Paul Rodzianko, then a captain in the Tsar's cavalry. After receiving a grounding in horsemastership from James Fillis, Rodzianko had joined the Italian Cavalry school at Pinerolo and Tor di Quinto. Returning to Russia he prepared himself and his compatriots for the run of successes which was to make them outright winners of the King Edward VII Cup which returned with them to Russia and has not been seen since.

The first year of the Russians' success, 1912, was even more notable for the introduction of equestrian events into the Olympic Games. After the failure of his attempt to hold them in London in 1908, Count von Rosen had renewed his efforts when it was decided that the following Games should be in Sweden, his home country. In 1909 a committee was set up, under the honorary presidency of Prince Carl of Sweden, with von Rosen as secretary general, to draw up a fresh set of events for inclusion in the 1912 Games.

The result was three events which, in essence, were as they are now: a three-day event, otherwise known as a military; dressage; and show jumping. Awards were given both for team and individual achievements.

Schmidt-Jensen, in his invaluable history of the Equestrian Olympic Games, describes the course at Stockholm as 'a very difficult one at the time'. Obviously the severity of the course must be taken in context with the comparative lack of development of the men and horses involved. In Stockholm the maximum height of the fences was about 4 ft 6 in; in Mexico in 1968 it had gone up to 5 ft 7 in. Height alone, of course, is little indication of the severity of a course: the placing of fences in correlation to each other is the true arbiter.

There were fifteen fences in Stockholm, of which four had to be jumped twice, including a 13 ft water jump. Ten marks were given for each fence with marks deducted for faults as follows:
first refusal, 2 marks; second or fall of rider and horse 4; third, or fall of rider only, 6.
High jumps: touching with hind legs or fore legs, 1 mark; knock down with hind legs 2; knock down with fore or fore and hind legs, 4.
Spread jumps: hind legs on demarcation line, 1 mark; fore legs on demarcation line or hind legs within demarcation line, 2; fore legs within demarcation line, 4.
Exceeding the time limit penalised 2 marks for each 5 seconds.
Jumping a fence in the wrong order, or any other deviation from the course, elimination.

These have been listed in detail to show just how much reliance was placed on the judges' sight. The simplification of judging in recent years, with the exception of the water jump which often remains a bone of contention, has done

Caprilli at Florence, 1907

H. Willet and Heatherbloom, 1902

much to improve the situation, and is surely responsible for the popular appeal of show jumping as a spectator sport.

Each country could enter six competitors in the individual and four, of whom the best three counted, for the team competition. Now, of course, they are only allowed three in each, though there have been moves to return to four for the team prize. In the individual event eight countries, Belgium, Chile, France, Germany, Britain, Norway, Russia and Sweden, entered 31 competitors. The gold medal was won by Captain Cariou, who also won a bronze in the three-day event, riding Mignon, for France; second was Lieut. von Kroecher of Germany on Dohna; third the Belgian Captain de Blommaert on Clonmore. In the team competition the finishing order was: Sweden, France, Germany, the United States, Russia and Belgium.

The following year the Germans, perhaps foreseeing the prestige to be won at what was to become one of the most popular spectator sports, created their own Olympic Committee for equestrian events. But in 1914 the First World War brought sporting ambition of all sorts to a standstill.

Between the wars

Despite the horror of the First World War, or perhaps because it could serve as a vehicle in which people could escape, sport revived fairly quickly afterwards, and show jumping with it.

International show jumping in the two decades between the World Wars was almost entirely confined to military men: cavalries were engaged in their final fling before mechanization made them obsolete.

Domestically, of course, it was a different matter. In Britain, names which were to have considerable bearing on the sport came to the fore: Fred Foster, whose horse Swank, ridden by Donald Beard, still holds the British high jump record of 7 ft $6\frac{1}{4}$ in, Tommy Glencross, Joe and Tommy Taylor, Sam Marsh, Phil Blackmore, Lady Wright, forerunner of the many top-class British women riders that Britain has produced, and others. Tommy Glencross had been only a couple of inches below Swank in his victory at the first International Show in Olympia, jumping 7 ft 4 in on All Fours. Glencross, who believed in giving his jumpers a thorough training on the ground, imported a number of Australian Walers, now a common trend among horse trainers.

Across the Atlantic the United States began organising a horse show circuit with the foundation in 1917 of what became known as the American Horse Shows Association. Formed by Reginald C. Vanderbilt, it attracted the representatives of no fewer than 50 shows to its first meeting, and was in later years to become the organising and official body for that country.

The first post-war Olympic Games were held at Antwerp in 1920. There were no British or

Lt. G. Crousse on Conspirateur salutes King Alfonso XIII of Spain

Henry Leclerc and Lady-Belle, Lucerne 1909

Swiss competitors in the show jumping—kept away because of a cattle-disease ban. The team event went to Sweden, Belgium took the silver medal and Italy the bronze, with France fourth and the United States fifth and last. As they were still working under the system of training men and horses separately their lowly place was fairly predictable.

Rather more comment was aroused by the Italians who took the first two places in the individual. The gold medal went to Lt Tommaso Lequio on Trebecco, who beat his compatriot Major Valerio, riding Cento. Both riders were products of the Caprilli system of training, the merits of which were beginning to attract many horsemen.

In London, unable to compete in the Games, the British employed themselves at the International Horse Show, which reopened in Olympia in 1920, again under the guidance of Lord Lonsdale.

In the following year came perhaps the most important single event in the history of the sport, the foundation of the *Federation Equestre Inter-*

Ernst Haccius and Utopie, 1907

nationale. Baron de Coubertin, who had revived the Olympic Games, thought that the rules for the sports involved in the Games should be standardised, and the only way to achieve this was by the creation of world federations for the various sports. At the International Olympic Congress in Lausanne, de Coubertin set about bringing together the leading horsemen of the various countries.

The Swedish, naturally, having been mainly responsible for bringing equestrian events into the Games, and the French, with their strong tradition of horse shows, were the prime movers in bringing about the establishment of the F.E.I., which was founded in May, 1921. The Statutes of the Federation were drawn up by Commandant Georges Hector, who for long acted as secretary-general, and adopted at a Congress in Paris on November 24th and 25th of that year.

In addition to France and Sweden, the six countries who were founder-members of the Federation were Belgium, Denmark, Italy, Japan, Norway and the United States.

Japan, the only country outside Europe or the Americas to be involved in horse sport for many years, had a well-established base long before 1920. The first military and civilian riding clubs had been formed towards the end of the previous century after a French cavalry officer had spent some time in the country instructing. The Japanese Military Attache at their Paris Embassy, Colonel Tatekawa, accordingly represented his country at that important meeting. A year later the Japanese formed a national Riding Association, and had their first Olympic equestrian team at the 1928 Games.

Of the other founder-members, Belgium had been the initiators of the three-day event, with a similarly arranged championship in 1905, and had an extremely successful show jumping team which won on the Continent, in Britain and North America; Norway had, and has, a sparse horse population and little chance of serious competition, and Denmark has been more interested in dressage and eventing than show jumping. They did not have an Olympic show jumping team until 1948 in London. Germany became affiliated to the F.E.I. in the year of its

Georges Crousse and Conspirateur jump 2·35 m in 1904

H. Poudret and Betty, 1910

creation and Switzerland followed in 1922. By 1947 twenty-nine countries were members of the Federation, and twenty years later the number had risen to about fifty.

Show jumping had also found favour in parts of South America. The first international show was held in Buenos Aires in 1910, with riders from Italy, Spain and France as well as the countries of South America. Chile had sent two riders to the International in London in 1912, and to the Olympic Games that same year—their first and last sortie on the Games until forty years later in Helsinki. The Argentinians, who of recent years have furnished so many of the top European show jumping horses, did not send a team abroad until 1922, and then only to neighbouring Brazil.

In Canada the Toronto Winter Fair was started in 1922. The Fair is now a well established part of the show jumping scene, following the United States shows at New York, Washington and Harrisburg to complete the autumn tour for a number of European teams. The first Nations Cup team event, in Toronto in 1925, was won by the Belgians.

Meanwhile in Britain a group of interested and dedicated men got together to produce order out of near chaos, and in 1923 the British Show Jumping Association was formed. The great problem with British show jumping in the early days was that there were no rules by which to judge it other than those which the judge might evolve for himself. These could be, and sometimes undoubtedly were 'adjusted' to cope with any given situation. Fences tended to be monotonous to an extreme, gates and walls, several plain hurdles, perhaps a triple bar and a water-jump; most of the shows had a water-jump to ensure that the crowd received its money's-worth. The judge could decide how the jumping of the particular fences should be marked, and there were marks for style as well, which could be useful in arriving at the most diplomatic result!

Even at the exotic International, in Olympia, the judges, one at each fence, decided what mark each horse achieved at his assigned fence, and sent it back to 'headquarters', at the ringside, where the marks were added and the winner decided. Small wonder that in the early represented by 99 riders on 110 horses. These were the first Olympic competitions to be held under F.E.I. Rules, and Sweden repeated its victory of 1920, ahead of Switzerland and Portugal; following them, in order, were Belgium, Italy, Poland, Britain and Spain. France, the U.S.A. and Czechoslovakia did not have three horses finish and so were eliminated from the team placings. The Antwerp gold medallists Lequio and Trebecco for Italy, this time had to be satisfied with the silver, behind the Swiss Lieut. Gemuseus.

For their successes the Swiss had to give much credit to their chef d'equipe, Col. Haccius, who, having seen the state of the ground, foretold that they would probably have to jump off and onto gravel, and schooled his horses on such a surface. When the day came, after much rain, he proved to be right, for Gemuseus on Lucette, a small Irish mare bought for the Swiss Army, jumped round with only six faults, to Lequio and Trebecco's $8\frac{3}{4}$. The bronze individual medal went to Poland, through Lieut. Krolikiewicz and Picador, who, with 10 faults beat Britain's Bowden-Smith (later a member of the Organising Committee when the Olympics came to London in 1948) by just half a fault on Rozzer.

Poland, who were affiliated to the F.E.I. that same year, sent teams with some success all over

René Ricard and Montjoie III, jump 2m in 1910

twenties those riders, civilian and military, who had the true interests of the sport and its future at heart met to do something about it.

Lord Lonsdale accepted the position as president of the B.S.J.A., and the secretary was Colonel V. D. S. Williams, who was associated with equestrian sport for many decades. His son, Dorian, is the best-known of present-day television commentators. Most of the top civilian riders, Glencross, Taylor, Marsh, Blackmore and the others helped form the new Association, along with such as Colonel C. T. Walwyn, and Colonel Joe Hume Dudgeon, who became a master trainer of horses and men.

The Association produced improved standards, in both courses and judging, which in turn attracted more and better riders, so that in the 1930s, Britain was able to produce capable riders and horses at any standard of international competition.

The equestrian events in Paris in 1924—three-day event, dressage and show jumping, the pattern which has continued until the present—had the biggest entry of any Olympics up until that time. Seventeen nations were

Lt. Haccius and Coeur de Moireau, 1910

Xavier Bizard and TicTac, 1929

Europe, to London and to the U.S.A. throughout the 1920s and 30s but have yet to recover from the desolation of the Second World War. Britain joined the F.E.I. in 1925. In addition, Britain was to restrict team membership for overseas shows to the military, a monopoly that was not broken until after the 1939-45 war. In New York, show jumping returned to Madison Square Garden, where it continued uninterrupted until 1939, while in Ireland, The Royal Dublin Society, never a body to rush in without giving a matter searching consideration, introduced international jumping to their most attractive showground at Ballsbridge in 1926.

For some years the Swiss had been buying hundreds of Irish horses each year for their Army remount depots, and it was one of the officers responsible for these purchases, Colonel Ziegler, who suggested to Judge Wylie that the Irish should further advertise the undoubted abilities of their horses by having international jumping in their own 'shop window'. The Judge, until his death in 1964 the father-figure of the Dublin Horse Show, saw the merits of this, and five foreign teams took on the Irish in 1926.

It was fairly appropriate that the Swiss, under the redoubtable Colonel Ernst Haccius were the first winners of the Nations Cup. They repeated this in 1927 and with a third victory three years later became outright winners of the Aga Khan Trophy. In those days the Irish banks, single and double, for which the Ballsbridge arena is famous, were included in the international competitions; but they were the cause of a number of accidents, including one fatality to a French rider, especially among competitors not accustomed to such obstacles, and eventually in 1948 the F.E.I. ruled them out. They are, of course, still used for the national competitions.

The United States teams of that period, although they often had good horses and accomplished riders, met with much less success than they have known in the last two decades, again primarily the result of training men and horses separately instead of as a combination.

A notable exception, however, was Fred Bontecou, a junior army officer and rich enough to try his hand at all manner of equestrian sports: he played polo, hunted and rode in races, and was in the American team in the Paris Olympics in 1924. That team met with little success, but Bontecou saw enough to make him think he could beat the Europeans at their own game. In 1926 he brought two horses, Ballymacshane and Little Canada, both Canadian-bred, to the International Horse Show in Olympia, and on the grey Ballymacshane became the first American ever to win the coveted King George V Gold Cup.

What is more, joined by just one compatriot, Major George with Morgan, Bontecou rode his two horses in the Prince of Wales Cup, the team competition, and lost to the British by only half a fault. At present, each rider in a Nations Cup can ride only one horse.

The King George V Cup has been won by some of the greatest horses and riders in the sport, and the year after Bontecou's triumph it went to the elegant Frenchman Xavier Bizard. A product of Saumur, Bizard rode Quinine in 1927, and ten years later scored again on Honduras. Always monocled and dapper, Bizard, who won well over 100 international cups, was French chef d'équipe from the mid-1930s and after the Second World War played a major part in the rebuilding of the sport.

The 1928 Olympic Games in Amsterdam were notable for the breaking of the Swedish grip on the team competition, which went to Spain, and for the presence of the first competitors from Japan. The Dutch Colonel Maris, who was also president of the F.E.I., was President of the organising committee of the Games, which produced an increase over the Paris games: 20 countries sent 114 riders and 120 horses. Britain, because of a lack of the necessary funds, was not among them. These were also the first Games at which countries were allowed to enter no more than three competitors in each of the three equestrian events. The ruling still applies to show jumping, although where individual and team events are held separately the three riders in each need not necessarily be the same.

Spain took the team gold medal from Poland, with the dethroned Swedish third; Italy, France and Portugal tied for fourth place, ahead of Germany, Switzerland, the U.S.A., Holland, Norway, Argentina, with Hungary and Belgium equal 13th and last. Japan could not compete for the team prize, having only one rider, who was in any case eliminated so the only team who suffered from having one rider eliminated was Czechoslovakia. They had ample compensation, however, through the individual gold medal of Captain Ventura on Eliot. There were six clear rounds initially, three of which were faultless a second time. Jumping off, only Ventura was clear again, to beat Captain Bertran de Balanda of France on Papillon, who had two faults, and the Swiss Major Kuhn, with Pepita, who collected four.

The dressage gold medal at Amsterdam went to the versatile German rider Baron von Langen, who that same year won for the third time the Hamburg Jumping Derby, one of the most arduous competitions in the whole calendar and the precursor of many other jumping derbies all

Pierre Clavé and Irish Boy, Nice 1928

over the world. Von Langen, who achieved the unusual double of a show jumping and dressage Grand Prix on the same day in Sweden, was also an accomplished cross-country rider. A great trainer of horses, he was killed in 1934 when schooling a young horse for the 1936 Olympics.

Well behind von Langen when he won his dressage gold medal in Amsterdam came the Japanese Major Kohei Yusa. A samurai, Yusa joined the Officers Training Corps of the Japanese cavalry at 14, devoted himself to horses and was the inspiration of Japanese equestrians, helping to build their team into a force of international strength, until he died, aged 83, in 1966.

Argentina's team which finished twelfth in Amsterdam was the first from that country in the Olympic Games. A team from Chile toured Europe that year, and with some success, but did not try its hand in the Olympics.

At about this time Mike Ansell, who was to be the architect of Britain's rise to the top of world show jumping, was having his first taste of international competition. Then a captain in the Royal Inniskillings, Ansell won at the International in Olympia on his horse Mousie in 1930. The next year, he went to the International in New York, where he triumphed as a member of the British Army team, which also included the late Jack Talbot-Ponsonby, another important figure in British show jumping.

In 1930 Talbot-Ponsonby won the first of his three King George V Cups. Born in County Kildare the son of a British Army officer, he followed in his father's footsteps, and it was at Sandhurst that he first became interested in show jumping. Commissioned into the 7th Queen's Own Hussars, Lieut. Talbot-Ponsonby had his first taste of international jumping at Olympia in 1928 on Chelsea, a mare who had been taken out of the 12th Lancers after they had become mechanised. Chelsea was ridden at first by the 7th Hussars' rough-riding Sgt. Major Wallis, but as an N.C.O. Wallis was unable to ride her at the International. Two years after their debut at Olympia, Talbot-Ponsonby and Chelsea won the King George V Gold Cup; they won it again in 1932, and Talbot-Ponsonby was successful again, and so won the Cup outright on Best Girl in 1934.

In 1932 the Olympic Games were held outside Europe for the first time, at Los Angeles. Under the presidency of General Guy Henry, President of the F.E.I. from 1931-35, they contrasted sharply with Amsterdam in that only six countries competed in the equestrian events, with a total of 34 riders. France, Holland and Sweden sent competitors to take on the Americans, Mexico and Japan. Travel in those days was long, arduous and expensive, and the West Coast of the United States was more than many Europeans could afford.

There were no team awards because none of the four teams—France and Holland had no show jumpers there—had three finishers. All three of the Mexicans, and one each from the U.S.A., Sweden and Japan were eliminated. The 18-fence course was a good deal bigger than in Amsterdam, with a maximum height of 5 ft 3 in compared with 4 ft 7 in, and the water, at more than 16 ft, was 3 ft more than the 1928 jump. The individual gold medal was won, for the first and to the present day only time, by a Japanese, Baron Takeichi Nishi, riding Uranus, an Anglo-Normand that he had bought from the Italians during a tour of Europe in 1930. Uranus was a headstrong horse, not easy to control, but Nishi himself, though he enjoyed every moment of the social life that accompanied horse shows then even more than now, was not a man to give in easily.

In this competition, Lieut. Count von Rosen, son of the man who had done so much to get the equestrian events into the Olympic Games, and who had already won the individual bronze medal for the three-day event in Los Angeles, was leading for the gold with only two more competitors to go. Von Rosen and Empire had gone round the stiff course with a total of sixteen faults. The last to go for the United States was Major (later General) Harry Chamberlin, perhaps the most brilliant horseman his country has ever produced. A student at both Saumur and Tor di Quinto, Chamberlin's books, *Riding and Schooling Horses* and *Training Hunters, Jumpers and Hacks*, rank among the classics of equestrian literature, while the Army team he trained was probably the U.S.A's best before the advent of Bertalan de Nemethy.

Chamberlin and Show Girl, an attractive grey

Lt.-Col. Chamberlin and Pleasant Smile

mare schooled as one would expect from such a rider, went around for just twelve faults and with only the unconsidered Japanese to come the United States looked assured of a gold. But one of the supreme joys of show jumping is its uncertainty until the very end, and the U.S.A. had to wait another 36 years, until Mexico 1968, before getting their first Olympic gold medal for show jumping. Uranus may not have been as stylish as his predecessor in the ring, but he started off jumping everything with room to spare and with two-thirds of the course behind him had made only one mistake. Over the final few fences Uranus was pulling his rider's arms out by the roots, he ploughed through the last scattering bricks in all directions and came through the finish with just eight faults, the winner.

Nishi, promoted to captain, rode in the Berlin Olympics in 1936 and served with his embassies in the United States and Canada. Strangely, both he and his great rival Harry Chamberlin died in the same year, 1944, during the Second World War.

The Japanese Racing Association, perhaps inspired by Nishi's Los Angeles achievement, soon afterwards set about creating an equestrian centre near Tokyo, for the training of riders and jockeys, which, despite the war, is still going strong and was the venue of part of the 1964 Olympic Games. Uranus, hero of 1932, is buried there.

Ireland became affiliated to the F.E.I. in 1933, at the start of a period which has not since been equalled in that country's show jumping history. The man behind this success was Col. Paul Rodzianko who had already shown himself a superlative horseman to the British audiences at the International in Olympia.

Rodzianko was at the Russian Embassy in Rome when he heard of the revolution in his country. He came to England, where he had left his children en route from St Petersburg to Rome, joined the British army (as a private) but was later transferred to the Cavalry as an honorary colonel, and was sent with the Expeditionary force to Russia. After the War he started a training school at Windsor, which was successful enough at first but suffered, along with much else in Britain, during the years of the depression. It was then that Rodzianko was invited to Dublin to become director of the Cavalry School of the Irish Army, a position he held for nearly five years, during which time he welded together what was probably the best military show jumping team of all.

The names of the principal members of that team are still ones to conjure with: Col. Fred Ahern, who commanded the Army Equitation School in Dublin until he died in 1958; Colonel Jack Lewis, Colonel Dan Corry, who at Rotterdam only a few years ago rode in the Nations Cup when one of his team was hurt; Commandant Neylon and Major Ged O'Dwyer. They won the Aga Khan cup within weeks of Rodzianko taking over, and rode in triumph throughout Europe and North America. They won the Prince of Wales Cup at Olympia in 1937; Lewis, on Tramore Bay, and O'Dwyer, with Limerick Lace, took the King George V Cup in successive years, 1935 and 1936. This team, horsemen all of them, with their early training in that best of all schoolrooms, the hunting field, was not, unfortunately sent to the 1936 Olympic Games in Berlin, where, even on their home ground the Germans would have had a struggle, though Corry, Lewis and Aherne were still riding after the War, and rode for their country in the London Olympics in 1948.

In the 1936 Games, the Germans won the individual and team gold medals in all three equestrian sports: the three-day event, dressage and, in the vast arena bursting with some hundred and twenty thousand people, the show jumping. In common with all else in this vast display, there was a record entry in the equestrian events, 21 nations and 133 riders.

In the three-day event the British team, Captain Scott on Bob Clive, Captain Fanshawe with Bowie Knife and Lieut. Howard-Vyse with Blue Steel, became the first Britons ever to win an Olympic equestrian medal, taking the bronze behind Germany and Poland. This was not, however, an omen for the show jumpers, for not one of the three of them finished the course. The riders, Lieut. Jack Talbot-Ponsonby, Captain Brunker, one of the original supporters of the B.S.J.A., and Captain Bill Carr, were all competent enough but their horses were not up to Olympic standard.

The course, though no higher than in Los Angeles, was a difficult one, with a double and three combinations, the final treble being Nos 11, 12 and 13 jumped in the reverse order; an open ditch and bush at 4 ft 3 in, followed at two strides by a similar fence in reverse, then one stride to an upright post and rails at 4 ft 7 in. The marking of penalties was almost exactly as it is now, with three faults for the first refusal, six for the second and elimination for the third; knock down of a fence, irrespective of whether by fore or hind legs, or landing within the demarcation line, four faults; fall of horse and rider six faults, of rider only ten faults. Now, of course, eight faults are given for fall of horse and/or rider.

Kurt Hasse and Tora, 1939

Col. X. Bizard at 1936 Olympics

Eighteen countries started for the show jumping, each of them fielding a team of three; sixteen of the fifty-four riders did not finish, Britain being the only country to be completely 'wiped out'. After the first round Germany's Lieut. Kurt Hasse on Tora and Lieut. Henry Rang, from Rumania, with Delphis were jointly at the head of the placings, with four faults apiece. Tora went first in the timed jump-off, and clipped a pole at the final parallels in 59.5 sec. Delphis, that year's Aachen Grand Prix winner, was taken round carefully, needing only a clear round to win, but the same pole came down, and in a time more than 13 sec slower.

There was also a jump-off for the bronze medal, which finally went to the Hungarian Captain von Platthy with Selloe, who was clear and too fast for Captain van der Meersch of Belgium on Ibrahim; America's Captain Raguse, the only other involved in the jump-off, had the fastest time on Dakota but had one fence down.

Germany's Hasse and Tora, Brandt with Alchimist and von Barnekow on Nordland, each of whom had twenty faults, took the team gold with a total of 44 faults; Holland won the silver, with $51\frac{1}{2}$ faults and Portugal the bronze with 56. Following them, in order, came the U.S.A., $72\frac{1}{2}$; Switzerland, $74\frac{1}{2}$; Japan, 75; and France, $75\frac{1}{4}$. Austria, Belgium, Czechoslovakia, Britain, Hungary, Italy, Norway, Poland, Rumania, Sweden and Turkey were all eliminated. That same year a British team under the captaincy of Jack Talbot-Ponsonby went to the New York show and triumphed in the Nations Cup there. A year

Dan Corry and Red Hugh, Nice 1939

T. Lequio and Ronco, 1939

later it was won by Canada, who yet had to wait nearly another thirty years before they were finally recognised as a world-class show jumping nation, beating the Belgium team led by the Chevalier de Menten de Horne, still secretary-general of the F.E.I., a post he has held since 1956.

1937 was an important year in the development of show jumping in the United States: it was the year that the American Horse Shows Association took over the U.S. Cavalry Association's membership of the F.E.I., with the subsequent and inevitable decrease of military influence in the sport. Development was rapid, for two years later the first authoritative rules for jumping in the country were formulated, while in 1940 the F.E.I. rules were adopted. A further development in 1937 was the division of the United States into five zones (there are now eleven) to facilitate the control of all to do with the sport in such a large and diverse country.

At Olympia Don Beard and Fred Foster's Swank set their British high jump record of 7 ft $6\frac{1}{4}$ in, which has possibly not been exceeded anywhere in the world in an indoor arena. But such highlights were rare in a round of show jumping unimaginatively presented and attracting little in the way of public interest. Fortunately, the man who was to alter all this, Mike Ansell, was becoming ever more engrossed in the sport. Trips to the continent had whetted his international appetite: at Nice in 1939 he and Teddy, though young and comparatively inexperienced, were placed every day of the ten-day show.

Aachen, 1939, attracted a formidable concourse of top class jumpers, headed by Hans Brinckmann, for many years on the highest rung of his sport and the builder of the courses for which Aachen is now famous. Brinckmann, who has been appointed to supervise the building of the courses for the Olympic Games at Munich in 1972, won the Grand Prix of that year, and his team took the Nations Cup by what is almost certainly a world record margin, nine faults to the second-placed Rumanians' 87.

International sport was forgotten with the outbreak of war. Show jumping continued in a local, desultory way, but without the glamour of foreign competition; the F.E.I. lay dormant and the prime objects of the shows were to raise funds for charity or to provide a little light relief. But for those with the vision to see it, show jumping's brightest days were ahead, and no one saw this more clearly, despite the tragic accident which left him blind, than Britain's Colonel Mike Ansell.

After the war

Britain had played only a minor part in international show jumping before the outbreak of hostilities, but that was to change after the War. The change started in 1942, in a prisoner-of-war camp in Spanenburg, Germany. In that camp were three men who had been in British show jumping teams, Mike Ansell, Nat Kindersley and Bede Cameron. These men helped to pass the time by giving lectures on horses, and hunting and, of course, show jumping. Out of all their talk there grew an idea, a dream of putting Britain at the top of this comparatively new-born tree; of putting on jumping shows to rank with any in the world, and of beating the continentals at their own game.

When Ansell was repatriated in 1944 he soon set about making his dream become a reality. The B.S.J.A. had been kept going, though only at a low key, and although jumping had started again it was just as dull and unimaginative as it had been before the War. But in December, 1944, 'Colonel Mike' was invited to be chairman of the Association, and swung into action almost before he had taken his seat. Choosing a committee with men like Tom Taylor, Phil Blackmore, the secretary of the B.S.J.A. during its moribund years of war, and Brigadier John Allen, he set out to improve the standards of jumping, to instil into it the verve and excitement he had experienced on his trips abroad. For he knew that if he could do this, the public would come to see it.

The first thing to do was to set about altering the rules. At that time in Britain there was virtually no limit to the time a rider could take to complete the course, which did not exactly make for slick production. Indeed, the slats (thin laths of wood on top of the poles, which if knocked down cost half a fault) put a premium

Harry Llewellyn and Foxhunter

H. C. Cameron, M. P. Ansell, R. F. W. How and J. A. Talbot-Ponsonby

on accuracy at the expense of speed. Riders could circle if they wanted, to make sure that their horses were on the right stride, a tactic used invariably when coming to a water-jump; there was, too, the distinction between hitting a fence with fore or hind legs. Gradually these impediments to the presentation of show jumping as a popular spectacle were abolished, though the slats took long in being removed.

In order to encourage riders to introduce young horses a system of grading was started, whereby horses who had won more than £100 were put into Grade A, and could not thereafter compete in events confined to the less experienced horses. There are, throughout the world, various systems of grading horses, a subject which will later be discussed at greater length.

Having separated at least some of the chaff from the wheat, Mike Ansell and his committee now needed to put it on public show, and John Allen suggested that the Greyhound Racing Association, with which he had some connections, should be approached to see if they would allow a show to be held at the White City Stadium, one of London's largest. A meeting with Frank Gentle, chairman of the G.R.A., brought immediate and enthusiastic support for the idea. So it was that on September 1st, 1945, six years to the day after the outbreak of war, the National Championship was held, and a show jumping association with White City was begun which was to last until 1967.

The National Championship, with a first prize of £100, a useful sum in those days, was confined to horses which had won at least that amount in competitions during the current season.

Mike Ansell, in the short time leading up to the show, had already shown his flair for publicity, trying to attract both the country people who usually supported jumping at their local shows, and the Londoners, whose 'local' show this now was. His efforts were rewarded by a crowd of about 8,000, not big by present standards, and minute for the vast stadium that contained them, but an extremely healthy beginning. Ansell was also determined that, having got them there, he would make sure they got their money's-worth, and supervised the building of the fences and designing of courses with characteristic efficiency. Had he been able to write a script for the National Championship, Ansell could not have produced a better competition than the one that took place.

Tom Taylor, stalwart of the B.S.J.A. had been having a good season on his little Jorrocks, but this 14-year-old put in a stop; with but three horses to go Ted Williams's horses, Umbo, Huntsman and Leicestershire Lad, were lying first, second and third. But for so many of those 8,000 spectators this show was something of a thanksgiving for having survived the dark years, so when Nat Kindersley, returned from his P.O.W. days, appeared on his ex-Army horse Maguire, then 18 years old, he had many supporters.

Ted Williams and Umbo finished with only half a fault (for a displaced slat) leaving Kindersley and Maguire with nothing to spare. They timed the gate badly, and looked sure to stop or hit it, but the clever old horse somehow twisted over and the first National Championship had its storybook ending.

The following year there were two shows at the White City, the second National Show, for three days in June, and a Victory Show in September. The National show, run in the sunny

Hans Brinkmann and Wotansbruder

P. J. d'Oriola with King George V cup, 1947

weather which has become almost a tradition, was so successful that it was soon agreed that the time was ripe to reintroduce the International. The September Victory Championship was won by the man most commonly associated with show jumping, Colonel Harry Llewellyn, who rode Kilgeddin in the jump-off to defeat Douglas Bunn, then only 18, who has since become chairman of the B.S.J.A. and founded Hickstead, one of the most important international developments in British show jumping.

Show jumping had staged a revival in other parts of the globe as well. In 1945 the New York show reopened at Madison Square Garden, while in Lausanne the I.O.C. met and decided that the 1948 Olympic Games should be held in London. The F.E.I. resumed their activities in 1946, the Canadian Horse Shows Association was founded on the U.S.A. pattern of zones and delegated authority and the French recommenced their successes on the international scene. They travelled to Dublin to win the Aga Khan Trophy from the Irish and Swedish, and went, too, to the three Internationals staged in Switzerland, at Berne, Geneva, and Zurich. France had broken with tradition by now, and included civilians in her team, among them one of the great riders of the sport, Pierre Jonqueres d'Oriola, who won the Grand Prix in Zurich on L'Historiette.

Those Swiss shows were something of a preview of the giants, for numbered among the Italians was Piero d'Inzeo, then a Lieutenant, who with his brother Raimondo, were to win just about every major prize in the show jumping calendar. Britain was represented by officers from the B.A.O.R., who managed to take back a few first prizes with them to Germany.

In 1947 teams were sent out from Britain, and for the first time they too included civilians: Harry Llewellyn, who had quickly been co-opted by Mike Ansell into the B.S.J.A. organisation, 'Curly' Beard, Tom Brake, Bay Lane and Bobbie Hall were invited to go on the spring tour to Nice and Rome. Though they jumped well in Nice, the British were well out of their depth when it came to jumping off 'against the clock'. This rapier-thrust of competition was something outside their experience. In Rome things went rather better: Llewellyn and Kilgeddin, a big, fine stamp of horse, won the Premio di Campidoglio, but this was a *puissance* competition, in which fences were raised in successive barrages, or jump-offs, without recourse to the clock for a decision. 'Curly' Beard finished runner-up in the Grand Prix, the show's major competition, but still, quite evidently, the British had a long way to go, even if the comment they aroused in Nice that 'the British would do better to stick to riding bicycles' was an unkind exaggeration.

That same year saw also the rebirth of the International, in July, again at the White City, and despite much prejudice and criticism, remained there until building developments made its demise a necessity twenty years later. That five-day show gave the British public a glimpse of what is now, thanks to television, familiar fare in millions of homes. Several of the competitions were run under F.E.I. Rules, with riders from France, Belgium and Ireland challenging the British.

Pierre Jonqueres d'Oriola, the volatile Frenchman from the Pyrenees, later to win two individual gold medals at the Helsinki and Tokyo Olympics, won the King George V Gold Cup on a small, elegant Anglo-Arab named Marquis III. The Prince of Wales Cup also went to France.

The balance was at least partly redressed, however, in the Daily Mail Cup, the *victor ludorum*, which brought together more than a score of the most successful horses of the show. Brian Butler, a Hampshire farmer, and his nine-year-old Tankard were the only ones to go clear. Pat Smythe, who was to become the undisputed 'Queen' of show jumping, made her first international appearance at that show, aged only 18, riding Finality, who stood scarcely 15 hands

John Lewis and Limerick Lace, Nice 1939

high, and had been bought by her mother as a three-year-old. Pat taught her to jump, and won many local jumping competitions on her, but the mare was put out of action before the 1946 Victory Championship with a cut leg. Two wins at the Bath and West show, one of the most important on the British circuit, preceded her appearance at the White City. Throughout the show they went consistently, tying with none other than d'Oriola for a place in the Moss Bros. *puissance*, and at the end of the show were invited to join the team for Ostend and Le Zuote. In the same team was another who had made his first appearance at the White City, Harry Llewellyn's Foxhunter, destined to become perhaps the most famous horse in the history of show jumping.

Bred in Norfolk by a Mr Millard, by Erehwemos, Foxhunter had been bought by Llewellyn in Leicestershire from Mr. J. N. Holmes. He had been foaled in 1941, stood just under 17 hands when he came to White City and had enough quality to make people take notice even before he jumped. Pat Smythe and Harry

Llewellyn were joined on the team by Brian Butler and Toby Robeson, father of Tokyo bronze medallist Peter. They tied for second place with the Swiss behind the unbeatable French in Ostend. Pat won cups for the best performance by a lady rider at both Ostend and Le Zoute, and Foxhunter was acclaimed the best novice horse in Europe.

Civilians were not yet allowed to ride in the Aga Khan Cup in Dublin, but Britain sent a Military team: Alec Scott on Notar and Arthur Carr with Lucky Dip, both Hanoverian-bred horses captured in Germany, and Henry Nicoll with the brilliant 15·1 hands Pepper Pot, captured in Austria, Britain took the Cup, for the first time since 1931, from France, Switzerland, Italy and Sweden as well as the Irish. So Britain's first post-war international year had brought some measure of success, but, in 1948, the scene was set for the pinnacle of sporting endeavour, the Olympic Games.

No competition of this standard had ever been staged in Britain before, so the first thing to organise was the course and the building of the fences. Colonel Mike Ansell put in his customary thorough staff work, and, working all night at the B.S.J.A. Sloane Street headquarters, he, Captain Jack Webber, secretary general of the Association, and Phil Blackmore, the senior course builder, planned the course. They finally came to an agreement and Mr. Bill Rodwell, from Hampshire, was asked to build the fences in the utmost secrecy. A typical Ansell touch was to have them erected, again with deadly secrecy, on a field in Hampshire, where they were inspected and approved, and in due course brought to Wembley.

Meanwhile the B.S.J.A. was doing its utmost to ensure that the British team should not let down the supporters who would be there in their thousands on their home ground. Llewellyn's Foxhunter and Kilgeddin had been, during the winter, for a course in dressage at Col. Joe Dudgeon's school just outside Dublin; after a trial trip to Lucerne with several other possibles, they were both selected. Henry Nicoll was to be

The Duke of Beaufort presents the King George V Cup to Llewellyn, 1949

Llewellyn and Foxhunter, 1949

on Kilgeddin and Llewellyn himself would ride Foxhunter; the third member was Arthur Carr on Monty, a brilliant speed horse at that time owned by Mr. Eddie Broad but subsequently leased to Llewellyn.

The weather was wet for much of the Games, and when it came to the Grand Prix show jumping, traditionally the final event before the closing ceremony, the ground was soggy and badly cut up. Just to get the course erected, fences put up, ditches and the 16 ft 3 in water jump dug, was a herculean task, for work could not start until well after 10 o'clock the night before. Course inspection by the two F.E.I. technical delegates, Switzerland's Haccius and Moeremans d'Emaus from Belgium was due at 8.30 a.m. and only fractionally later all was ready for them.

Fifteen teams of three started for the event, before a crowd of about 85,000, and of the first twenty horses through there were eight eliminations. The best of these was the eight faults of Frenchman Chevalier 'Paqui' d'Orgeix and Sucre de Pomme. Kilgeddin had double that.

There was no shortage of problems on that course, and they were being progressively increased by the shortage of water in the ditches; although they had been carefully dug and lined, a succession of splashing by horses and falling by men had lowered the water level. They could not be refilled, as Water Board officials had turned off the supply and gone for the weekend. A small style and ditch, the insignificance of which caused some to stop and stare, and a treble consisting of a glaring white gate, followed at two strides by a ditch, now nearly dry, then two more strides to another gate. Both had their share of casualties, but the most difficult fences were the last two: the water, followed all too soon, perhaps a dozen strides, by a 5 ft 3 in wall jumped off ground which got gradually worse as the competition went on.

Arthur Carr and Monty had a fairly disastrous round; a stop and then headstrong carelessness took Monty's total for the round to 35; but at least he finished. Foxhunter, like Kilgeddin, collected 16 faults, while Mexico's Ruben Uriza and Hatvey and Colonel Wing of the United States with Democrat each had only eight, the day's lowest total, with only one rider left: Mariles of Mexico with Arete. Mariles, an experienced and brilliant horseman, and indeed the whole Mexican

Iris Kellett and Rusty, 1949

team while in training at Aldershot, had shown all the quality of potential Olympic champions, but could he and the one-eyed Arete, a smallish horse and no longer young, succeed where so many others of the best in the world had failed?

If Mariles had any doubts he, at least, did not show them. Most of those who had gone before him had had time faults, but the Mexican did not let this fluster him. He started off with a slow but calm assurance and had Arete placed exactly right at fence after fence. Arete almost stepped over the style, came to the treble in the same unhurried manner, and through it immaculately. Only two fences to go and still faultless save only for time; up to the water, but not over it, not even trying to get over it, slap in the middle but cantering on, up to the final wall, and over it perfectly. Just four jumping faults, and though he had to add two and a quarter for time the gold medal was his, and the team gold Mexico's.

This was the culmination of what Mariles had planned twelve years earlier in Berlin. There he had been a spectator, but an observant one, studying each of the best riders and deciding how much of that rider's technique he could use or adapt for himself. Back in Mexico, he started to put his theories into practice, developing what was good, rejecting the rest.

After Mariles had assured himself of the gold, the three men who had each collected eight faults had to jump again, this time against the clock, to lay claim to the silver and bronze medals. This time Uriza and Hatvey, of the Morgan horse breed, though bred in Mexico, had the only clear round, to take the silver medal. D'Orgeix and Sucre de Pomme and Wing with Democrat each had a fence down, but the Frenchman was 1·2 sec faster.

Democrat was in many ways an unlucky horse, for he had shown great promise under Franklin Wing in 1941, and was still extremely good in 1948, but the War had robbed him of what might have been world-beating years. He was Bill Steinkraus's second horse, to Hollandia, although eventually ridden by John Russell, in the 1952 Games, and at Harrisburg, New York and Toronto that year, for all his nineteen years, he won all the eight classes he jumped in.

The team silver went to Spain, through Garcia Cruz on Bizarro, Morenes with Quorum and Ponce de Leon with Foratido, who totalled $56\frac{1}{2}$ to the Mexicans' $34\frac{1}{4}$. Third came Britain, the only other of the 15 nations to finish with a complete team, with an aggregate of 67 faults. This was Britain's first Olympic medal for show jumping, but they have won at least one at every Games since then.

For the Irish military team, Corry on Tramore

Llewellyn and Foxhunter, Helsinki 1952

P. J. d'Oriola and Ali Baba, Helsinki 1952

J. F. d'Orgeix and Reine Margot, 1946

Bay, Aherne on Aherlow and Lewis on Lough Neagh, eliminated when Lough Neagh, their last to go, had three refusals, this was very nearly the end of an era; but for the Italian d'Inzeo brothers it was just the beginning. Raimondo had made his debut in the three-day event, finishing 30th individually, while Piero had been eliminated in the show jumping when Briacone stopped three times. An inauspicious beginning but there was time enough yet.

Scarcely was the Olympic course dismantled than another was being erected only a few miles across London, at White City, for the International Horse Show followed the next week. The Mexicans did not stay on for this, but there was a strong turn-out of international talent: the Americans, Italy, France, Spain, Sweden and Turkey. The U.S. team, a military one based in Germany, had won in the Nations Cup at Lucerne, and they did so again at White City, before going on to complete the hat-trick in Dublin.

The entries for the King George V Cup were so numerous that it had to be run in three sections, the first five from each going into the final. For the first, and last time women riders were allowed in the King's Cup—from 1949 they had their own Princess (later Queen) Elizabeth Cup—and Pat Smythe on Finality and Lulu Rochford on Ladybird, both fifth in their sections, went through to the final.

The first section had been won by Colonel Wing on the American Olympic reserve horse Tortilla, another American, Rattler, took the third; and in between them came Foxhunter. In the final the two women were disposed of fairly unceremoniously, for Ladybird, only 15 hands, found it all rather beyond her and refused, while Finality, a bit off colour, stopped in the double three from home and parted with her rider. Finality no longer belonged to Pat Smythe; earlier in the season they had beaten Seamus Hayes and a horse of Tommy Makin's at the Royal Counties, and Mr. Makin, for whom Hayes had been riding with tremendous success for several years, replied by buying Finality.

In the first round of the final for the King's Cup Foxhunter went clear and into the jump-off: this time he had a brick out of the wall, but no one else could get round for less than eight faults, though Tortilla's second mistake was not until the last fence.

So Foxhunter won his first King George V Gold Cup; only seven, he was to win it again in 1950 and 1953, the only horse ever to triumph three times in this, one of the most coveted individual trophies in the world. And much more glory was to be his before he retired to his Welsh home. For Llewellyn, too, this had been a remarkable year, for as well as his exploits in the show ring he was an accomplished amateur N.H. rider,

Peter Robeson and Craven A

totalling some 60 victories, and in March 1948 he brought off a rare double at the National Hunt Festival at Cheltenham, winning both the Foxhunters and the United Hunts' Chases.

The time had begun for the British show jumpers to spread their wings; there is no tutor like experience and in 1949 teams were sent to a round dozen shows, with nine riders sharing the honours between them. The first tour went to Nice and Rome, and numbered among the team was another British combination destined to play an important part on the international scene, Wilf White and Nizefela.

Foaled in 1942 by a Shire out of a thoroughbred mare, in Lincolnshire, Nizefela worked on a farm before being bought for £100 as a four-year-old by Wilf White, who had been a successful show jump rider in pre-War days, from a Mr. Harrison of Bridgnorth. Upgraded after only seven shows, Nizefela was an enormously powerful horse with a characteristic kick-back for which there were many theories but never one really satisfactory explanation. Though Nizefela's performances in Nice and Rome were of a modest character he was in the team which won the Nations Cup in Geneva that year, beating France and Italy. This was Britain's first Nations Cup victory on the Continent.

Also making his debut in 1949 was the 17-year-old Peter Robeson, following in his father's international footsteps, riding a home-bred mare Craven A, bred the 'opposite' way to Nizefela, by a thoroughbred stallion, Victory, out of a Shire mare. She only started jumping in 1947, and in 1949 was invited on the late-season tour to Ostend and Le Zoute, where she jumped 6 ft 3 in to take the *puissance*, with King's Cup victor Marquis III among her victims. Just a few weeks after that Robeson and Craven A were runners-up for the Grand Prix de Paris, behind Llewellyn and Foxhunter. The great horse, who had started the European season by winning three times in Nice, where Britain were runners-up for the Nations Cup, had a triumphant year.

At the International Horse Show, with teams from Ireland, France, Holland and Belgium, Brian Butler had the only two clear rounds in the whole of the King George Cup on Tankard and Bruto, nominating his consistently successful Tankard as the winner. Nizefela, too, had jumped round without fault, but collected three-quarters of a time fault. Though so near many times, Nizefela was never to win this classic prize.

Iris Kellett won the first of her two Princess Elizabeth Cups on Rusty; the second time was two years later in 1951. Exactly twenty years after her first triumph she was to break her run of ill-luck which had for so long dogged her to take the European Championship before her home crowd at Dublin.

The British team had its first post-War success in the Prince of Wales Cup, starting a run of victories in the competition which lasted until 1955. British riders' 'bag' of European Grand Prix that year was five: Paris, Nice, Ostend, Brussels and Rotterdam. In September the season was brought to a triumphal conclusion by the first Horse of the Year Show.

It was the idea of Captain Tony Collings, a brilliant horseman and winner of the Badminton three-day event in 1950, that there should be a championship show to wind up the season. Collings himself was killed in an aircrash, but not until he had seen his idea brought to fruition. A visit by Mike Ansell and Col. V. D. S. Williams to the indoor show in Paris, where Foxhunter won the Grand Prix, convinced them such an event could be staged successfully in London. The atmosphere, totally unlike the traditional outdoor show, was an exciting and lively one, and scarcely were they back in London before plans were being evolved.

Not just a jumping show, but a championship for every type of show horse, hunter, hack, cob, child's pony—truly a 'Horse of the Year Show'. But where to put it? There were not many alternatives, and the final decision fell on Harringay. The show was put on for three days, September 13th–15th, and had riders from France, Belgium and Ireland as well as some 250 jumpers. There was a qualification of £75 in winnings during the season for the jumpers.

The attractive, very feminine 18-year-old French rider Michele Cancre soon became a favourite with the crowd, and won two competitions to show she was not simply decorative, Iris Kellett took the Ladies' class, with Foxhunter ridden by Mrs Llewellyn in third place, and Pat Smythe rode Finality to victory in the Leading Show Jumper of the Year competition. Finality had shown that she would go for no one as well as for Pat Smythe. Tommy Makin had sold her on to a Mr. Snodgrass, who asked Pat to ride the mare at Harringay. In the jump-off Finality beat Ted Williams, who was subsequently to take the title no fewer than four times.

In the United States, show jumping was being reorganised and in 1950 the United States Equestrian Team was formed, under the captaincy of their former military Olympic rider Col. John Wofford, who has had three sons in American Olympic teams, either show jumping or in the three-day event. Wofford was succeeded by Arthur McCashin, a former steeplechase rider, who led the team from the saddle into third place in the Helsinki Olympics, and is now international course builder at Madison Square Garden, New York. In 1955 Bill Steinkraus took over as captain, and, with Bertalan de Nemethy as coach, created a truly formidable team.

The first German teams since the War also started to travel the circuit, working their way up to a monopoly of Olympic team gold medals from 1956 to 1964. But in the meantime the British star was still very much in the ascendancy.

In 1950 the British team won the Nations Cup in Lucerne, London and Dublin, and were second to the French in France. At the White City,

Wilf White and Nizefela, Helsinki 1952

Llewellyn and Foxhunter took their second King George Cup. Llewellyn had both Foxhunter and Kilgeddin through to the final and they and the Irish Captain Michael Tubridy on Kinsale were the only ones to go clear. Kilgeddin hit the first fence and Kinsale the last element of the treble; Foxhunter needed a clear round, and in characteristically immaculate form, he jumped it. Foxhunter won the Moss Bros. *puissance*, jumping 6 ft 6 in, at the same show.

In the autumn the British team went on the North American tour. At Harrisburg they were beaten for the Nations Cup by the Olympic gold medallists, Mexico, and finished third in Toronto. Stars of the tour, undoubtedly, were Wilf White and Nizefela who had two outright wins in Harrisburg, three in Toronto, and were equal first in two other competitions. Foxhunter had three successes on the tour, and jumped two clear rounds in the Toronto Nations Cup.

On the other side of the world, too, there was action in equestrian circles. Both the Equestrian Federation of Australia and the New Zealand Horse Society were formed in 1950. With the vast distances involved to compete in Europe both countries tended to take on each other. New Zealand, which had a Hungarian trainer, sent a team to win at the Sydney Royal in 1952, but three years later the Australians had more than made up the deficit.

In the final pre-Olympic season of 1951 the British team was sent to try their strength in eight Nations Cups. They won in London, Dublin and Rotterdam, were beaten by Spain in Nice and then went under by just one fault to the Italians on their home ground in Rome. Teams of less experienced performers were second in Le Zoute, third in Madrid and fifth in Geneva. In both Nice and Rome, where Colonel Jaime Garcia Cruz of the London silver medal team had taken the Grand Prix, the Spanish had showed themselves to be a strong and talented team, though perhaps just past their best.

The British team's performance in London was especially encouraging: it consisted of Nizefela and Foxhunter, of course, and Alan Oliver, then only 18, on Red Star II. Oliver, for all his unorthodox style (which has since been changed to conform more closely to what the purists consider 'correct') was the leading rider of the season. For the Prince of Wales Cup all three horses jumped double clear rounds, to finish with a total of no faults. Foxhunter took most of the individual prizes of the show for himself, but this time the King's Cup evaded him. Some of the best horses in the competition, including Foxhunter, Craven A and Piero d'Inzeo's Brando hit a fairly insignificant style, possibly upset by a flickering neon light which distracted them. Whatever the reason, they hit it, while Captain Kevin Barry and Ballyneety for Ireland jumped the only clear round to win.

In Rotterdam a significant newcomer to the British team was Colonel Duggie Stewart, who had been in the three-day event team in the 1948 Olympics. An accomplished horseman, he had jumped with some success in Germany, and on the German-bred Bones was a member of the

Peter Robeson and Firecrest

Pat Smythe and Flanagan

team which won the Nations Cup in Rotterdam.

So, with Helsinki only months away, expectations were justifiably high that winter.

Helsinki—Britain victorious

Nor were the only serious preparations going on in Europe, for across the Atlantic major threats were developing. The United States were making their first preparations for an Olympic Games since the foundation of the civilian United States Equestrian Team Inc., under the captaincy of Arthur McCashin. The team they finally selected was McCashin with Miss Budweiser, Bill Steinkraus at the start of a brilliant international career, with the late Colonel John Wofford's Hollandia, and John Russell with Democrat, the horse on which Colonel Wing had jumped off for the silver and bronze medals in London.

The first Pan American Games were held in Buenos Aires in that pre-Olympic year of 1951, and though, for the only time, the U.S.A. had no team, Chile, Argentina, Mexico and Brazil got together to show the high quality of show jumping in the South American continent. Chile's cavalry, unlike its European and North American counterparts had not been disbanded. On the contrary, it was flourishing with two well-equipped schools in Santiago, the capital, and Quillota. Captain Alberto Larraguibel on Huaso had leaped 8 ft $1\frac{1}{2}$ in in 1948, still the official world high jump record, and in Buenos Aires he rode Julepe to win the individual competition from the experienced Argentinian Carlos Delia on El Linyera. Two other Chileans, Joaquin Larrain on Pillan and Ricardo Echeverria with Bambi, were equal third, and the Chilean team had nearly forty faults to spare over Argentina, with Mexico and Brazil third and fourth.

There was no clear line to form between Europe and the Americas, but clearly the transatlantic threat was one to be taken seriously.

In England there were selection problems. Not so much whom to put in but whom to leave out. There was only one place to spare, for Harry Llewellyn and Foxhunter, the king of European show jumping, and Wilf White with Nizefela, his 'prime minister', were certainties. Had either of them been left out the B.S.J.A., selection committee and all, would have been annihilated overnight. But who would join them? Logically, the choice boiled down to two: Colonel Duggie Stewart and Alan Oliver. Stewart, commanding the Scots Greys in Germany, had, because of his military duties, less time than most, either for competition or training, but had Olympic experience in the three-day team event in London. And he had been in triumphant form in Germany in 1951.

Oliver had been even more successful that year, the start of a period which saw him leading rider in 1951, 1953 and 1954, and second in 1952 and 1956. A brilliant youngster, even if his style of flinging himself in the air over the jumps did not endear him to some of the purists; though that great trainer Rodzianko, perhaps the greatest of all, did not condemn him for it. For, despite his acrobatics, he did not unbalance his horses, and, the only criterion which really mattered, he did win.

Oliver, Stewart and young Peter Robeson, as well as Llewellyn and White, were invited to take part in the training; the horses in the squad, Foxhunter, Nizefela, Aherlow, who was lent to the team by Mr. Holland-Martin, Nobbler, lent by Mary Whitehead (now Mrs. Bryan Marshall), Prince Hal, lent by Pat Smythe, for women were still not eligible for the Games, and Red Star and Talisman, belonging to Mr. A. H. Payne, who owned so many of the good and the great horses that Alan Oliver rode.

A plan of preparation had been thought out most carefully. The Games were to be held in August, so the horses were let down until the beginning of February, then brought up and given hours of road work to build stamina into them for the gruelling task ahead. Then they went to Aldershot in April, for preliminary schooling, and then some loosening-up competition at the Dublin Spring Show in May, primarily an agricultural affair but coming at just the right time for a little 'sorting out'. Later that same month the squad went to the International show in Lucerne, the oldest of its status in the world. Foxhunter and Nizefela did not jump, for what did they have to prove, apart from their wellbeing? The team for the Nations Cup was Stewart on Aherlow, Oliver on Talisman, Robeson with Craven A and White on Nobbler. They finished second to Argentina—at last an indication of inter-continental form—with France and Italy among those behind.

The final 'pre-race gallop' was held at Aldershot in June, with Stewart still heavily engaged in Germany. But it was decided that he had the better claim and that in any case Oliver's horses were not quite up to an Olympic course, and so Robeson was announced as the reserve rider.

Air travel for horses, commonplace now, was quite rare in those times, but it was decided that

Winkler and Halla, World Champions in Madrid, 1959

Fritz Thiedemann and Meteor

flying the horses to Helsinki would vastly improve their chances, rather than have them face a week-long trip by boat. Several thousand pounds had already been spent on the training, so why risk everything for the sake of saving money at the last minute. And so, just four days before they were to go into action, the team flew out.

With 16 teams, a total of 48 riders, due to go round twice, the accepted Nations Cup pattern, the competition was obviously going to go on for a long time and the start of the first round was due at 8 a.m. The riders were up by 6 o'clock and an hour later had their first sight of the scene of battle. There were thirteen fences, totalling nineteen elements with the combination fences. The first impressions were that the width of the fences took away from their height, but they were big, there was no doubt about that. The distances between some of the fences was even more disturbing, for it is the approach which governs how well, or badly, one jumps. Between the double of parallels and a wall at 5 ft 3 in there was only about 30 feet; there was an unusual treble of a gate at 4 ft 7 in, a 9 ft open water, then logs 5 ft high.

The spirits of the British camp as a whole were not exactly high, quite apart from the early hour. There had not been one British success during the Games, and the three-day event team had suffered the most atrocious luck when Lawrence Rook's horse, Starlight, a last-minute substitute when the originally-chosen rider fell ill, put a foot in a ditch while making a sharp turn. Semi-conscious, Rook was put back into the saddle, jumped the last fence and then went the wrong side of the final flag, and so was eliminated, and with him the almost certain chance of a team medal.

But the overture had been played; now it was on stage for the first act. At that time of the morning the 70,000-seat stand was rather less than half-full, but the sun was shining and the course, though riding difficult as an Olympic course should, was not proving quite as tricky as many had feared.

Duggie Stewart and Aherlow were the first to go for Britain, and when they went, after about a dozen others, the best score was eight. So Aherlow's twelve was no cause for dismay. Aherlow had hit the big parallel poles, 4 ft 8 in with a spread of 5 ft, at Number 3, and again at the difficult double of parallels.

Nizefela, for all his undistinguished background was a true Olympic horse and he showed it that morning. Not until the last gate did he have a touch; it was no more than that, but four faults put Britain right in the picture. Indeed, with two horses from each team gone, Britain, with a total of 16 faults, was second to Italy's 12. Italy had Piero d'Inzeo and Uruguay to go, Britain had Foxhunter. Then disaster for both, but worse for Italy, for they had no chance to recover.

Apparently d'Inzeo was outside arguing a technical point with an official when his turn came. His name was called, but nothing happened. At last, after giving him as much time as they reasonably could, the jury announced that he was eliminated. So the leaders were out of it, years of work thrown away in a few excitable moments. Now Britain were ahead, and with Foxhunter to come, the mighty, the infallible Foxhunter. It was time for more hopes to be dashed.

To give Foxhunter as much chance as possible in his two rounds over this huge course Llewellyn had deliberately not worked him beforehand as much as was his custom, and the moment they came into the ring it was clear to all, but especially to Llewellyn himself, that this had been an error of judgement, for Foxhunter was as fidgety as a cricket, shying at fences and patently in no mood for the necessary concentration for the job.

The first mistake came at the double of parallels; this brought Foxhunter into the wall on the wrong stride and for one awful moment he almost stopped. Gathering himself up he hurled himself over almost from a standstill, took a brick out of it, and landed with his rider sprawling desperately round the underside of his neck.

Surely Llewellyn must come off, but for what seemed like hours, as British fingers crossed and British voices breathed prayers, he struggled slowly but surely back into the saddle. In an effort to make up time they went too fast at the next, and hit it, and there were, also, the three faults for a circle while Llewellyn was righting himself, and time faults for a grand total of $16\frac{3}{4}$ faults.

When all the horses had gone round once Britain had slumped to sixth place, with $32\frac{3}{4}$ faults: the United States led, with 23, followed by Portugal, Argentina, Chile, and France. Germany's Fritz Thiedemann on Meteor, with the only clear round, led the individual.

There was a few hours respite before the battle recommenced at just after 3 o'clock in the afternoon; time to relax, or to work oneself up into a state of nervousness. The calming, inspiring influence of Mike Ansell helped a lot during those vital hours.

Portugal, whose Carvalhosa on Mondina had twenty faults, and Argentina, for whom Sagasta and Don Juan, who finished the course lame, collected $20\frac{3}{4}$, were out of the running soon after the start of the second round, but Stewart inspired Aherlow to get round with only one fence down. Chile, too, were riding superbly, and with one horse from each team gone were ahead of the United States, with Britain pulled up to third. Now it was Nizefela's turn, and never was a horse

H. G. Winkler and Halla, Stockholm 1956

of his calibre more needed. Wilf White had the experience and the temperament, Nizefela had the ability, and round they went, magnificently. Checked after the water, to meet the final fence, a wall, on the right stride, Nizefela put himself right so quickly that White lost a stirrup iron, but still they went clear of it. Then it was seen that one of the two judges at the water jump had raised his flag. Many impartial men still swear that Nizefela had cleared the water, but, inevitably, the judge's decision was final. But for this Nizefela would have won the individual gold medal without more ado, but still his eight-fault total had put Britain right back into the hunt.

The Chileans, too, were going strong for the finishing line; Oscar Christi and Bambi had gone round twice with only one fence down in each round, and in the second his compatriot, Mendoza with Pillan, had gone clear. Eccheverria and Lindo Pearl, $17\frac{3}{4}$ first time, cut this to eight in the second round, and at the end of their two rounds the Chileans' aggregate was just $45\frac{3}{4}$ faults. Britain, with Foxhunter to go, were five faults less than this. So Foxhunter could afford one fence down, but only one, not a repeat of that morning's sad display.

Llewellyn knew it; maybe Foxhunter knew it too, or sensed it at least, for this time, well worked before and obviously happy with himself he set about the job with the determination which had been sadly lacking in the morning. And this time he jumped as everyone knew he could: clear, and the team gold medal was Britain's.

Nor was the excitement yet over, for now there had to be a jump-off for the individual medals among the five who had finished with eight-faults totals. The quintet involved were Pierre Jonqueres d'Oriola and Ali Baba, one of the three clear in the second round, Thiedemann and Meteor, who had lost their lead with two down second time, White with Nizefela, Christi with Bambi and de Menezes of Brazil on Bigua, who had had four each time.

The Olympic Games marked only the third time that d'Oriola had ridden Ali Baba, a smallish Anglo-Arab, one-time polo pony and now in the French cavalry, in competition. Colonel Cavaillé, himself a talented show jumping rider, had seen d'Oriola ride the horse once, and promptly took Ali Baba away, giving him to other Army officers to ride, having told d'Oriola that he should have him back for the Olympic Games. This ploy, presumably designed to keep d'Oriola's concentration needle sharp, for it is not the volatile though brilliant Frenchman's strong suit, worked wonderfully well. D'Oriola and Ali Baba went first in the timed jump-off, flashing round the shortened course clear in exactly forty seconds.

Christi and Bambi had four faults, in 44 sec, to take the silver for Chile, while Thiedemann and Meteor, though they cut the time to 38.5 sec, hit two fences. This gave them the bronze, for Bigua also hit two, but at a much slower pace, and poor Nizefela, not at his best against the clock, especially in this sort of company, had three down. With just a little luck, or, some would say, with only reasonable justice, Nizefela would have won the individual gold without any need for a jump-off. For all his fine achievements he must rank altogether as one of the unluckiest of the truly great horses of show jumping.

That team gold medal aroused tremendous interest in the sport in Britain, but now, in all parts of the world, the international impact was growing.

Digging in

The F.E.I., realising the need to encourage younger riders, started the European Junior Championship in 1952, for teams of riders, four from each country, between the ages of 14 and 18 years. The first competition was held in Ostend, when Italy beat the home team. The Federation's aim, that of encouraging youngsters who might go on to make the grade in senior competition was rapidly justified, for in that initial winning team was Graziano Mancinelli, who was to become Italy's consistent No. 3 to the d'Inzeo brothers as well as winning the men's European Championship in 1963.

Mancinelli was in the Italian team for the first three years of the championship, and in 1954, when they won in Rotterdam the runners-up, Germany, numbered among their quartet Herman Schridde, the senior European champion in 1965, and Alwin Schockemohle, who has been twice second and twice third for the title. Another German rider destined to even greater things and even more quickly than his two young compatriots who made his international debut in 1952 was Hans Gunter Winkler. He had his first taste of foreign competition at Bilbao, only two years before he first won the World Championship, which was to be inaugurated in 1953.

Pat Smythe, unable to jump in the Olympics, had been carving a successful niche for herself on the domestic scene. Her Tosca was the season's leading horse, and, with Tosca and Prince Hal jointly, she won the premier championship at the Royal for the third successive year.

The International Horse Show at the White

Pat Smythe and Scorchin

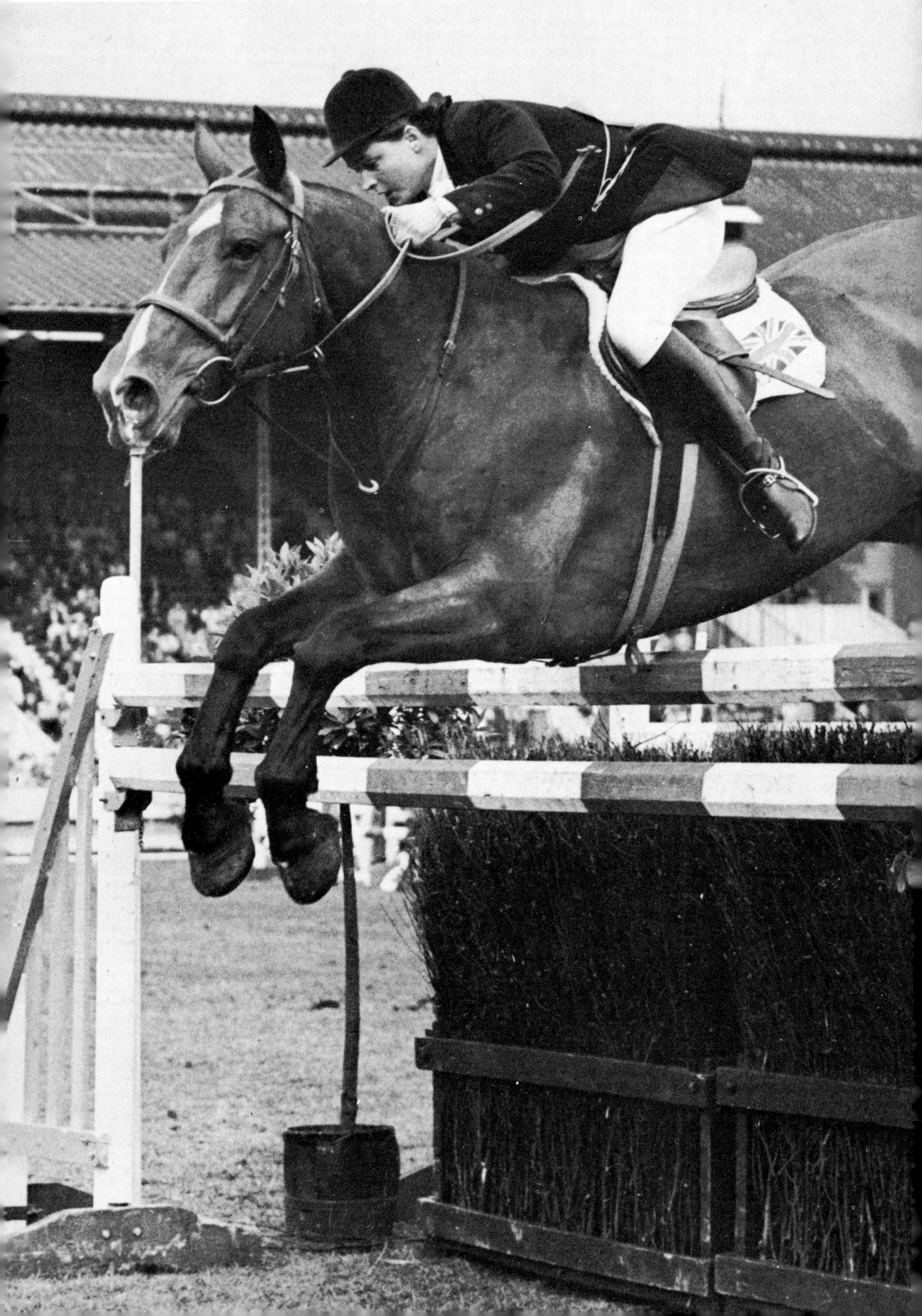

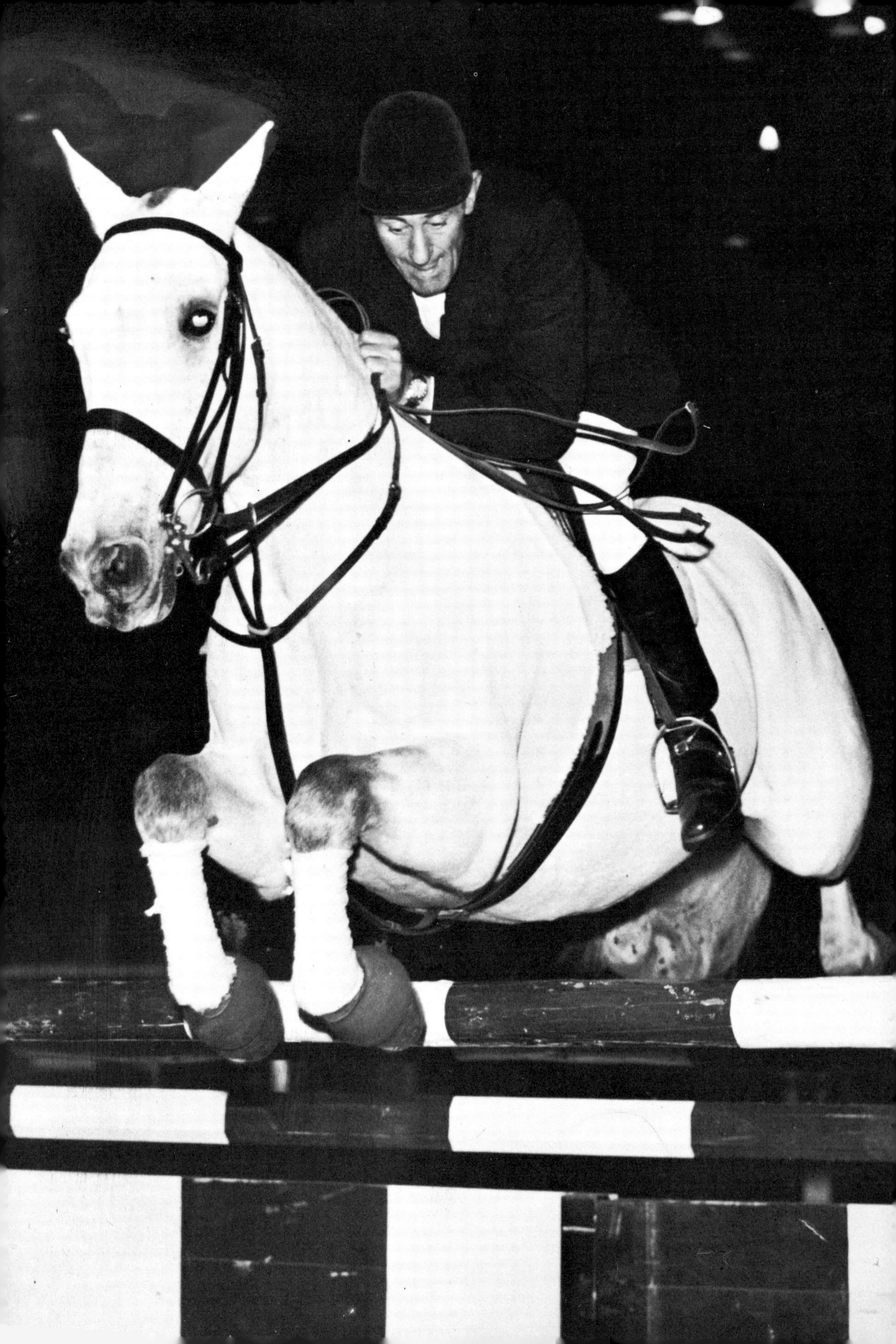

City followed all too soon on the heels of the Olympic Games for the comfort of the Olympic horses, and Foxhunter, as well as Aherlow, failed to qualify for the final of the King George V Cup; and the gallant Nizefela put up a showing far below his usual form. Harry Llewellyn, however, had another threat in Bob Hanson's The Monarch, who was to be ridden to victory in the following year's Rome Grand Prix by the owner's son, William Hanson. The 14ft water-jump, made more difficult than it should have been by a spooky shadow, caused a lot of trouble to the King's Cup finalists, and only The Monarch and the excitable, aristocratic young Spaniard Don Carlos Figueroa with his Anglo-Arab Gracieux could jump clear rounds. Jumping off first, The Monarch hit two fences, leaving the eight-year-old Gracieux to jump clear and win, to date the only Spanish horse and rider ever to take this Cup.

The Spaniards were not, as a team, as strong as they had been in their heyday, such as that which won the 1928 Olympic Gold medal. However, there were a few talented individuals, and it was one of them, Francisco Goyoaga, who took the first World Championship, organised by the F.E.I. in Paris in 1953. Goyoaga's father, Pedro, had been one of the leaders of Spanish show jumping in its early days. His own father had run a riding school, and Pedro Goyoaga brought together a few enthusiasts in 1907 to start a club. He himself won numerous international competitions. So Francisco 'Paco' Goyoaga had been jumping since an early age, and with no little success. For the World Championship Goyoaga was alloted by his Federation the horse Quorum, which Morenes had ridden in the silver medal team in London five years earlier. Those intervening five years had not been happy ones for the French-bred, however. He had taken a distinct dislike to the game, and in addition had a tendency to go lame. So the Spaniard's hopes were not very high.

His pessimism looked likely to be well-founded in the first of the qualifying rounds, for they only just squeezed through. But Goyoaga was a determined and persuasive rider, and so they went through to the final.

In the final in Paris, Goyoaga finished with a total of eight faults, just a half in front of Thiedemann, who had been on Diamant, with d'Oriola, who had been riding his Olympic gold medal winner Ali Baba, third with 16 and Piero d'Inzeo, who was on Uruguay, fourth with 24.

The World Championships, which started by

Ted Williams and Pegasus, Wembley 1963

being run every year but now are held only every four years, have an unusual formula and one which does not have universal approval. After three qualifying rounds the top four riders pool their horses, and all of them ride each horse. This can be, and sometimes is, a distinct advantage to a rider with a horse that may be difficult to ride except by his regular jockey, but generally it does level things out, and can certainly produce an interesting display of horsemanship.

The Italian Grand Prix, in the lovely, cypress-edged Piazza de Sienna, had fallen to William Hanson and The Monarch, the first British victory in this competition. The only other one to date occurred ten years later when Harvey Smith and O'Malley, who was also owned by Bob Hanson, William's father, triumphed. William Hanson and the Irish-bred The Monarch won again for Britain in Dublin and, that autumn, in New York, but Hanson became seriously ill the following year and died, a great loss to the sport.

At the International Horse show in the summer of 1953 Foxhunter completed his unique treble victory in the classic King George V Gold Cup. After his exhaustion in 1952 Foxhunter was not brought out for the season until June, went extremely well throughout the tough Aachen show, and came back to London at the peak of his form as he showed by winning the first major competition of the week: and this time he made no mistake about qualifying for the King's Cup.

Late in the afternoon of the competition it looked distinctly possible that there would be no King George Cup, for the rain came down in such torrents that, almost within minutes the ring looked more suitable for a sailing gala than a show jumping competition. But show director Mike Ansell thrives on such situations—only once, in 1965, has the International been delayed by bad weather, and then but briefly—and within an hour some forty tons of sand was spread liberally round the arena.

The show had to go on, and though the ground was far from perfect for jumping, on it did indeed go, and on time too. The fifteen-fence course had been modified, but at first it looked still too difficult. Even Nizefela found it beyond him, but the popular young Irish Captain Michael Tubridy broke the spell on Red Castle. Altogether there were five clears, two others from Ireland, Piero d'Inzeo on Merano and Foxhunter.

The first jump-off: the brilliant Merano just touched a wall, but Red Castle and Foxhunter went clear again. Two left to jump a last time, and Red Castle was first. This time he had two fences down. Just as in Helsinki, Foxhunter could afford just one fence down, and this time he had it, a brick from the wall, now raised to 5 ft 6 in, which had foiled Merano. But that was all, home with four faults to victory and a record in the King George V Cup which has yet to be equalled.

Foxhunter continued his path of triumph throughout the show, including a clear to help Britain retain the Prince of Wales Cup, failing only, and narrowly, to hold off the future World Champions Raimondo d'Inzeo and Merano in the Daily Mail Cup, the Grand Prix. A couple of weeks later he helped the British team to a third successive victory in the Aga Khan Trophy, which they thus won outright, in Dublin. But at the Horse of the Year Show he had a heavy fall which probably did little for the horse's confidence. Although he went on another two and a half years, winning his last international competition in Dublin in 1956, his 78th international victory, Foxhunter rarely again showed his most brilliant form. But he had done enough to be, even today, the show jumper most people remember.

Unhappily, Michael Tubridy, who had made Llewellyn and Foxhunter fight hard for their King's Cup record, and who had appeared to have brilliant prospects, was killed in a schooling accident the following spring.

1954 may be regarded as the year in which German ascendancy in show jumping finally came to fruition. Fritz Thiedemann, individual bronze medallist in Helsinki and second to Goyoaga for the World Championship, had led the way. He was a rider of the old German school, demanding complete obedience from his horse. In the massive Meteor, of Holstein breeding, Thiedemann had a horse with which he could beat anyone, and in the 1954 King George Cup he and Alan Oliver on Red Admiral fought as breathless a finish as one could wish for. Completely contrasting in style they matched strides until, at last the German got his head in front.

In Madrid, Hans Gunter Winkler was winning the first of his two successive World Championships. Winkler and Halla, were as untypical of the characteristic stolid Teutonic show jumping combination as one could imagine. Winkler had not been taught how to show jump. His father, a riding school master, taught him dressage, but he learned about jumping by watching others. He went to endless trouble to improve his style, even to tying his stirrups to the girth of his saddle to keep his legs in the right position. Although he did not make his international debut until 1952 he learned fast.

For the only time in a World Championship it was decided that the holder should not have to qualify, but be immediately eligible for the final. So Goyoaga joined his uncle Colonel Jaime Gracia Cruz, on the Helsinki Olympic horse Quoniam, d'Oriola, with Arlequin, Salvatore Oppes of Italy on Pagoro and Winkler. In the final Winkler showed the way he has with horses by finishing with just four faults to win from d'Oriola, who had eight, and Goyoago, twelve. Oppes took fourth place with sixteen, ahead of Garcia Cruz, who had thirty.

The following year on his home ground in Aachen Winkler retained his title, but Raimondo d'Inzeo made him fight until the last ditch to do so. The two of them were still level at the end of the final, and had a jump-off on their 'reserve' horses. Raimondo d'Inzeo, riding his brother Piero's Nadir, hit the sunken ditch, and Winkler and Halla also went round with one error so they changed horses and jumped again. Winkler with

(L to R) Carol Hofmann, Mary Chapot and Kathy Kusner

Nadir were clear, but d'Inzeo, with Halla, again faulted at the sunken ditch. Third place went, no doubt much to the surprise of the experienced internationals, to Britain's Major Ronnie Dallas, riding Bones, the huge German horse that Duggie Stewart had been so successful on before Helsinki.

The United States team made their Pan American debut in 1955, but it was not an auspicious one, finishing fourth and last behind the Mexicans in Mexico City. The course must have been a formidable one, for the Mexicans' winning score was $71\frac{1}{4}$ faults. Argentina, with $89\frac{3}{4}$, were runners-up, ahead of Chile's $122\frac{1}{2}$. The individual competition was won by Lieut. Ricardo Vinals, who had been in the Mexican Helsinki team, on Acapulco, with $10\frac{3}{4}$ faults, from Argentina's Jorge Lucardi on Baturro, who had eighteen.

In Europe, the Italians and Germans were having things very much their own way. Italy took the Prince of Wales Cup, the Aga Khan Trophy and the Nations Cup in Paris, with Britain second each time; while at Aachen the Italians had in turn been beaten by the Germans, who, with Thiedemann and Winkler as a nucleus, were developing a squad of immense strength.

The British team did not win one Nations Cup that season, and one of the few bright spots was the appearance on the international scene of Dawn Palethorpe. The previous year, on her first appearance at the White City, Miss Palethorpe had finished third, behind Jose Bonnaud of

Harvey Smith and O'Malley, Rome 1967

France and Pat Smythe in the Queen Elizabeth Cup, and went on to take the National Ladies' Championship and the Leading Show Jumper title at Harringay. In the spring of 1955 Miss Palethorpe and Earlsrath Rambler, an Irish half-bred, were selected for the British team for Paris. At the International in July they won the first of two successive Queen Elizabeth Cups.

Two other horses who were to remain long and honourably on the scene achieved prominence at that time and pre-Olympic consideration. The first, Flanagan, had been brought over from Ireland by Brigadier Lyndon Bolton as an event horse. He went round both Badminton and Harewood before being bought by Bob Hanson and given to Pat Smythe to ride. She rode him with such effect that they won three classes at the Paris international.

Scorchin, owned by the late Miss Dorothy Paget, had been brought out by Ted Williams, then ridden effectively in international competition by Sue Whitehead. For the first time women riders were to be allowed into the show jumping in the Olympic Games, and Miss Whitehead and Scorchin were among those selected for the training squad, but Sue Whitehead had the bad luck to break an arm right at the beginning of training.

When the team for Stockholm was announced it was Wilf White and Nizefela, Pat Smythe with Flanagan and Peter Robeson on Scorchin. Dawn Palethorpe and Earlsrath Rambler were the reserves. A good team, a balance of experience and youthful ability, but at Stockholm they were to meet, in Germany and Italy, two great teams.

Stockholm

Although the Olympic Games of 1956 were held in Melbourne the strict Australian quarantine regulations meant that the equestrian events had to be staged elsewhere. It was decided to return to where they had begun in 1912: Stockholm. These were Halla's Games. Hans Gunter Winkler and Halla had twice won the World Championship, in 1954 and 1955, and, unlike many of their compatriots, they were a partnership, with perfect co-operation between horse and rider. As a result, when Winkler needed help most, Halla gave it to him, and two gold medals were the result.

The Stockholm arena, which had been built for the 1912 Games, was not as big as those of Helsinki and London; the early morning inspection gave an impression of too many fences, big fences and many of them not particularly solid. Heavy rain had left the ground sticky and slippery for the 66 starters. A double of big parallels with 28 ft in between (an awkward distance), followed soon after by 5 ft of poles over a seven-foot water, looked especially difficult; as did the treble, consisting of parallel poles, an upright, then parallel gates, which followed a 5 ft wall that was preceded at fairly close range by the 16 ft 3 in water.

Alfred Lutke-Westhues, the weakest member of the German team went first on Ala, a consistent mare, who knocked up sixteen faults; Piero d'Inzeo and Uruguay went round for half this, while Peter Robeson and Scorchin, after faulting at the water, proceeded to 'score' at the last three, the third element of the treble, the parallel gates, and two uprights. Thiedemann and Meteor pulled their team up as they were expected to do, round for eight faults, as did Pat Smythe on Flanagan. Flanagan, a comparatively small horse probably without truly Olympic scope found the parallel gates coming out of both the double and the treble just more than he could cope with.

The Italians had put their 'weak link' Salvatore Oppes on Pagoro, to go second, and he set them right back, with a total of 23 faults, which included a refusal in the double. Winkler and Halla jumped superbly, indeed almost too well for, clear until the last but one, a fairly narrow upright, the mare stood off much too far, made a courageous effort to clear it, and only just failed. They came home for four faults, the best of the first round, but in the process Halla's prodigious leap had strained Winkler's riding muscle and he was soon in the utmost agony.

Raimondo d'Inzeo and Merano, possibly his best horse ever, went round for eight faults, then Wilf White put up another of his consistent rounds to notch the same for Britain, faulting at the parallel gates out of the treble and then just nudging the last.

After all 66 horses had gone round once Germany led with 28 faults to Britain's 32 and Italy's 39. Argentina, for whom Carlos Delia and Discutido had had an unexpectedly poor round, for 15 faults, were next best with 47. Lying second to Winkler for the individual awards was d'Oriola, gold medallist four years earlier, on another of the little Anglo-Arabs with which he was able to produce such good results, perhaps because their temperament was so much akin to his own. Voulette, who stood only a fraction over 15 h.h., had burst round the course, stopped at the wall after the water and hit the middle of the treble, for a total of seven faults. Her second round for eight, however, left her only sixth.

Between rounds the main, almost the only, topic of conversation was whether or not Winkler would be able to ride in the second round. If not, then Germany would be out of the running; but Winkler himself, though eventually he had to be carried from the stand where he was watching the early part of the second round to be put into the saddle, had no thoughts of retiring.

Nelson Pessoa and Gran Geste at Hickstead

Lutke-Weshues and Ala cut their first round sixteen by half in the second, then Piero d'Inzeo took Uruguay round without hitting a fence but collecting three faults for a stop. Robeson and Scorchin collected twenty, but Oppes and Pagoro went for twenty-four. A battle was developing for second place, but an almost immaculate round by Meteor, for just four faults, left the Germans in a commanding position. Pat Smythe and Flanagan hit the first element of the treble and stopped at the second, hit the parallel gates going through it a second time and were given two time faults as well. So, with one horse each to go, Germany were well in front with 40 faults: Britain had 65 and Italy just one more. And the last of the Germans to go was Winkler and Halla.

Possibly there has never been a braver piece of riding in any show jumping championship than this. Winkler, in immense pain and in greater agony each time Halla jumped, could do nothing to help her. It took all his concentration to sit in the saddle and point the way. And that was all he needed to do, for Halla did the rest. Each fence she measured and leaped, clearing one after another and finally, still clear, through the finish. The first faultless round of the competition, and for Winkler both the individual and team gold medals.

Then, as is often the way in all levels of competition, after one, long-awaited clear round another comes immediately. From Raimondo d'Inzeo and Merano. If Wilf White and Nizefela too could go clear Britain would take the silver team medal and White and d'Inzeo would have to jump-off for the individual. Consistent as ever, Nizefela nearly did it, but the first big spread,

Princess Grace of Monaco and Anneli Drummond-Hay

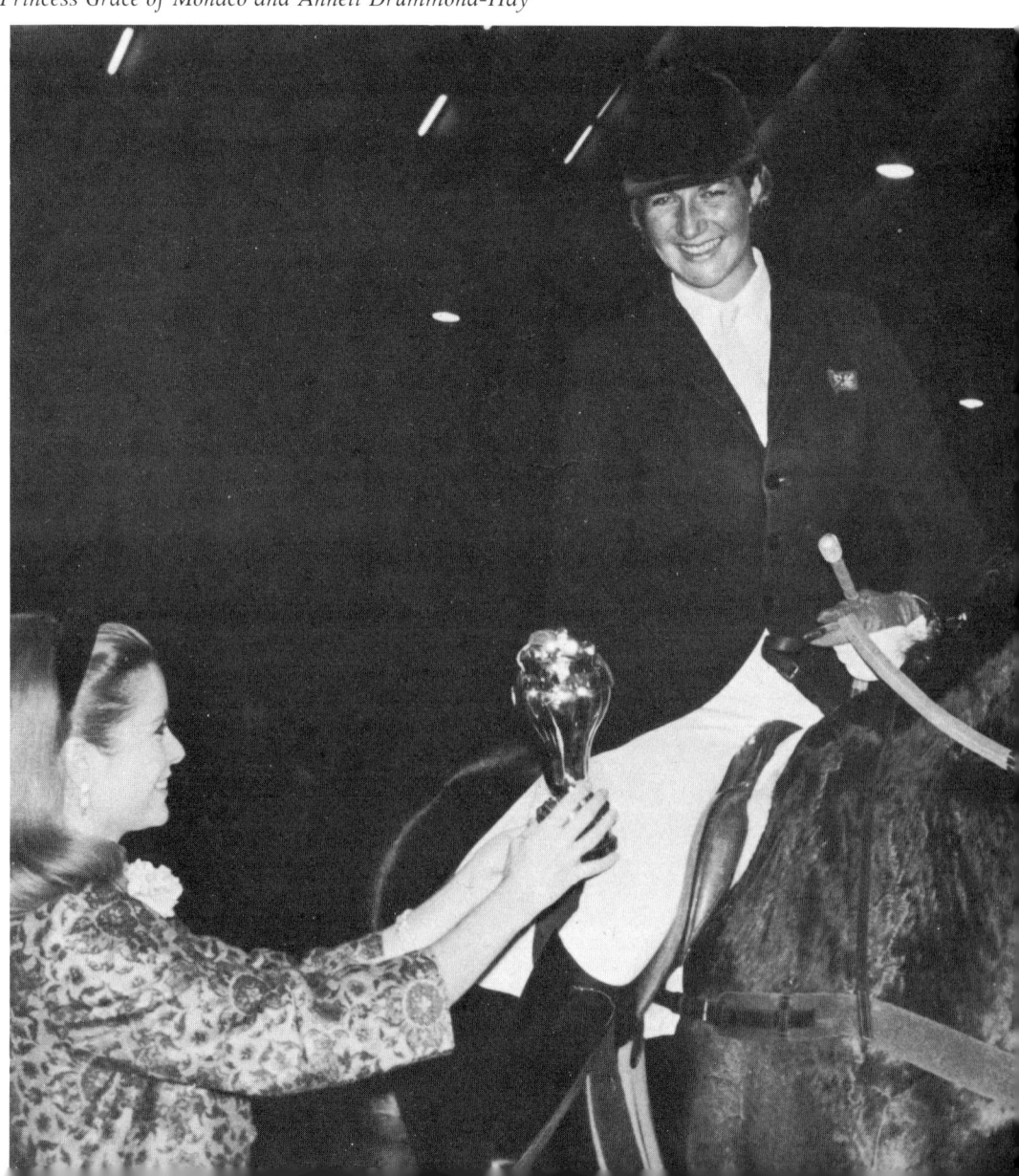

walls with parallel poles on top, foiled him. So Germany took the team gold, the first of a hat-trick, with Italy holding off Britain for second place by just three faults.

Although the event had, almost throughout, been the concern of just three teams, Stockholm contained a few significant pointers for what was to come, the most important of them coming from the United States. Their young team, Bill Steinkraus, who had been in the Helsinki bronze medal team, Frank Chapot and Hugh Wiley were the first to represent the U.S.E.T. since Bertalan de Nemethy, one-time Hungarian cavalry officer, had been appointed trainer. He was, in just a few years, to produce what is generally reckoned the most stylish team in the world, and one, moreover, which combines style with effectiveness. In Stockholm they were fifth, with $104\frac{1}{4}$ faults; four years later in Rome with George Morris in for Wiley, they took the silver behind Germany, and in Mexico Steinkraus won the individual gold.

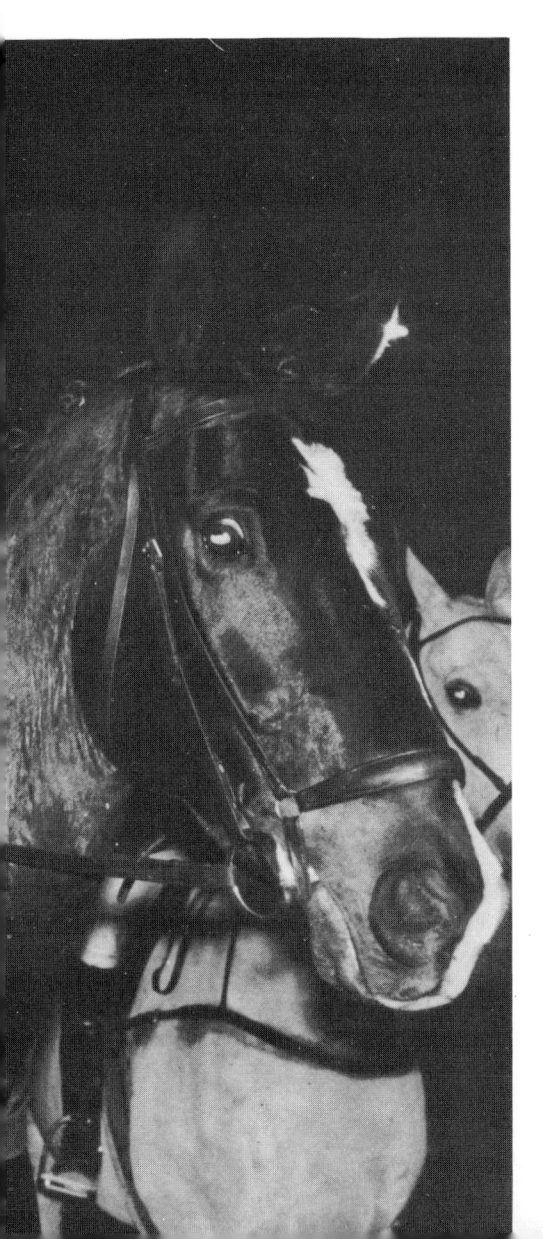

Stockholm also had the first competitor from 'Down Under', the Australian Bert Jacobs with Dumbell. They did not finish, but it was at least a start.

Winkler's injury in the Olympics meant that he was unable to defend his world title when it was held in Aachen where, for the first time in its short history, the World Championship really lived up to its title, with competitors from the United States, South America, Japan and the Middle East. Still Europe provided three of the four finalists, Goyoaga of Spain, winner of the first championship, on Fahnenkonig, Raimondo d'Inzeo of Italy with Merano and Germany's Thiedemann and Meteor, joined by the Argentinian rider, Carlos Delia with Discutido.

Delia, going first, on his own horse, was obviously not at ease with the formula of the World Championship, and lost his chance straight away. D'Inzeo and Merano had just half a time fault, while the other two were clear. Goyoaga had a stop at the awkwardly-placed parallels on Merano, d'Inzeo was nearly in trouble with Meteor, but came home clear, as did Thiedemann and Discutido. But Thiedemann collected four faults on Fahnenkonig, a German-bred horse and probably the best Goyoaga ever had, at the parallels.

Both Goyoaga, with a three-fault total, and Thiedemann, who had four, were clear in the last round, in which d'Inzeo, who had only his half a time fault, had to ride Fahnenkonig. The big horse was not the sort he most favoured, but d'Inzeo rode him round steadily and slowly, jumping clear. They collected one and a quarter time faults, and with the half gained earlier, d'Inzeo had won the world title with one and a quarter faults to spare.

Although beaten in the Olympic Games, the British team, which was opened up to include a number of less experienced riders, had a good record in 1956, winning five out of the six Nations Cups in which they started: Lucerne, Stockholm, London, Dublin and Rotterdam. In Aachen a Brazilian team which included Nelson Pessoa won its first ever Nations Cup in Europe.

For the first time a British team, Mary Barnes, Chris Middleton, Jan White and Michael Freer, was entered for the European Junior Championship, at Spa, Belgium, and won. It had been felt that the British children, mounted as they habitually were on ponies, would be at a considerable disadvantage with their continental rivals who, having no indigenous pony breeds, primarily rode horses. The fallacy of this theory was ex-

Winkler, Schockemohle, Schridde and Jarasinski of 1962 German Nations Cup team

ploded immediately, and thoroughly, for Britain won every European Junior Championship until 1961, and of the fourteen championships which have been held from 1956 to 1969 have won no fewer than ten.

At the International Horse Show in London, Bill Steinkraus won the first of his two King George Cups (he won again in 1964 with Sinjon) when he had the only two clear rounds, an achievement previously attained only by Brian Butler in 1949, on First Boy and his Olympic horse Night Owl. Steinkraus nominated as the winner Miss Joan Magid's brilliant, but temperamental First Boy rather than his own horse.

Foxhunter won his last international competition in Dublin that summer, his 78th in all, then retired to his owner's Welsh farm, where he was a hunter until he died of a ruptured kidney in 1959.

The World Championship was renamed European Championship in 1957, but the formula remained unchanged for that year, and it was still open to riders from any part of the world. Only recently have the F.E.I. decided, quite correctly, that continental championships should be confined to riders from that continent, otherwise the name would be meaningless.

Winkler, fit again, regained the title, though without his great mare Halla. Instead he rode Sonnenglanz, a half-brother to Halla, out of the half-bred mare Helene by a trotting stallion, but without Halla's calm temperament. Indeed, Sonnenglanz's intractability played a big part in Winkler's victory in Rotterdam, for when they got through to the final the other three riders found him no easy horse to cope with. Italy's Marquis de Medici retired into fourth place after Sonnenglanz had had him on the ground twice.

Winkler, with an aggregate of 8 faults, won from the French Captain de Fombelle, who rode Bucephale, with Oppes, the second Italian in the final, third with 24. Oppes's horse, Pagoro, had the best record in the competition, going clear with each rider. Winkler also won the German International Jumping championship that year, the first time it was held, in Aachen, with Halla.

Veteran British rider Ted Williams, who had started his career with horses riding for a horse dealer, was given his amateur licence, which made him eligible for all official events under F.E.I. rules except the Olympic Games, in the winter of 1956, and the following spring was off with the British team in Nice and Rome. There was no Nations Cup in Nice, but at Rome the British team, consisting of Williams, riding the ex-Australian Dumbell, along with Llewellyn on Aherlow, Dawn Palethorpe on Earlsrath Rambler and Tom Barnes with Sudden, finished second to Italy. They had their revenge, with Nizefela and Flanagan in for Aherlow and Sudden, in the Prince of Wales Cup.

In Spa Pat Smythe won the first women's European Championship, the first of four times she took the title. In a jump-off she and Flanagan beat Italy's Giulia Serventi on Doly, a French-bred by that great sire of show jumpers, Furioso.

When the European season was over Williams, Pat Smythe and Dawn Palethorpe went on the North American circuit, where they took on riders from Argentina, Chile, Mexico, Canada, Ireland and the United States, but still won a total of twelve competitions, more than any other country, at the three shows, Harrisburg, New York and Toronto.

Ted Williams and Pegasus, leading horse in Britain no fewer than five times and one of the

53

David Broome and Mister Softee in the 1967 European Championship

great characters of the sport, showed that they were not only a superlative national combination by winning the Grand Prix at all three shows. The following year, when riding for Britain at Aachen, Williams had a nasty fall from Dumbell and broke a bone in his neck. This put him out of action for a time and left the British team much the weaker: in the Nations Cup, won by Spain from the United States and Germany, Britain was only sixth.

The European Championship, on a new formula, with points towards the final title being accumulated in a series of competitions, was also held at Aachen. It stayed in Germany through the agency of Thiedemann and Meteor, who totalled 106 points to beat Piero d'Inzeo and The Rock, with 98·3 pts. The holder Winkler, with Halla, was third, only 0·3 point behind the Italian.

Nizefela, eighth in the European Championship, jumped in his ninth Prince of Wales Cup, and had two clear rounds, when the United States team just held the British, with four faults to eight. The King's Cup went to Hugh Wiley, on Master William. The Americans were now really beginning to feel their strength, though they received a salutory lesson on the unpredictability of show jumping when beaten in Dublin by a scratch team of Britons, George Hobbs, with Royal Lord, Jill Banks, on her sister's Earlsrath Rambler, Marshall Charlesworth with Smokey Bob and Harvey Smith on the horse which first brought him to the top, Farmer's Boy.

In the absence of Pat Smythe, or of any other British competitor, Giulia Serventi, who had been runner-up for the women's European Championship in 1957, won the title on Doly in Palermo. She beat Anna Clement, one of remarkably few top class women riders from Germany, on Nico, winners of the 1959 Queen Elizabeth II Cup, with Irene Jansen of Holland third with Adelbloom.

In 1958 the first, and so far the only official team from South Africa came to Europe. It was a young team, and finished second to Britain in the European Junior Championship, but Gonda

Butters, although she was only fourteen years old, rode her three horses, of whom the best was Oorskiet, with remarkable success against senior riders.

Although other South African riders, notably Bob Grayston and Mickey Louw, have come to Europe and won in the highest company, the horse sickness ban which came into force about 1960, has prevented them bringing any South African horses since then. This ban is imposed autonomously by each country and there is, I understand, a chance that it may be lifted in some countries in the not too distant future, probably subject to a period of quarantine.

In the winter Chile staged an Inter-Continental championship, with several top European riders taking on those from the Americas. The horses were chosen from a pool of the top performers from Chile, Argentina and Colombia. Once again, Pierre Jonqueres d'Oriola showed his sympathetic touch on all four horses in the final to win from Britain's Col. C. H. 'Monkey' Blacker. Argentina's Hugo Arrambide and Captain Gaston Zuniga of Chile, though they had had the good fortune to draw their own horses, finished only third and fourth.

The United States team came back for another successful tour in 1959, the year before the Rome Olympics. In Rome they beat Italy for the Nations Cup, with a zero score to the home country's eight; were third in Paris, which was won, to the surprise of just about everybody concerned, by Russia; in Aachen Italy improved on their Rome form to beat the U.S. by seven faults to sixteen; then in London, the Americans last port of call before returning home, they won the Prince of Wales Cup for the second year running, though only narrowly from Spain and Britain. Hugh Wiley, this time riding Nautical, a palomino of tremendous scope, won his second successive King George V Cup, as well as taking both the Loriners' Cup and the Saddle of Honour, for the most successful rider at the International Horse Show.

Returning to the United States the team won the Pan American Games Championship in Chicago in August. The team was Bill Steinkraus and Riviera Wonder, Wiley on Nautical, who, in the second round had the only 'clear' of the competition, Frank Chapot on Diamant, the horse Thiedemann had ridden into second place in the 1953 World Championship, and George Morris with Night Owl. There was no individual classification, but if there had been the winner would have been Wiley and Nautical, with an aggregate of eight faults for the two rounds. Brazil, with a total of 59 faults to the winners' 32, were second; their team included the veteran Ferreira on Marengo, which was to be his Rome horse, and Nelson Pessoa (possibly the most brilliant rider Brazil has produced—certainly the one who has met with the most success in

G. Mancinelli and Rockette, Rome 1963

Europe). Third place, with $80\frac{3}{4}$ faults, went to Chile, for whom the Helsinki silver medal horse Pillan, now ridden by Gaston Zuniga, was still going strong. Argentina were fourth, ahead of Venezuela.

Ann Townsend and her German-bred horse Bandit IV, a Hanoverian that she had bought from Carlos Figueroa at the previous year's Horse of the Year Show, was having a great season, especially in *puissance* events. Miss Townsend started the season by being leading woman rider at the Lisbon, Madrid and Paris internationals; in London they tied for the *puissance* with Dawn Wofford—Miss Palethorpe had married American Warren Wofford—on the Olympic horse Hollandia, and Ann was runner-up to Wiley for the leading rider award. Then, in Rotterdam, she and Bandit just held off Pat Smythe and Flanagan for the European title, with 30 points to 29.33. The previous year's winner and runner-up, Giulia Serventi and Anna Clement, were equal third.

The men's championship, in Paris, reverted to the 'world' formula of finding four finalists who then ride each other's horses. Piero d'Inzeo with Uruguay, a French-bred then seventeen years old, broke the German domination of the title. In the final d'Inzeo totalled eight faults for his four rides, to beat d'Oriola, with $16\frac{1}{2}$ and Thiedemann, the title holder, who collected 24. Winkler, with half a fault more, was the fourth finalist.

In the spring of that year the B.S.J.A. had selected a dozen riders for training to decide on the Rome Olympic squad, including David Broome who showed how wise that selection had been by having his best season, especially on the ex-Army horse Wildfire that his father had bought in the autumn of 1957 for just £60.

Wildfire had, to say the least, a dubious reputation, but the Broomes, David and father Fred, wrought such a change that he finished up the season's leading horse in Britain. A trip to Rotterdam added international successes to the national ones.

Rome—d'Inzeo's day

In the spring of Olympic year the group from whom the team was to be selected was brought together for final training under Jack Talbot-Ponsonby: Pat Smythe, with Flanagan and Grand Manan, owned by the Hon. Mrs. Edward Kidd; Colonel Blacker and Workboy, formerly a steeplechaser; Ann Townsend and Bandit; Wilf White with Nizefela, still going, if not quite as strong as ever, and Scorchin; Marshall Charlesworth with Smokey Bob; David Barker with Franco; and David Broome with Wildfire. Franco, at seven, was the youngest horse of the squad. By the sprinter Como, he had trained as a racehorse as a youngster, but showed more aptitude for show jumping. In 1959 Barker had ridden him in the winning teams in Le Zoute and Rotterdam.

The British picture was changed, and remarkably improved only weeks before the Games were held, early in September. Mr. Oliver Anderson's Sunsalve, Queen's Cup winner with his daughter Elizabeth in 1957, had been given to Pat Smythe as a second horse but on a pre-Games trip with the team to Wiesbaden and Lucerne, where they finished second to the U.S.A., Pat Smythe realised Sunsalve was not her sort of horse, so he was given to Broome to ride. A long talk with the owner gave Broome the clue to Sunsalve's quirks. The chestnut proved a brilliant jumper once Broome had won his confidence, and within two weeks of coming together they had won the King George V Cup. Dublin showed the other side of the coin, but taught Broome a little more about his prospective Olympic mount.

The four riders finally named to travel were Broome, with Sunsalve and Wildfire, Pat Smythe, with Flanagan and Scorchin, Dawn Wofford with Hollandia, an addition to the original list, and David Barker with Franco.

Clearly the teams most highly rated for the gold medal were Germany, with Winkler's Halla and Thiedemann's Meteor still in form and a number of younger riders to join them, and the ever-improving Americans. Italy still had not found a third rider on a par with the brothers d'Inzeo, while France, tied up with military troubles, had no one to match up to d'Oriola.

For the first time since Antwerp in 1920 (Stockholm in 1912 had been the only other occasion), there were to be two separate jumping competitions, the individual in the Piazza di Sienna, home of the Italian official international show, and the team competition, according to tradition, in the Olympic Stadium on the closing day. The course for the individual was not, at first sight, an inviting one, the fences were without much substance, and often had false ground lines, or none at all. The treble at No. 7 looked a particularly tricky customer, a wall, then 23 ft 9 in to a triple bar, followed, at 29 ft 6 in, by parallel poles. The long double at No. 11, coming soon after a high upright, was another likely to cause trouble.

It began just after seven o'clock in the morning, and Raimondo d'Inzeo, to the delight of thousands of his fellow countrymen, showed early on how it should be done, clear with his ten-year-old Posillipo in superb style; but it was an example

Mary Chapot and White Lightning winning the Queen Elizabeth Cup in 1968

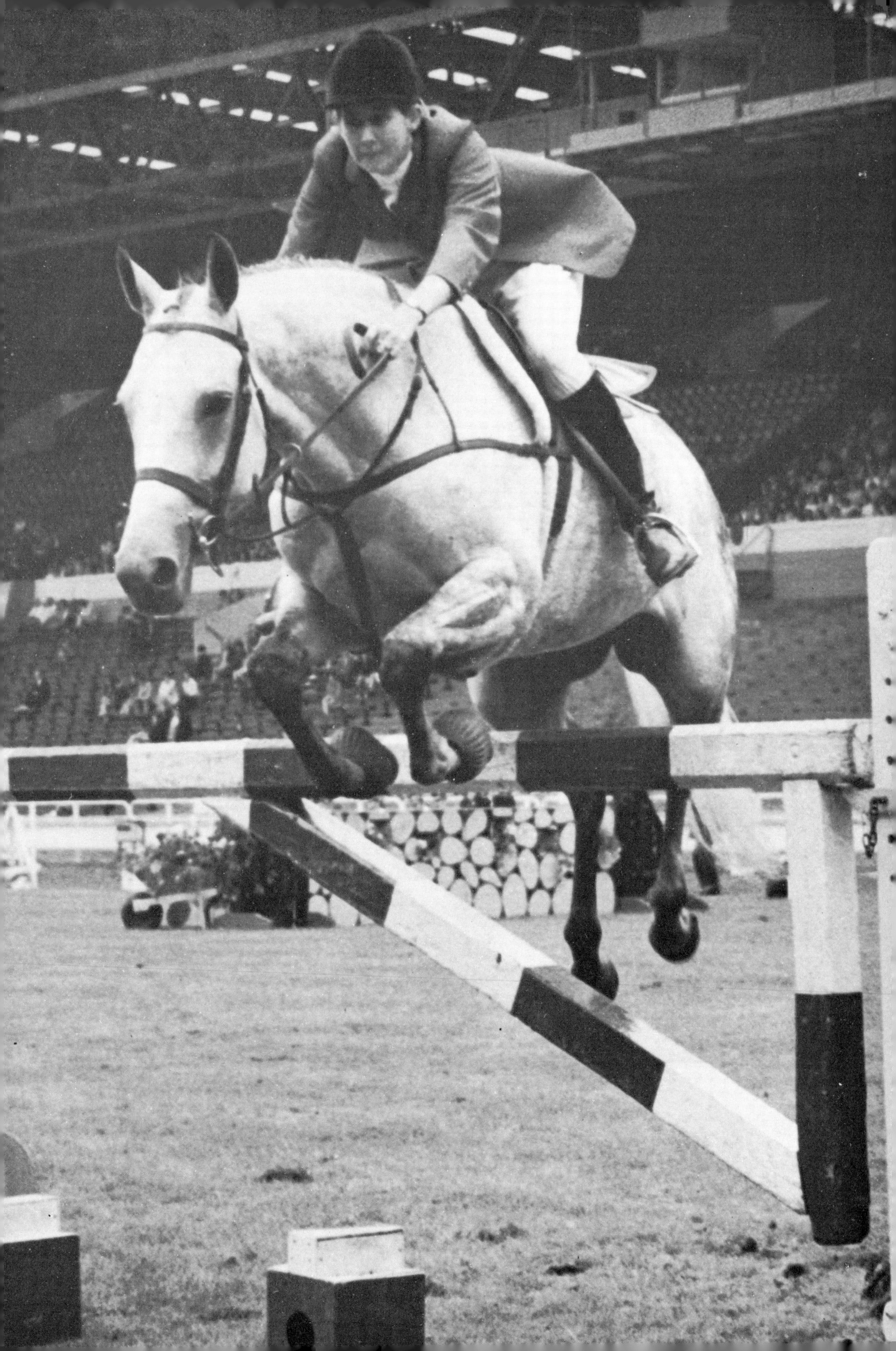

no other could follow, not even Raimondo in his second round. It was the only clear of the entire competition. Winkler and Halla had a rare off-day, seventeen faults, while Thiedemann with Meteor could do no better than $13\frac{1}{2}$. At the end of the first round second place was held by the Argentinian rider Dasso on Final, with just four faults. Lying third, with eight faults apiece were Piero d'Inzeo on the massive Irish-bred grey The Rock, hero of so many *puissance* competitions, and Max Fresson of France on Grand Veneur. Broome and Sunsalve had collected sixteen faults, with the chestnut still inclined to go at some of his fences like a runaway Ferrari.

second the young Welshman showed something of the brilliance that was to rocket him to the top of international show jumping. Sunsalve, perhaps being overchecked, had a stop at the wall, but otherwise clear for fence after fence until the last, a big parallel in the shadow of one of the cypress trees which abound in the Piazza di Sienna. There a clip, for a total of seven and a grand, two-round aggregate of 23. The third best so far, and there it stayed. Dasso appeared to go to pieces after a fine start to his second round when Final faulted at the water and finished with 24 faults. So it was the d'Inzeos, Raimondo and Piero, first and second, with Broome, whose

Alwin Schockemohle and Ferdl

In blazing hot sun for the second round Raimondo d'Inzeo and Posillipo could not quite maintain their early morning precision, and had three down for a grand total of twelve: beatable by three horses, had they gone clear. Piero d'Inzeo and The Rock repeated their first round eight, while Fresson and Grand Veneur added a disastrous $29\frac{1}{4}$ to his. Broome and Sunsalve were well back in the first round placings, but in the

second-round score was the best of all, taking the bronze.

Pat Smythe on Flanagan, who finished 11th equal, and Dawn Wofford, on that game old American veteran Hollandia, joint 20th, had been the other British in the individual, but David Barker and Franco were brought in to replace Hollandia for the team. Had Barker had his baptism of fire in the individual, the story of the team competition might have been a different one.

Eighteen teams lined up for the Prix des Nations, in the 100,000 capacity stadium, with only a sprinkling of spectators for the start. For nearly an hour the competitors are kept waiting to start, then the first man in, from the Turkish team, ended up being carried from the ring.

Hardly the sort of atmosphere in which to make one's Olympic debut, but in, at No. 2, came David Barker. It was soon clear that all was not well with the young Yorkshireman and his thoroughbred. Franco was jumping, but without the impulse he was going to need. At the treble,

calculations could have been no more than hypothetical.

For the rest, however, the competition was going very much to form. The water, at No. 7, was causing most of the faults: Thiedemann and Meteor and Germany's No. 3, Alwin Schockemohle with Ferdl, went into it both times. America's Bill Steinkraus with Ksar d'Esprit, one of the best *puissance* horses of all time, were slightly below their best, hitting the water and both elements of the double at 10.

At the end of the first round Germany, with $25\frac{3}{4}$ faults, led from the U.S.A. at 29. Italy, though third, were trailing with $52\frac{1}{2}$; Posillipo had been

Ted Williams and Pegasus

No. 5, Franco stopped after going over the first two parts; round again, and another stop. The third time Barker got him over, then clear right until the last of the fourteen fences, then another refusal. So Barker and Franco were eliminated, and with them went the chances of the British team, for even though the jury decided that eliminated riders should be credited with the worse score in the round plus 20 the ensuing

as consistent as ever, hitting only the first part of 10, but Oppes with The Scholar had $24\frac{1}{2}$, and incredibly, The Rock was only half a fault less.

Second time round, save only for Ksar d'Esprit, who after early faults at four and the first part of five pulled himself together, the Americans slipped slightly. Not so the German team, with victory now well in their grasp. Meteor again had only the water and one fence down, as did

Elizabeth Anderson and Sunsalve

Ferdl, plus the three-quarters of a time fault, and the marvellous Halla went round with just a nick at the last, to give the Germans a total of $46\frac{1}{2}$ to the U.S.A's 66.

Italy, for whom Posillipo, with another four-fault round had the best score of the competition, totalled $80\frac{1}{2}$, ahead of the United Arab Republic, $135\frac{1}{2}$; France, $168\frac{3}{4}$ and Rumania, the only other to finish, at $174\frac{1}{2}$. Altogether twelve of the eighteen countries had been eliminated, nine of them in the first round.

The record books show no clear rounds throughout the team competition, but if David Broome and Sunsalve did not get one they came extremely close to doing so. By the time they came in for the second round they had nothing to lose, and a good deal of kudos to gain if they could jump the only clear. Sunsalve was in his best possible mood, jumping exuberantly and exactly as his rider was asking him. Clear of the first six, approaching the water just right and soaring over; through the finish with still not a pole down, a zero flicked up on the board, then down again to be replaced by a four. A foot in the water was the explanation; there was no way of proving anything one way or the other, but at least the consolation, unlike poor Wilf White in Helsinki, that nothing depended on it other than the personal satisfaction of jumping the only clear round.

A few days after the Olympic Games the World Championship was held in Venice, on the usual pattern. Through to the final went Raimondo d'Inzeo with Gowran Girl, Broome and Sunsalve, Bill Steinkraus on Ksar d'Esprit and Huipil ridden by Carlos Delia, from whom the Broomes had bought his Helsinki and Stockholm Olympic veteran Discutido. D'Inzeo had made a clever choice in riding Gowran Girl in the championship for this eight-year-old by Water Serpent, which he had brought out only the year previously was, to say the least of it, a difficult ride. When the other riders came to try their skill on her Delia collected twelve faults, Broome and Steinkraus sixteen apiece, and d'Inzeo collected the world title, or rather kept the one he had won in Aachen four years earlier.

Broome and Sunsalve had their revenge the following year when the European Championship was held in Aachen. Throughout the preliminary rounds the Welshman and Piero d'Inzeo, with Pioneer, battled it out, and when it came to the final Broome had to finish in the first two to take the title. Five of them went through to the timed jump-off. Callado of Portugal, on Konak, was round in 39·1 sec, Winkler with Romanus (Halla had now retired to stud), was also clear in a second longer, then Italy's Mancinelli, in an endeavour to help his compatriot, though he himself had no chance of the title, took Rockette round in 37·1 sec. Broome and Sunsalve came into the ring, before a packed 35,000 crowd, tense as only an Aachen crowd can be. They could not afford one mistake, and at the treble, where the great chestnut was almost down on his nose, at least one fence down seemed certain. But two great leaps took them clear, and home in 36·7 sec. Unable either to beat Broome or to drop below second place, d'Inzeo and Pioneer opted out of the barrage. Winkler took third place overall.

In Deauville, Pat Smythe regained the European title she had won in 1957, with more than ten points to spare over her nearest rival, the Dutch girl Irene Jansen. Later that year Miss Smythe was invited to jump in Australia, evidence of the growing interest in the sport in that country.

At the All-England Jumping Course at Hickstead, Sussex, which had been started by Douglas Bunn the previous year, the European Junior Championships were won by Germany, bringing to an end a five-year run by the British, who that year could finish no higher than third, behind Holland. Also at Hickstead, which has been financed from the start by W. D. & H. O. Wills, Seamus Hayes with Goodbye won the first British Jumping Derby with the only clear round in an event which soon became a classic in its field.

As always after an Olympic season, the subsequent year was used to try out new riders and horses. Germany had the edge in the Nations Cups of 1961, winning its own show in Aachen and then at Dublin and Geneva, each time with the Italians runners-up, and in Ostend, beating Ireland; however, with the exception of Sunsalve, probably the outstanding horse that season was Piero d'Inzeo's The Rock. Since his international debut just over four years earlier, The Rock, a massive grey bred in Ireland by Water Serpent, had won major competitions all over Europe; in only his second full season he had taken the 1958 Italian Grand Prix, and in 1961 he and d'Inzeo won the first of two consecutive King George V Cups and the Grand Prix in Aachen.

In contrast to The Rock, the Queen's Cup winner that year was the 14·3 h.h. Oorskiet, brought over by Gonda Butters from South Africa and now being ridden successfully by Lady Sarah Fitzalan-Howard, daughter of the Duke and Duchess of Norfolk.

Although The Rock was so successful, Italy's own Grand Prix went to Ireland. The Irish team had won the Nations Cup in Nice and when they went on to Rome, Captain Billy Ringrose and Loch an Easpaig beat the home team for their most coveted individual prize. Loch an Easpaig, the best Irish Army horse since the War, won a great number of important prizes both on the

Janou Lefebvre and Rocket

Continent and in North America until he dropped dead in the ring during the 1967 Nations Cup in Ostend.

The only Nations Cup victory for Britain came in Rotterdam, when Valerie Clark (who became Mrs. David Barker) won the Grand Prix on Atalanta in her first overseas international. Atalanta had only been upgraded the previous year, and in the intense heat had to go first in the 15-horse jump-off. They went clear, and none of those who followed, including Sunsalve, could emulate them.

In Britain, the B.S.J.A., finally accepting that competitions resulting in a dead-heat of any number of horses were not calculated to appeal to the public, brought in a change of rule so that in any competition worth £50 or more, the second jump-off had to be timed.

In New York, the Argentinian team won the Nations Cup, but the U.S.A. made no mistake in Toronto; the outstanding horse, however, was Canada's O'Malley, ridden by Jimmy Elder. O'Malley, by an American thoroughbred, Peep Show, was only six when he won the individual championship, and was bought for a reputed 30,000 dollars by Yorkshire businessman Bob Hanson and brought to England.

Because of Broome's triumph in Aachen the European Championship of 1962 came to London, to be incorporated in the Royal International at the White City, but the holder was not given the chance to defend it. The great Sunsalve had died of a heart attack, and although Broome's Wildfire ended the season leading money winner and National Champion he was not thought of a high enough standard for a European Championship. Broome had a second string to his bow, too, in Mrs. Edward Kidd's Grand Manan, who had jumped two clear rounds in Barcelona only the month before to help Britain beat Spain by 12 faults to sixteen in the Nations Cup.

Britain's choice for the championship fell on Peter Robeson with Firecrest, a horse of exceptional promise that he had bought from leading Scottish rider Duggie Iggulden some years before, and David Barker with Mister Softee, who had been bought by the Massarella family in Dublin. Robeson and Barker had been

Frank Chapot and San Lucas

The final parade at the Horse of the Year Show

in the team which went to Nice and Rome, both times finishing second to the Italians. Going on to Lucerne the British team, Barker on Mister Softee, Robeson on Firecrest, Pat Smythe with Flanagan and Valerie Clark on Franco—as her own horse was a last-minute casualty—beat a German team which included Winkler, Schridde and Schockemohle.

The Nations Cup went to a jump-off, and Mister Softee jumped three clear rounds, his third the fastest of all. Riders are allowed two horses in the preliminary rounds of a European Championship, the highest placed one counting towards the rider's total, and Barker concentrated on Franco in the 'preliminaries'. The championship rules can vary, sometimes the points gained in the preliminary rounds count towards the title, but in 1962 they only decided the finalists.

The final event was run in Nations Cup style, two rounds over a big, 14-fence course up to 5 ft 6 in. First time round only Mister Softee and Piero d'Inzeo with the Rock were clear, with Winkler and Schockemohle on four faults. Second time round The Rock had two fences down, Mister Softee flattened at the 13th, but cleared the final double of parallels to keep the title in Britain. The Rock and Winkler's Romanus finished equal second, on eight, with Peter Robeson and Firecrest, who had had twelve the first time followed by a clear round, equal fourth with Raimondo d'Inzeo and Posillipo.

The United States team was making a short

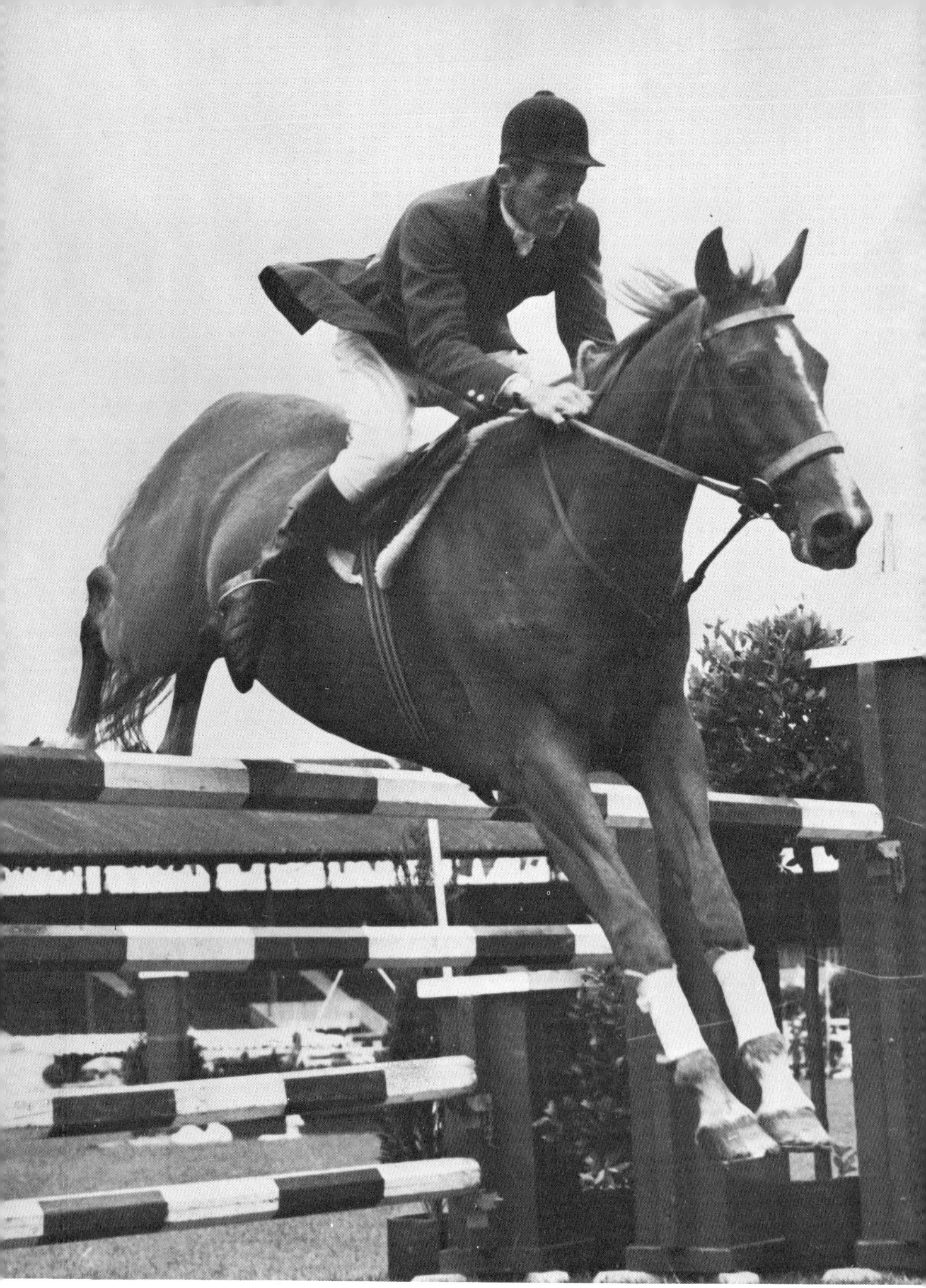

European tour, with the experienced Bill Steinkraus, Hugh Wiley and Frank Chapot joined by Kathy Kusner, who had already made her name as a steeplechase rider as well as a show jumper, Bill Robertson and one of the most stylish riders of all, Mary Mairs. They won the Nations Cup in Aachen, beating Germany, but the tables were turned on them in London when Germany won and the U.S.A. and Italy were equal second. In Dublin, Italy won from the U.S.A. with Britain third; clearly none of the teams that season was dominant.

The Brazilian Nelson Pessoa started a run in 1961 which had him labelled 'Derby specialist': in Hamburg that year he won on Espartaco, was equal first with the only two clear rounds in 1963 on Espartaco and Gran Geste and won again on Gran Geste in 1965. And in both 1963 and 1965 he and Gran Geste also won the British Jumping Derby at Hickstead.

Japan and Korea, preparing for the Tokyo Games, had a match, riding New Zealand and Australian-bred horses.

The British junior team journeyed to Berlin to regain the European title: a team notable for the international debut of Marion Coakes and Stroller, just six years before Miss Coakes, still riding her fantastic pony Stroller, was to become the first woman ever to win an individual Olympic show jumping medal.

Mancinelli, having tried so hard to help Piero d'Inzeo win the European Championship in 1961, took the title himself when it was fought out on the Piazza di Sienna in 1963. With Rockette, reputed to be a full-sister to The Rock, he finished the championship with just six points, two in front of Alwin Schockemohle of Germany on Freiherr, with Harvey Smith and O'Malley third.

Smith, who had taken to the great Canadian horse so quickly that only a month after he first had him he won the John Players Trophy, the most valuable competition at the Royal International Horse Show, was only the second Briton to win the Rome Grand Prix, just ten years after Bill Hanson had won it on The Monarch.

Piero d'Inzeo, having 'domestic troubles' with his National Federation, was dropped from the Italian team that year, and the strong British team took full advantage of his absence to beat the home side in Rome. It was a team which included not only Mister Softee but a horse and rider whose rise had been nothing short of meteoric. Anneli Drummond-Hay and Merely-a-Monarch, a horse of such quality that one well-known National Hunt trainer was sure he could have trained him to win the Grand National, had won the Burghley three-day event in 1961, Badminton the following spring and then, as women were not at that time allowed in the Olympic three-day event, turned to show jumping. Within weeks they won the Imperial Cup, one of the oldest at the Royal International, and at Rome in 1963 they jumped two clear rounds to contribute to Britain's Nations Cup victory. Later that summer they finished third when Pat Smythe completed her unique hat-trick of victories in the European Women's Championship at Hickstead, a feat which will not soon be equalled.

British teams had a successful time in 1963, winning four of the six Nations Cups they contested—Rome, London, Ostend and Rotterdam—with a total of thirteen different riders, of whom, strangely enough, David Broome was not one. Their victory in London, at the expense of Ireland and Italy, was Britain's first Prince of Wales win since 1957.

The Irish, too, were able to please their home crowd when they took the Aga Khan Trophy, the first time since 1949. Led by Ringrose and Loch an Easpaig, the team also included Diana Conolly-Carew's Barrymore, making his international debut that year. The Irish grey and his dashing rider have since won all over Europe and North America. Tommy Wade and Dundrum, one of the most popular combinations ever to come out of Ireland took the King George Cup, and were the only ones to jump two clear rounds in the Aga Khan.

Raimondo d'Inzeo and Posillipo won the Aachen Grand Prix with, in second place, France's Janou Lefebvre and Kenavo. A graduate of the junior team, this was Miss Lefebvre's first year in senior internationals but her victories that season included the Grand Prix in Dinard and the French Jumping Derby, held at La Baule.

O'Malley finished the season leading horse in Britain, while that year Mr. Frank Smith bought the first two horses from Nelson Pessoa, Carnaval and Careta, of the string that Ted Williams was to ride with such startling success.

In Sao Paolo the United States team were having a tune-up for the Tokyo Olympics by winning both the team and the individual competitions in the Pan American Games. Mary Mairs and Tomboy, a versatile mare then eight years old, by Wait-a-Bit, who had made their international debut in the previous year's European tour were trailing the experienced Argentinian Carlos Delia on Popin at the end of the first round, with a total of $5\frac{3}{4}$ faults to $4\frac{1}{4}$. Next time round, however, the nineteen-year-old American girl went round with just one fence down, and no time faults, while Delia had two

Alan Oliver and Red Admiral

Lucia Faria and Rush du Camp

down and a quarter for time. With an aggregate $9\frac{3}{4}$ Miss Mairs had $2\frac{3}{4}$ to spare, with the Chilean Americo Simonetti and El Gitano, who had also notched a four-fault second circuit, one fault behind Delia in third place. For the team prize Tomboy, Bill Steinkraus on Sinjon, Kathy Kusner on Unusual and Frank Chapot with San Lucas totalled $44\frac{1}{4}$ faults; Argentina, on $52\frac{1}{2}$, were second, ahead of Chile, with 69. Mexico were fourth, Brazil fifth and Uruguay eliminated.

At the New York show Gail Ross and Tom Gayford gave warning of the growing strength of Canadian show jumping. Miss Ross won the Grand Prix on her seven-year-old Thunderbird, who went on to score in the international championship in Toronto, while Gayford and Blue Beau established a new high-jump record for the show of 7 ft 1 in.

The Olympic Games in Tokyo in 1964 were not due to be held until October, after the European season was over. This gave plenty of time to make the team selections, too much probably, and raised the problem of having horses fit at the right time. The B.S.J.A. announced at the end of 1963 their intention of having a series of 'trials' during the ensuing season, which turned out to be a disastrous move with only one of the twelve named for the short list making the team: Peter Robeson's Firecrest. Barker and Mister Softee looked assured of their place in the team, but the rock-hard going at the first trial, at Windsor, put 'Softee' out for the season. The most impressive horse in the second trial was Andrew Fielder's huge Vibart, and as Fielder was only seventeen he was too young for the Games, though they were included in the team which went to Aachen.

At this, the toughest show of the year, Britain's Olympic hopes could hardly have been more thoroughly dashed: only Harvey Smith, with the brilliant speed horse The Sea Hawk, brought from South Africa by Bob Grayston, got into the winner's enclosure, twice, and in the Nations Cup Britain were only fifth, behind Italy, Germany, Spain and France. Germany, like Britain, had to field a reserve horse, but improved in the second round to be beaten only narrowly. The outstanding individual was Nelson

Pessoa, who with Gran Geste won both the Grand Prix d'Europe, a substitute for the European Championship, which was not held that year, and the Aachen Grand Prix.

The U.S.A. team had arrived in Europe in time for the International at White City, where Bill Steinkraus won his second King George Cup on Sinjon, who had been the team's leading horse in Europe in 1962 and was in the Rome silver medal team ridden by George Morris.

With Italy, winners in Rome as well as Aachen, also at the show, British hopes in the Prince of Wales Cup were not high, but the team, Harvey Smith on O'Malley, David Boston Barker, cousin of the 1962 European champion, on North Riding, Elizabeth Broome, David's sister, on Jacopo and Peter Robeson with Firecrest, produced a two-round total of no faults. Only O'Malley disappointed, with eight faults first time; the other three had double clears. The only others to go round twice without fault were Steinkraus on Sinjon and Seamus Hayes with Goodbye for Ireland, but Italy, with Piero d'Inzeo having rejoined his brother and Mancinelli in the team finished second ahead of the United States.

In Dublin, where Kathy Kusner and Untouchable won the first of two successive Grand Prix, the U.S.A. finished first ahead of Britain, and at Rotterdam Germany beat them both, with $6\tfrac{3}{4}$ faults to America's $7\tfrac{1}{2}$ and Britain's $16\tfrac{1}{2}$.

The experiment of trying David Broome on Merely-a-Monarch, who seemed completely to have lost his form, was short-lived, but Jacopo, ridden to victory by Elizabeth Edgar, Broome's sister, in the National Championship and the Lonsdale championship, the *puissance*, at the White City was finally chosen as the Welshman's ride for Tokyo. The others in the British team were Peter Robeson on Firecrest, and David Boston Barker on North Riding, with Barker's younger brother William and North Flight, a good but inexperienced mare, as reserve.

Tokyo—d'Oriola again

The Olympic Games in Tokyo were masterfully organised, well repaying the years that the Japanese had spent in preparing for them. For the show jumpers there was to be only one competition, the grand finale to the Games, with the individual medals going to those best placed in the team competition.

The Americans suffered a vital last-minute disaster when Steinkraus's Sinjon, the most consistent member of the team, went lame and could not start. This still left three top class riders and horses, Chapot with San Lucas, Mary Mairs on Tomboy and Kathy Kusner with Untouchable, but the loss of their captain and his

Sophie Joncquez and Kelbia

Princess Anne and Col. Sir Michael Ansell celebrate the 21st anniversary of the Horse of the Year Show

fine horse did little for their peace of mind.

Winners of the two previous team gold medals, the Germans were not fielding a team of comparable quality: Winkler's Fidelitas was no Halla, Kurt Jarasinski had only started riding Torro, a nine-year-old Holstein, the year before; probably the best of them was Herman Schridde's Dozent, a Hanoverian who had won that year's Hamburg Derby.

A good deal of rain had made the ground soggy, and in the comparatively small ring the fourteen fences had a formidable look: the triple bar at No. 6, 4 ft 11 in high with a 7 ft spread, the treble at No. 8, with big spread fences as the first and third elements, and especially the last fence, parallel poles 4 ft 11 in high with a 5 ft 9 in spread, made more difficult by the wall in the middle which created a false ground line, all looked like problems.

The great surprise was that somehow the Italians had persuaded the Olympic Committee that Mancinelli, though he had started his career in a stable, had never been a professional, and he was allowed to join the d'Inzeos in the Italian team. In the field were fourteen teams, including for the first time one from Australia, and four individual riders. The course rode as difficult as it looked, and in the first round no one could get round for less than eight faults, the three sharing first place being Peter Robeson and Firecrest, John Fahey from Australia on his diminutive Bonvale and Duarte Silva of Portugal with Jeune France. Pierre Jonqueres d'Oriola and Lutteur had hit only the last two fences—thirteen was the water—but also had one time fault. Mary Mairs and Tomboy had had an utterly disastrous round, collecting no fewer than $44\frac{1}{2}$ faults which put the U.S.A. right out of the running. Pessoa and Huipil, whom most people expected to come near winning the individual, had collected twelve faults. Broome had got Jacopo round for sixteen faults, but North Riding's $28\frac{1}{4}$ was a severe burden for Britain.

At the halfway mark Germany led with $39\frac{3}{4}$ faults from Italy on 44, France, one fault behind; Britain with $52\frac{1}{4}$ were fourth and Australia fifth, with $53\frac{1}{2}$. In the second round Schridde and Dozent, who had $12\frac{1}{2}$ faults first time, jumped clear but with one and a quarter time faults, Firecrest and Bonvale again had eight faults, while Jeune France hit three.

Still there was no clear round when d'Oriola, gold medal winner way back in 1952 came in on Lutteur, a nine-year-old son of that amazing sire of jumpers, Furioso. Lutteur had made his international debut only that year, but his early training, as a three-year-old in the French Cavalry school, and the inestimable advantage of being ridden by d'Oriola was such that he had won the Spanish Grand Prix and the French Jumping Derby. The ground was well cut up by the time Lutteur came into the ring in Tokyo, but nothing could shake d'Oriola's confidence. Round they went, brilliantly clear and in the time, though with only half a second to spare. Another individual gold for d'Oriola and the team silver for France. Schridde and Dozent took the silver, but Robeson's Firecrest and Fahey's Bonvale, with sixteen faults apiece, were equal third. In the jump off for the bronze Firecrest was clear and slightly faster than Bonvale, who had two down again after a marvellous exhibition for a horse of his size. Da Silva's Jeune France and Pessoa with Huipil shared fifth place individually, while in the teams Britain finished fourth, ahead of Argentina and the U.S.A.

Following the Tokyo Games the F.E.I. instituted the President's Cup, a world team championship based on points won in Nations Cups. Because of the difficulties some countries experienced in travelling to a great number of official international horse shows it was decided that only each country's best six performances should count. Appropriately, as Prince Philip was President of the F.E.I., Britain won the first President's Cup. A general outbreak of equine 'flu' kept them away from the Nice and Rome shows, both won by Italy, but thereafter they won six Nations Cups, in Dublin, Madrid, Copenhagen, Ostend, Rotterdam and in Olsztyn, the first time a British team had been sent to Poland. Italy, winning in Aachen, Nice and Rome, gained an early lead for the Cup, which was consolidated when they came to London and won the Prince of Wales Cup. Britain's chance went when bronze medallist Firecrest had a crashing fall on the slippery going. The damage proved no worse than muscular, but it kept Firecrest on the sidelines until near the end of the season.

Italy, including Mancinelli on The Rock and Piero d'Inzeo with his Aachen Grand Prix winner Ballyblack, totalled 24 faults to beat Ireland by only one and quarter, with the Australians, touring Europe during their quarantine period before they were allowed to return home, third with 44. John Fahey's little Bonvale did particularly well for the Australians that season, especially at Hickstead, where Judy Crago and Spring Fever won the gold medal for the season's leading rider on the course for the second successive year.

Hickstead's owner Douglas Bunn with Beethoven had a jump-off duel for the King

George Cup, which went to Hans Gunter Winkler and Fortun, while Marion Coakes and Stroller won the Queen Elizabeth Cup by one-tenth of a second from Alison Westwood and The Maverick, who that year was the leading horse in London, Aachen, Geneva, Rotterdam and Enschede. Miss Coakes, at 18, and Stroller, standing $14 \cdot 1\frac{1}{2}$ h.h. were the youngest rider and smallest horse to take the Queen's Cup. The first World Championship for women was held at Hickstead, and this too fell to Stroller's mighty leap and his young rider's skill.

America's Kathy Kusner and the former racehorse Untouchable, owned by Mr. and Mrs. Paul Butler, were favourites for the title on the strength of their second Dublin Grand Prix and the tremendous form they had shown on the current European tour, but in the first competition they finished only fourth to Stroller, The Maverick and Miss Coakes's second horse Little Fellow. In the second round, a Nations Cup-type, Stroller and Little Fellow finished equal first, ahead of Untouchable, and though the American girl won the third competition, Miss Coakes's early lead brought her the championship.

The men's European Championship in Aachen went to Herman Schridde and Dozent, though they had luck on their side, for both Pessoa and d'Oriola took the wrong course and were automatically eliminated. Narrowly beaten, in second place came Spain's Alfonso Queipo de Llano and Infernal, the 1964 Rome Grand Prix winners, with Alwin Schockemohle and Exakt third. In Cologne that year Exakt set a German high-jump record of 7 ft 4 in.

De Llano's compatriot, 'Paco' Goyoaga, World Champion twelve years earlier, retired that year. After a heart operation he returned to lead his country to victory in the Geneva Nations Cup, but then decided to call it a day. He sold his horse Kif-Kif to the Spanish Federation for £20,000.

The Geneva Nations Cup, which was expected to be the crowning glory of Britain's President's Cup victory turned out to be an utter farce. Because the course was mis-measured by eighty yards only four horses got round without time faults, and the fences were so easy time faults were all that many of them had. This 'steeplechase' suited the Spanish horses, who won from Italy and Germany. Brazil and Switzerland were equal fourth ahead of Britain, but still Britain had gained enough points to ensure taking the President's Cup, with Germany second and Italy third.

Following the course taken by other sport federations, the F.E.I. gave official recognition to East Germany, enabling it to send its own teams abroad and hold its own C.H.I.O. The Federation also introduced a rule whereby riders could only compete at a show outside their own country which was either a C.H.I. or C.H.I.O., unless they had been resident in that country for thirty days. The rule, since reduced to fourteen days, was intended to prevent certain riders, such as Pessoa who was based in Geneva, and Seamus Hayes from popping over the border into neighbouring countries and raiding their rich prizes. This rule proved a retrogressive step in the internationalism of the sport.

In Britain, Harvey Smith was parted from O'Malley after a difference of opinion with owner Bob Hanson. O'Malley went first to David Barker and then to Alison Westwood, but Smith, who could get much more out of him than anyone else, had the great horse back for 1967. Meanwhile, he was with Harvester, the season's leading money winner.

On the North American autumn circuit the U.S.A. won the Nations Cups in New York, Harrisburg and Toronto. Bill Steinkraus's Snowbound, who had made his international debut the previous season, his first in show jumping, took the New York Grand Prix. Frank Chapot's San Lucas won the North American Championship in Toronto, where Douglas Bunn, on a solo tour, won the Grand Prix with Beethoven.

Following the 1965 epidemic of equine 'flu', which caused lasting damage to a number of horses, the 1966 European season was even more devastated by swamp fever in France. The British team had visited only Paris, in March, before the swamp fever outbreak. As World Champions they went with high hopes, which were gradually whittled away as day after day passed without one success. But they made up for it all in the Nations Cup, especially Ted Williams and Carnaval, who had been hopping lame only days before, when ramming a nail in his foot in the collecting ring. Williams spent sleepless hours nursing him back to health, and they were the only ones in the Nations Cup to jump round twice without hitting a fence. France, including gold medallist d'Oriola on Lutteur, pulled up into second place ahead of Spain, with Germany, Italy and Holland behind.

D'Oriola showed his genius yet again later in the season when he went to Buenos Aires and took the World Championship, the first time it had been held outside Europe. The Frenchman was much criticised for his decision to take Pomone, a young and inexperienced half-sister to his Tokyo hero Lutteur to Buenos Aires, but his confidence was justified. Through to the final were d'Oriola, Raimondo d'Inzeo with Bowjack, Nelson Pessoa with Huipil and the

Capt. Billy Ringrose and Loch An Easpaig

Spaniard Alvarez de Bohorquez on the Anglo-Arab Quizas. Clear on Pomone, d'Oriola found Bowjack the most difficult and had two fences down; one mistake on each of the other two left him a total of sixteen faults, three ahead of de Bohorques, with d'Inzeo, on thirty, third ahead of Pessoa, who had $35\frac{1}{4}$.

Pessoa, himself, at last won a title, however, in Lucerne when he and Gran Geste took the European. They were just too consistent for Frank Chapot and San Lucas, finishing with six points to nine and a half, with the Argentinian Hugo Arrambide on Chimbote, the previous year's Rome Grand Prix victor, third with eleven. Although this was a 'European' championship the nearest from the host continent was Switzerland's Paul Weier, who finished fourth on Satan.

For the first time since Palermo in 1958 there were no British riders in the European Women's Championship, held in Gijon, and for the first time since that year it was won by a non-British rider, Janou Lefebvre. This brilliant French girl, who had been in the Tokyo silver medal team, won from Monica Bachmann, that season's Swiss champion, ahead of all the male riders, and Italy's Lalla Novo.

The American team made a European tour which, because of the swamp fever restrictions, avoided England and Ireland. They won the Nations Cup in Lucerne and were second to Italy in Aachen, where a newcomer to their team, Neal Shapiro, riding Jacks or Better had his first ever international success, and that in the Grand Prix.

Neither London nor Dublin could stage a Nations Cup, as a minimum of three nations are needed and they were restricted to each other's country. In Britain it was Mister Softee's year, but no longer partnered by David Barker. In 1965 Barker, having married Valerie Clark, had moved to Buckinghamshire. At first the Massarella family had kept Mister Softee in their home county, Yorkshire, but after a short, unprofitable interim the chestnut had gone to David Broome's stable.

In 1966 Broome and Mister Softee were unbeatable in the major events: they won the King George V Cup, with South African rider Mickey Louw on Trigger Hill second, they had the only clear round in the British Jumping Derby, won the Olympic Trial at the British Timken show, and finally triumphed in the Ronson Trophy, the *victor ludorum* of the Horse of the Year Show.

After 22 years in office Colonel Mike Ansell, the inspiration of British show jumping, retired as President of the B.S.J.A., though he continued as director of both the Royal International and the Horse of the Year Show, and as guiding light of the sport.

The United States, building on their Lucerne Nations Cup victory with two more at New York and Harrisburg won the President's Cup, but

Piero d'Inzeo and Uruguay

were surprisingly beaten in Toronto by Canada. The Canadians administered an even greater shock the following season in Winnipeg, when Jimmy Day, at 21 the 'baby' of their team, took the Pan American individual gold medal with his great horse Canadian Club. An impressive-looking horse, standing 16·2 h.h. Canadian Club was then only seven, but he had already given car salesman Day an idea of his ability. For the individual award Canadian Club had a double clear round but so had the more experienced Nelson Pessoa with Gran Geste, and the two of them had to jump-off. This time both horses had two fences down, but Canadian Club, in 38·7 sec, had 1·1 sec to spare over the Brazilian, with Mexican Manuel Mendivil Yocupicio on Veracruz, with just one mistake in his first round, third.

The U.S.A. could not find much consolation in the team result, for the Brazilian team, Pessoa, two of his pupils Simoes and Fernandez, and Ferreira, finished with a total of just eight faults, half the Americans' aggregate. The American team consisted of Kathy Kusner with Untouchable, Frank and Mary Chapot on San Lucas and White Lightning and Bill Steinkraus with Bold Minstrel. The Canadians, whose first venture in the Pan American Games this was, were third, totalling 24 faults, and so their team of Day, Tommy Gayford with Big Dee, Moffat Dunlop with Argyll and Jim Elder with Pieces of Eight, convinced their Federation they were worth sending to the Olympic Games.

In Europe in 1967, Britain made a determined and successful effort to regain the President's Cup, winning six out of eight Nations Cups, in Nice, Aachen, Olsztyn, Leipzig, London and Rotterdam. Second to Switzerland in Rome, they should have been third to Brazil, for Pessoa approached the last two fences on Gran Geste with two fences in hand, hit the last but one, asked far too much of his great horse, who stopped: and in the ensuing altercation the Brazilian team's lead disappeared in time faults.

It was a young British team, including Caroline Bradley in her international debut, which made the long trip to Olsztyn and the East German show in Leipzig, but the mood of adventurous triumph was contagious. The hair's-breadth victory in Aachen was a triumph for sheer determination. As had happened in Paris, the team came to the Nations Cup without a win to their name, and, as there, Ted Williams and Carnaval came into the ring needing a clear round for victory. Guts as well as skill have kept Williams at the top for so long, and clear they went. Althea Roger Smith and Havana Royal jumped two clear rounds, while John Baillie's Dominic and Andrew Fielder's Vibart also did their share. Germany lost their chance when Schockemohle's Donald Rex, just beginning a brilliant career, fell at the water, leaving Italy to take second place, with $4\frac{3}{4}$ faults to Britain's $4\frac{1}{4}$, with the United States a well-beaten third with 17.

Fielder and Vibart had a solo triumph the next day when they became the first British combination to win the Aachen Grand Prix—in which Mancinelli's No. 1 horse Turvey collapsed with heart failure and died—and a week later Vibart became the first British horse to win the Hamburg Jumping Derby, with Winkler falling and badly breaking an arm.

The British selectors, in their wisdom, left Marion Coakes and Stroller out of the British challenge for the European Championship, choosing instead Anneli Drummond-Hay with Merely-a-Monarch, who had shown revived form in 1966, and Alison Westwood with the Maverick. But neither of them proved any match for Kathy Kusner and Untouchable.

Miss Kusner won the first competition from Diana Conolly-Carew, was surprisingly beaten by the Belgian Francoise Thiry in the second, almost missed the third when Untouchable had an attack of colic, but had him fit enough to finish second to Lalla Novo. The American girl's consistency earned the title, with Miss Novo second and Monica Bachmann third. Miss Westwood was fifth and Miss Drummond-Hay eleventh.

There was a much happier ending to the men's championship in Rotterdam, however, from a British viewpoint, with David Broome and Harvey Smith finishing first and second. Once again Pessoa's temperament let him down, for he came to the final competition needing only to finish in the first three to be sure of keeping the title. Broome and Mister Softee were at their best in the final, run in two rounds, over eighteen and then over twelve fences, designed to test all the weapons in a show jumper's armoury. Schockemohle, with Donald Rex, had been lying second to Pessoa at the start of the competition, but a fence down in the first round and a stop in the second put them behind Harvey Smith. While Pessoa, who finished only fifteenth in the final competition, dropped to fourth over-all.

Britain had a resounding victory over the Italians in the Prince of Wales Cup, with Althea Roger Smith and Havana Royal again jumping a double clear—the only ones to do so. In a high class, all-British finish to the King's Cup Robeson and Firecrest defeated the holders, Broome and Mister Softee, with Smith and O'Malley third ahead of Alan Oliver and Sweep. The shock of the competition was when Seamus Hayes, after Goodbye had jumped a superb clear, completely missed out the last fence, a momentary aberration which put him right out of the competition.

In Dublin, Ireland scraped home gallantly ahead of Britain for the Aga Khan Trophy, and Mister Softee won the first of two successive Grand Prix. The following year's was rather more profitable, however, for then the Royal Dublin Society moved into the era of sponsorship to such effect that the Grand Prix carried a world record first prize of £1,650, with £5,000 over all.

At Hickstead, Marion Coakes and Stroller won the British Jumping Derby with the only clear round. Harvey Smith was the season's leading money winner for the fourth time in five years, on Harvester. After a decade Britain sent a team on the North American circuit, and though the United States again won the Nations Cup in New York and Toronto, Smith and O'Malley triumphed in the New York Grand Prix.

Mexico—Snowbound supreme

Around the world the 1968 season was geared to Mexico. The United States team was coming to Europe for a final tune-up, but not until July. When they did come they were unbeaten in Nations Cups, winning in London, Dublin, Ostend and Rotterdam and then, after the Games, at their own show in New York, in the new Madison Square Garden, and finally in Toronto. In doing so they walked away with the President's Cup for the second time.

Italy showed good early form with victories in Nice and Rome, where Anneli Drummond-Hay regained the women's European Championship for Britain. With Merely-a-Monarch having an off-day it was the grand little former hunter, Xanthos, who laid the foundation for this by taking the initial speed competition. Merely-a-Monarch tied with Giulia Serventi's Gay Monarch in the second round, and though only fourth to Gay Monarch in the final event, Miss Drummond-Hay's early lead was enough.

Piero d'Inzeo and the German-bred Fidux, which he was to ride in Mexico took the Grand Prix by a tenth of a second with Merely-a-Monarch and Peter Robeson's Firecrest equal second, probably a record close finish for a Grand Prix. Italy won again in Aachen, from Germany, but the real trial of strength was to come at the Royal International, which had moved to its new, though temporary, home in the Olympic Stadium at Wembley. It was an appropriate setting for this 'Olympic dress rehearsal'. Germany gave a taste of their strength by taking the first three places in the *puissance*, with Winkler's Enigk and Steenken's Porta Westfalica tying, then Enigk, by a thoroughbred out of a Hanoverian mare and winner of the Aachen Grand Prix the previous month, took the King George V Cup, beating off a surprise challenge from John Kidd and Grey Owl.

Italy made a disastrous start to the Prince of Wales Cup, from which it never recovered, but throughout the first round Britain and United States fought neck and neck until Bill Steinkraus and Snowbound came in to jump the first clear. The Germans were not going well, and at half-way the U.S.A. led with eight faults to Britain's twelve, with the Irish a gallant third on 20, a form which they were unable to maintain next time round.

Mary Chapot and White Lightning, winners of the Queen's Cup two days earlier, then jumped a clear to start the U.S. off with an advantage in the second round. A clear from Mister Softee put Britain back in the running, but then Steinkraus and Snowbound administered the *coup de grâce* with another faultless circuit. At the finish the U.S.A. had twelve faults to Britain's 28, with Germany 36, Italy 51 and Ireland 55½.

Snowbound finished the show with an impressive victory in the Grand Prix for the Daily Mail Cup, and two weeks later in Dublin again jumped two clear rounds to guide his team to victory over Britain. Although the Americans went on to victory in Ostend and Rotterdam their mood was not one of unimpaired confidence, for Snowbound was lame and had to miss both these last two Nations Cups.

Britain's Olympic team was reasonably clear: Broome and Mister Softee, Marion Coakes with Stroller and Harvey Smith, taking both O'Malley and Madison Time. After an abortive Olympic Trial, which produced only two starters, Alison Westwood and The Maverick, the 1968 Derby winners, were chosen to go as reserves, but they never made the arena.

There had been a lot of pre-Olympic worry about the possible effect of the altitude in Mexico City, 7,000 ft, but it did not apparently affect any of the show jumpers. There were again two competitions, with 42 starters, including Snowbound, lining up in the attractive Campo Marte, for the individual, which was being run under a new formula, with one round over fourteen fences of Nations Cup size, followed by a round for roughly the best third—it turned out to be eighteen—over six fences of *puissance* dimensions. The second six were indeed big, with a 5 ft 11 in wall at No. 3, huge parallel poles 5 ft 7 in high with a spread of over 7 ft at No. 5 and finally a big double with an upright in and an oxer out.

Australia's Kevin Bacon was the first to show up prominently in the first round, galloping the inexperienced Chichester round and faulting only

David Broome and Mister Softee

at No. 12, crossed-poles 5 ft high with a 6 ft 6 in spread. Chapot and San Lucas also hit only one fence, but there was no clear round until, nearly half-way through the competition, Marion Coakes and Stroller bounced round with the elasticity for which they had become famous. Broome's Mister Softee, Piero d'Inzeo's Fidux and Day's Canadian Club all had one fence down, but not until near the end was Stroller's clear equalled, by Bill Steinkraus and Snowbound, in impeccable style.

Over the *puissance* fences the triple bar proved too much for the headstrong Chichester; San Lucas hit the parallels at Nos. 3 and 5, and though Winkler's Enigk hit only one he had had eight faults first time. Stroller, chirpy and determined as ever, cleared the first four, came into the insuperable number five on a perfect stride, but just clipped a back pole coming down. He collected another four at the oxer coming out of the last fence. Mister Softee hit the last two fences and Jim Elder's The Immigrant just one to join the twelve-faulters.

Then Bill Steinkraus's Snowbound jumped the round of his life. The parallels at No. 5 proved beyond him too, but that was his only fault and they came home with a four-fault total, the winners.

In a jump-off of four for the bronze San Lucas went clear over the seven-fence course—fences from the first course—in 36·8, surprisingly fast for such a big horse, Enigk was clear in 37·5, the Immigrant in 39·2, then Broome shot Mister Softee through the starting gate, made an impossible-looking turn into the parallels, and was clear in 35·3.

How near Snowbound had been to losing the gold medal was realised when it was seen that, so lame was he immediately after the event that Steinkraus had to come in for his medal riding a Canadian horse, The Immigrant. And this, of course, put Snowbound out of the team competition, Mary Chapot on White Lightning coming in to join her husband on San Lucas and Kathy Kusner with Untouchable.

The course for the Grand Prix des Nations was slightly bigger than the individual, and much more difficult because of the awkward placing of several of the 14 fences. The sixth, a triple bar 5 ft 1 in by 6 ft 6 in, was followed at only five strides by a treble, a wall at 4 ft 11 in, and two parallels, the first 4 ft 11 in by 5 ft 7 in, the second 4 ft 11 in by 5 ft 11 in. Only six strides after the 16 ft 3 in water, No. 11, came a double of true parallels, 4 ft 9 in by 5 ft 7 in and 4 ft 9 in by 5 ft 9 in. And, as was seen very soon after the competition started, the time for the course was desperately tight. Of the fifteen teams only three were eliminated, but the scores were astronomical.

Stroller was the first to clear the water, and though he stopped at the double finished with a respectable $21\frac{3}{4}$. The only four horses to get round with two fences down were San Lucas, Enigk, The Immigrant and Mister Softee, but of these only Mister Softee did not have time faults also. Harvey Smith and Madison Time were round for $18\frac{1}{4}$ faults, and at halfway Britain led with 48 faults, followed closely by Canada, on $49\frac{1}{2}$; France were third with $56\frac{1}{2}$, ahead of Germany, for whom Tokyo silver medallists Schridde and Dozent had gone very poorly, with $58\frac{1}{4}$, the U.S.A. on 63, were one ahead of Italy.

Britain's hopes crashed with Stroller in the second round. The gallant little pony, who had been suffering for some time with an abscess on a gum, and who had jumped his heart out in the individual, came slowly into the treble, over the wall and stopped. Round and over the wall again, and another stop, sending his rider crashing into the parallel poles. Dazed Marion Coakes got up slowly and remounted, but not until Harvey Smith had run up and told her to go again did she do so. Through the treble this time, but too late, the time limit had been passed, Stroller and Britain were eliminated.

Even with the last few horses to go, it was still a close thing. The Italians had a chance, but Fidux hit four, then Chichester fell at the water. The Canadians had been most consistent, and when Elder and The Immigrant came in they had five fences to spare. Four went down, but the Canadians were worthy winners of the team gold medal, with a massive score of $102\frac{3}{4}$ faults. France, with Janou Lefebvre and Rocket as their best performers, were second with $110\frac{1}{2}$, Donald Rex, with the best score of the day, four faults plus $1\frac{3}{4}$ for time, and Enigk's twelve placed Germany for the bronze, totalling $117\frac{1}{4}$. Broome and Mister Softee, giving a vain but brilliant display, got round for twelve, with the second best total of 20 to Donald Rex's $18\frac{3}{4}$. The last of the Americans, San Lucas, could have afforded three down for the team bronze if he had been fast enough, but three down and two faults for time gave the bronze to Germany by just a quarter of a fault.

The Canadians' individual scores, worth recording for their consistency, were: Tom Gayford and Big Dee, $39\frac{1}{2}$ faults, Jim Day and Canadian Club, 36, Jim Elder and The Immigrant, $27\frac{1}{4}$.

Broome's third

Highlight of the post-Mexico season in 1969 was the third European Championship for David Broome, in only three attempts, and also the third for Mister Softee. For both this was a unique treble, although Winkler did win two world titles and the first European, which differed only in name.

By 1969 the F.E.I. had at last got round to deciding that European titles should be contended for only by Europeans, a sensible decision even though it did exclude the touring Australians, and of course Pessoa. Without such an embargo on non-Europeans the world title must by comparison lose much of its importance. As Broome was the title-holder the championship was assigned to England, to Hickstead, which has now grown to be indisputably Britain's top venue for show jumping. It was timed for the week immediately before the Royal International Horse Show, to attract the greatest number of top riders.

Alwin Schockemohle had followed his fine performance in Mexico with an incredible run of success, both on Donald Rex, with whom he had won the German International Championship in Aachen, and Wimpel, equal first in the Aachen Grand Prix, with Winkler's Enigk, and, only a week before the championship, winner of the Hamburg Jumping Derby. For the first time there was official betting on show jumping in England, Ladbrokes representatives going to many shows, though not allowed to the two at Wembley, and in the ante post market on the European Championship Schockemohle was made favourite at 3–1, with Winkler at 7–2, d'Oriola 4–1 and the defending champion at 5–1. Broome had not had anywhere near as good a season as Schockemohle, but he made it no secret that he was aiming to produce Mister Softee at his peak at Hickstead.

Riders from eight countries started for the the championship, and Mister Softee showed brilliant speed to win the first, which was on time, in the first round, with Schockemohle second on Wimpel. Donald Rex had an uncharacteristic stop at the second element of the double, at No. 14, sending his rider out 'by the front door'. Broome also took third place, on his former Foxhunter champion Top of the Morning, with Winkler and Enigk fourth ahead of the Swedish lawyer Jan-Olof Johannsen (who soon afterwards changed his surname to Wannius) on Shalimar.

The second competition, run in two rounds over a Nations Cup type course, left Donald Rex, Enigk and d'Oriola's World Champion Pomone equal first, with Broome dropping to equal second over-all, with Winkler, one point behind Schockemohle.

The final leg of the championship was run, as it had been in Rotterdam, over two courses, the

Jim Elder and The Immigrant

first, with 18 fences of mixed speed, *puissance* and Nations Cup dimensions, the second over twelve fences. As in Rotterdam it was Mister Softee's brilliant jumping at speed which won the day. Softee and Donald Rex were both clear first time, but the German some three seconds slower. In the final round, again clear, Mister Softee clocked a lightning-fast 65·8 sec; Schockemohle and Donald Rex made a gallant effort to overcome their three-second deficit, but no horse in the world could have gone that much faster than Mister Softee, and in the attempt the German hit the middle of the treble and the following upright.

The women's title, which took place in Dublin, resulted in a major surprise when Ireland's Iris Kellett and Morning Light dethroned Anneli Drummond-Hay. Miss Drummond-Hay and Alison Westwood had looked odds on to finish first and second in the championship with only six competitors taking part: Miss Drummond-Hay set off, as she had in Rome, by winning the initial speed competition on Xanthos, from Morning Light and Miss Westwood's The Maverick. In the second round only Morning Light went twice round the 13-fence course without fault, putting Miss Kellett jointly in the lead with the holder. The final was run on the same lines as the men's: Morning Light faulted twice at the water, but Xanthos, ridden in preference to Merely-a-Monarch who was not going well, collected sixteen faults.

Miss Kellett was the first European Champion of either sex Ireland had produced, though Irish horses had been successful often enough. She had had a severe accident since her Queen Elizabeth Cup double nearly two decades earlier and, especially at Ballsbridge, no victory could have been more popular.

The destination of the President's Cup was not finally known until the last show of the European season, Geneva, but Germany showed its determination to break the Anglo-American domination of this championship throughout the season

Anneli Drummond-Hay and Merely-a-Monarch

and finally did so. After finishing second in Nice to France, that country's first Nations Cup victory since 1964, Germany won in Rome, with 16½ faults to Britain's 20. Miss Drummond-Hay and Xanthos won the inaugural running of the Trofeo Olgiata, on Jumping Derby lines, at the Olgiata stud just outside Rome. In Barcelona, Britain had a zero total, though both George Hobbs's War Lord and Paddy McMahon's Hideaway were making their Nations Cup debuts, and won narrowly from France and Germany. Then the Germans won in Aachen, their first home victory since 1963, in London, with a zero score, in Dublin, though there the British took them to a timed jump-off, and in Ostend, where Ann Moore, the former European junior champion, in her senior international debut, jumped two clear rounds on Psalm. Britain redressed the balance slightly with a victory in Rotterdam, with the Poles going surprisingly well for second place, and the Dutch team keeping Germany out of third by half a fault.

Janou Lefebvre and the thoroughbred Rocket, a high-class son of Le Tyrol, foaled in 1961 and winner of over £5,000 as a flat race horse, had a highly successful season, starting with the Grand Prix and the Championship at Nice, taking the Grand Prix in London, the Meisterspringen in Aachen and then jumping only the second clear round in the history of the French Jumping Derby at La Baule.

Ted Edgar and the American-bred Uncle Max, an ex-rodeo horse that he had bought the previous autumn from Neal Shapiro, after a disastrous time, including two falls, in the Aachen Nations Cup, won the King George V Cup, while the Queen Elizabeth went to Alison Westwood and The Maverick, with Anneli Drummond-Hay second for the fourth time on Merely-a-Monarch.

Although still cut off by the horse sickness ban, South Africa added a world-class touch to their indoor show in Johannesburg by 'importing' David Broome, d'Oriola, Schridde and Pessoa to compete against the locals, who by no means came off badly. The B.S.J.A.'s senior course builder John Gross, built the courses, a task which Jack Talbot-Ponsonby regularly performed at the Rand Easter Show and Pam Carruthers, of Hickstead fame, at the Rothmans Derby meeting. Good courses make good riders, and when the ban is lifted, as it may soon be in some countries, the South Africans will prove themselves not far behind European standards. At the same show Peter Levor, who had been awarded his Springbok Colours just two years before, raised the South African high jump record to 7ft 3in on Foormat, which he bought from Winkler.

In Geneva, Germany put the destination of the President's Cup beyond doubt with a narrow victory over the Italians, who led after the first round with a zero total, but could not quite maintain that form. Britain, equal third in Geneva, with the French, finished second for the President's Cup.

Anneli Drummond-Hay, winner of the Grand Prix on her previous visit to Geneva, in 1967, had a personal *tour de force*, winning four competitions on her own and two others, relays, in company with other members of the British team, which was not an especially strong one. In the Trophée de la Ville de Geneve, traditionally run over a massive course, Anneli and Merely-a-Monarch jumped superlatively for the only clear round.

In Britain Alan Oliver completed an extremely successful season, which included the National championship, by taking a second successive Ronson Trophy, the *victor ludorum* of the Horse of the Year Show, on Pitz Palu, the season's leading horse. This brought Oliver's number of first prizes for the season to 98. Paul Weier won the Swiss championship for the sixth time, at the expense of Arthur Blickenstorfer, with Monica Bachmann third.

After her triumphant season Janou Lefebvre did not contest the French women's title, which went to the talented 20-year-old Sophie Joncquez. With Kelbia, she alone went clear in the final of the championship at Fontainebleau to beat Mme. Iliane de Poumeyrol. The men's title went to Jerome Chabrol, who came out best in a four-rider final, on World Championship lines.

On the North American circuit, Jared Brinsmade won the Harrisburg Grand Prix, and was in all three of the U.S. Nations Cup teams, which won in Harrisburg and New York, and then were convincingly beaten by the Canadians in Toronto.

The quartet which won in Toronto was the Mexico gold medal team, Jimmy Day with Canadian Club, Tommy Gayford with Big Dee and Jimmy Elder on The Immigrant, who had a double clear round, plus Moffat Dunlap on Grand Nouvelle. Day with his very useful 'second string' Steelmaster, then a six-year-old, won the Rothman's Canadian Championship, the renamed North American Championship, in Toronto, beating Elder and The Immigrant and the Argentinian Juan Giralda, with El Ganso, winners of the Toronto Grand Prix and the President's Cup in Washington. The Argentinian team, which included a few brilliant horses, also added the New York Grand Prix to their tally, through the veteran Hugo Arrambide and Adagio. The Canadians Terrance Millar, on The Shoeman, and Jimmy Elder with Pieces of Eight, were second and third to him in New York.

Although they were well beaten in all three Nations Cups, finishing fourth behind Mexico in both Harrisburg and New York and third beating only the Mexicans in Toronto, the Argentinian team is obviously capable of more important individual triumphs. The United States team was rather disappointing, but introduced a few less experienced horses of considerable promise, and none more so than Kathy Kusner's Wicked City, whom she had brought over to Europe to gain experience at some of the French C.H.I.s, and whom she rode in the Nations Cups in both New York and Toronto.

The Canadian team confirmed that its Mexico Gold medal was no fluke, and although lack of funds prevents it making many tours of the European shows they obviously have both the riders and horses to play a major part in the scene when they can do so.

2 People in the Sport

Col. Sir Michael Ansell

Great Britain

Colonel Sir Michael Ansell (b. 1905) was knighted in 1968 for his services to show jumping, and no one deserved such an honour more, for without him show jumping in Britain would almost certainly not have reached the heights it has, and throughout the world the sport would have been poorer.

Michael Ansell turned his attentions to show jumping when an accident to a wrist stopped him playing polo for a while. An enthusiast for all sorts of equestrian sport; polo, hunting, racing, it was show jumping which took its firmest grip.

A course at Saumur and training under Paul Rodzianko brought Ansell to international standard, and in 1939, at Nice he and Teddy were placed on every day of the ten-day show.

The war put an end to his jumping. During the early days of the war, a Colonel in the Inniskillings, he received a wound which eventually robbed him of his sight, and was captured at St. Valery. The years in the prisoner-of-war camp, in company with his fellow show jumpers of pre-war days, Nat Kindersley and Bede Cameron, gave him plenty of time to think, and plan for the future.

In 1944 he was repatriated, and characteristically wasted no time in setting his ideas in motion. In December of 1944 he became chairman of the British Show Jumping Association under the Presidency of Col. Taffy Walwyn, appointed a committee of those he felt most likely to help him get things done, and started to improve British show jumping's standards, thereby increasing public interest.

Alterations to the rules, to cut out the endless time-wasting then permitted, and the grading of horses, so that the better horses should not compete against, and thus frighten off, the novices, took time, but he was persistent.

In 1945 the B.S.J.A. organised their National Championship, at White City, London, the start of a long association. Next year there were two shows there, and in 1947 the International reopened.

The 1948 Olympic Games in London were a masterpiece of planning. The course, which always has to be kept secret until the morning of the competition, was planned by Mike Ansell in co-operation with Phil Blackmore, the then-senior course builder. Under a blanket of secrecy the fences were built on a farm in Hampshire, where, with typical thoroughness, Ansell had the whole course set out and inspected.

Putting the course up in the Wembley Stadium was a mammoth task for it could not be started until very late the previous evening, and torrential rain left the ground so wet that lorries could not be taken on to the grass. So some 15 tons of fences had to be manhandled into place, but this was the sort of situation Ansell thrives on, and only seconds after the appointed time the course was ready for inspection.

In 1949 the Horse of the Year Show was created, at Harringay. Although both these great international shows have changed their homes since, Mike Ansell has continued to direct them, producing in each case out of the complex ingredients a masterpiece of split-second timing which is the essence of show jumping.

Throughout this time, too, 'Colonel Mike' has fervently injected into British teams his will-to-win internationally. Harry Llewellyn and Kilgeddin had Britain's first post-war victory, in Rome in 1947; and in 1952 Llewellyn, with Wilf White and Douglas Stewart, brought the Olympic Gold Medal back from Helsinki.

In 1965, when the first President's Cup, awarded by the F.E.I. to the country with the six best Nations Cup results, was contested, Mike Ansell determined that it should come to Britain. Teams were sent far and wide—as far indeed as Olsztyn, near Warsaw—in search of victory, and the President's Cup duly ended up in Britain.

In 1966, after twenty-two years as chairman and then as President of the B.S.J.A., Colonel Ansell retired, only to return as chairman in 1970; he is still chairman of the British Horse Society also, and has kept very much in touch with the affairs of British show jumping. Internationally he was for many years a member of the Bureau of the F.E.I., and, in recognition, when he retired from this the F.E.I. gave him the rare honour of honorary membership.

Hugo Arrambide and Chimbote

Monica Bachmann and Sandro

Dr. Hugo Arrambide

Argentina

Hugo Arrambide (b. 1930) is one of the most successful of recent Argentinian riders on Chimbote, foaled in 1958 by a thoroughbred stallion from a native mare.

In the 1964 Olympic Games Argentina's team finished fifth, only $3\frac{3}{4}$ faults behind Britain, with Arrambide and Chimbote 17th individually. The following year they had a successful tour of Europe, including in their triumphs the Grand Prix in Rome and tying in the Aachen Grand Prix with Italy's Captain Piero d'Inzeo on Ballyblack. In 1966 they finished third in an 'All American' finish to the European Championship, behind Nelson Pessoa of Brazil and the United States rider Frank Chapot. Arrambide produced a particularly useful horse for the 1969 North American circuit in Adagio, on which he won the Grand Prix in New York.

Major placing European Championship: 1966, third on Chimbote.

Monica Bachmann

Switzerland

Monica Bachmann (b. 1942) is the most successful woman show jumping rider Switzerland has produced since the war. Miss Bachmann was the over-all Swiss champion in 1966, when she beat Paul Weier, for whose stable she now works and rides.

In 1965 she contested the Women's World Championship at Hickstead, won by Marion Coakes, on her German-bred Sandro, finishing fourth. The following year, again with Sandro, she was runner-up in the European Championship to Janou Lefebvre at Gijon, just before winning her National title.

With Erbach she has been especially successful in Nations Cups and at Rotterdam in 1967 was the only one in the entire competition to jump the course twice without fault.

In the Mexico Olympics Miss Bachmann and Erbach finished equal seventh in the individual competition, with two eight-fault rounds, and rode in the team, with Switzerland finishing sixth.

Major placing European Championship: 1966, second with Sandro.

Ann Backhouse (nee Townsend)

Great Britain

Mrs. Backhouse (b. 1940) made her international debut in the team which retained the European Junior Championship when it was held in London in 1958. The following year, with Irish Lace and the German-bred Bandit IV she won the Women's European Championship in Rotterdam, beating Pat Smythe and Flanagan by less than a point.

Kevin Bacon and Chichester II

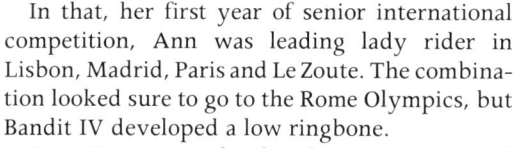

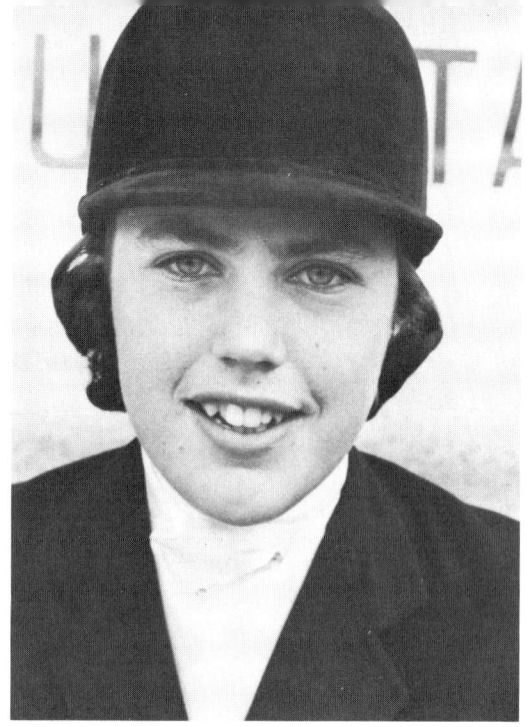

Ann Backhouse

In that, her first year of senior international competition, Ann was leading lady rider in Lisbon, Madrid, Paris and Le Zoute. The combination looked sure to go to the Rome Olympics, but Bandit IV developed a low ringbone.

In 1962 Ann rode the then eight-year-old Dunboyne to his first international victory in Rotterdam. The next season they won the National Championship, the Grand Prix at the Royal International and the £2,000 News of the World Championship at Ascot.

Another possible Olympic team place was thwarted when Dunboyne developed a habit of refusing, and though electrical treatment for the muscular trouble, which it was thought had caused this, brought some improvement, he is now mostly confined to small or speed classes.

Ann has, however, produced two extremely useful jumpers: the seven-year-old Cardinal, who won the Horse and Hound Cup at the 1969 Royal International, and The Brigadier, who won both there and at the Horse of the Year show.

Major placing European Championship: 1959, won with Bandit IV.

Kevin Bacon

Australia

Kevin Bacon (b. 1932) and Chichester, after a creditable performance in the Mexico Olympics were the sensation of the North American and European tours which followed the Games.

Bacon started show jumping in 1954 and has been the leading rider at the Sydney Royal Show 14 times, a position he also held at the New Zealand Horse of the Year Show in 1962.

The individual competition in Mexico was the then eight-year old Chichester's first major competition, yet he went round the first course with the fiery agility which has since endeared him to many crowds, with only one fence down. He found the *puissance*-type fences of the second round more than he could reasonably cope with, and eventually finished 18th, while the team was ninth.

At the New York International which followed soon afterwards Bacon and Chichester were, despite their inexperience, the leading combination. They then came to Europe, and won three competitions at the Berlin C.H.I. in February, 1969.

John Baillie

Great Britain

European junior champion in 1965, John Baillie (b. 1948) has successfully made the transition into senior internationals. The son of a Kinross farmer, Baillie started to ride when he was only twelve. Despite this tardy beginning, he had a successful career in junior jumping in Scotland.

He bought the grey Dominic, a free-going, adjustable sort, from Jack Barrie in 1964 and rode

David Barker and Mister Softee

John Baillie and Dominic

him when he went into senior classes and in the European Junior Championship in Salice Terme, Northern Italy, in 1965. That same year they won the Young Riders' Championship of Great Britain at Hickstead.

Baillie and Dominic were in the young British team which went to Poland and East Germany in 1967 and won the Nations Cups there, and then went straight on to join the 'No. 1' team for the much sterner tests at the West German C.H.I.O. in Aachen.

In the first qualifying round for the German Open Championship they beat all save Nelson Pessoa and his Olympic horse Huipil, finally finishing fifth in the Championship. And then they had just four faults in the two rounds of the Nations Cup to help Britain to a massive victory.

David Barker

Great Britain

David Barker (b. 1935), one of a large family of show jumpers, started riding in competitions when he was seven. His introduction to jumping was almost accidental, but with Springbok he was leading junior three years in succession.

In 1958 he bought the four-year-old Franco, by Como out of a Bellacose mare and the following year they went abroad with the British team, to Le Zoute, where they were second to the reigning European Woman Champion, Giulia Serventi of Italy with Doly, and to Rotterdam; Britain winning the Nations Cups at both.

Barker was chosen for the Rome Olympics, but he was left out of the individual competition, and in the team event Franco was eliminated at the last fence.

In 1961 Barker was offered the ride on the Massarellas' Irish-bred Mister Softee, and after a successful season at home they went with the team to Nice, Rome and Lucerne.

In 1962 Barker and Mister Softee were chosen with Peter Robeson on Firecrest to defend for Britain the European Championship that David Broome and Sunsalve, who had since died, had won in 1961. Barker won the title with just one fence to spare from the dead-heaters Hans Gunter Winkler and Piero d'Inzeo.

Barker had a phenomenally successful trip to Ostend and Rotterdam the following year: at the Belgian show he won three competitions on Mister Softee and two on Franco; and in Holland one on Franco and two, including the Grand Prix, on Softee.

Both Mister Softee and Franco have gone on to new riders, David Broome and Caroline Bradley, and David Barker prefers to spend more time now on his farm near Bletchley, Buckinghamshire, dealing with young horses, including a number of potential racehorses over from Ireland, and a good many successful show animals.

Major placing European Championship: 1962, won on Mister Softee.

David Boston Barker and Lucky Sam

Arthur Blickenstorfer and Marianka V.

David Boston Barker

Great Britain

David Boston Barker (b. 1943, the 'Boston' to distinguish him from his cousin, the former European champion) is the eldest of three show jumping brothers—their sister Anne preceded them but has given up the sport—to come out of Northallerton, Yorkshire. David Boston and his younger brother William were both in the Tokyo Olympic team, an achievement unique in British show jumping history.

In 1961 David Boston and Lucky Sam shared the Leading Rider title with Carol Beard and Mayfly. That same year Barker produced the then four-year-old North Riding. In 1964 North Riding jumped one clear round in the Nations Cup at Aachen and two in London, which clinched his place in the Tokyo team, which finished fourth, finishing 27th in the individual placings. Barker's 1965 wins included the Horse and Hound Cup on North Riding at the Royal International and sharing the *puissance* at Wembley on Lucky Sam with Seamus Hayes and Goodbye.

Valerie Barker (nee Clark)

Great Britain

Valerie Barker (b. 1940, wife of David Barker) made rapid headway in international show jumping. She lived until she was married at Wanstead, on the outskirts of London, and did well to produce the horses she did in the space available.

After winning several international competitions on the ex-hurdler Knight of the Wold, she produced the Irish-bred mare Atalanta as a three-year-old in 1959, and two years later, Atalanta's first season in Grade A, won a competition at the Royal International and was selected to go to the Dutch C.H.I.O. in Rotterdam, where they created a minor sensation by winning the Grand Prix.

In 1964 Valerie and Atalanta won the Leading Show Jumper competition at the Horse of the Year Show, as well as tying with George Hobbs for the richest prize then offered in British show jumping: the £2,000 News of the World Championship at Ascot.

After several years of winning consistently for the British team both in England and abroad, Atalanta was retired to stud when her owner had to give up temporarily, while she was adding to the Barker family. Atalanta, unhappily, died in 1969.

At the South of England show in 1969 Valerie Barker won the British National Ladies Championship on Brandy Jim. Her family duties keep her from jumping as much as she used to, though she does rather more than her husband.

William Barker

Great Britain

William Barker (b. 1946), born like his elder

William Barker and North Flight

brother David Boston, in Northallerton, Yorkshire, also started in the saddle at an early age. He has had his greatest successes on North Flight, a mare bred in 1958 by the Cleveland Bay stallion Lord Fairfax out of a thoroughbred mare. William Barker had her as an unbroken three-year-old. He broke and trained her himself, and in 1963, only her second season, won the Young Riders' Championship of Great Britain, which they repeated the following year, and helped the British Junior team to take the European Junior Championship in Rotterdam.

They made their senior international debut in Aachen the following year, and went well enough there and at home to be taken to Tokyo as a reserve. William Barker was not required to jump there; had he been, he would have been the youngest ever Olympic show jump rider—an honour which goes to Janou Lefebvre, who was nineteen in Tokyo.

1965 was an outstandingly successful year for William Barker and North Flight: as well as the Renault Grand Prix—which carried a car as first prize—at Ascot, they won the Grand Prix in Rotterdam, and then the *victor ludorum* for the Ronson Trophy at the Horse of the Year Show.

Taken along steadily with the 1968 Olympics in view, North Flight had the bad luck to cut a leg badly at the beginning of Mexico year, in Rome. She did not reappear for five weeks, when winning at the Royal Highland. This looked promising, but the mare could not find her true form again, and she had to be dropped as a Mexico possible.

Arthur Blickenstorfer
Switzerland

Arthur Blickenstorfer (b. 1935), who started jumping when he was eight years old, has been a stalwart of the Swiss team for several years. He was the Swiss champion in 1965 on Apache, a German-bred Hanoverian, then ten years old, which had been previously ridden by Alwin Schockemohle.

Blickenstorfer took him over after two other Swiss riders had tried their hands at him, and won with him in Aachen, Rotterdam and Amsterdam as well as the National Championship. He was second for the Swiss title in 1968 and 1969 and third in 1961 and 1962.

In 1967 Blickenstorfer won the Schlageter Cup, formerly the Baumgartner Cup, which is awarded annually to the Swiss rider with the best international record.

He made his Olympic debut in Mexico with the difficult Marianka, finishing equal thirteenth individually, with the team placed sixth.

Caroline Bradley
Great Britain

Caroline Bradley (b. 1946) has made her international mark with a variety of horses, and has

David Broome and Mister Softee

proved her ability to get a 'good tune' out of each of them. She made her international debut in the swamp-fever-restricted show at Dublin, in 1966, where she won two classes on the little Russian-bred chestnut Ivanovitch.

At the beginning of 1967 she was given the mount on Mr Robert Hanson's Franco, on which David Barker had had such an unhappy Olympic debut in Rome seven years earlier. That summer they went with a young British team to the internationals in Olsztyn, Poland, and Leipzig, East Germany, in both of which shows Britain, including Caroline and Franco, won the Nations Cups, and helped their country towards winning the World Championship for the President's Cup.

That autumn they went on the North American tour, and finished second to Harvey Smith and O'Malley in the Grand Prix in New York. Then in 1968 she went on the same circuit to augment the Olympic team, and in Toronto was allowed in, and proceeded to win, the Canadian National Championship.

With her dedication and ability Caroline Bradley looks set for many more international successes.

Jared Brinsmade

United States

Jared Brinsmade (b. 1946) is one of the United States team's brightest young hopes. A college student from Bethany, Connecticut, he was discovered by the U.S.E.T. trainer, Bert de Nemethy during one of the regular trials which de Nemethy holds all over the United States to find potential international riders, who then go to the U.S.E.T. headquarters for training.

Brinsmade made his debut at the Harrisburg show in 1968, while the No. 1 team were busy with the Olympic Games in Mexico, when he finished runner-up for the leading rider title. In 1969 he was in all three Nations Cup teams, riding his Harrisburg Grand Prix winner Triple Crown in Harrisburg and New York, where they had a double-clear, and Act I in Toronto. He and Act I also finished fourth to Jimmy Day and Steelmaster in the Rothman's Canadian Championship, formerly the North American Championship.

David Broome

Great Britain

David Broome (b. 1940) has the advantage of a father who had jumped himself and is one of the shrewdest men in the sport at spotting a potentially good horse. Young David, brought up on his father's farm near Chepstow, had his first experience in the ring when he was just nine years old, but, though he had plenty of success as a junior, it was not for another eight years that he was to get the horses that would take him on his way to the top.

In October, 1957, Fred Broome bought an ex-Army horse named Wildfire for just £60, and two

Douglas Bunn and Beethoven

years later he finished up as the season's leading money-winner; altogether he earned around £14,000 for the Broomes before being retired.

Broome later acquired Sunsalve, with whom he won a European Championship and an Olympic bronze medal. When Sunsalve died in 1962, Broome was without a truly great mount until 1966, when he first teamed with Mister Softee, with whom he has been equally successful.

In Rotterdam in 1967 both Broome and Mister Softee won their second European Championship, 'coming from behind' with two sparkling rounds in the final to dethrone Nelson Pessoa. Broome was 'robbed' of a North American tour, at least in the saddle, when Abelene fell with him at Wembley and broke his leg.

An automatic choice for the Mexico Olympics, Broome and Mister Softee won the bronze individual medal there after jumping off with three others, with another display of the brilliant jumping at speed which is their forte. It was this same formidable weapon which gave them their third European title at Hickstead in 1969; Alwin Schockemohle was ahead coming to the final competition, but two fast, faultless rounds by Mister Softee gave the German all too much to do. Mister Softee, who had won the Irish Trophy in Dublin in 1967 and 1968 went lame before he could try for a hat-trick in 1969.

Major Placings Olympic Games: 1960, individual bronze on Sunsalve; 1968, individual bronze on Mister Softee. World Championship: 1960, third on Sunsalve. European Championships: 1961, won on Sunsalve; 1967, won on Mister Softee; 1969, won on Mister Softee.

Douglas Bunn

Great Britain

Although he has made the international grade as a rider of show jumpers, it is for his work on the ground that Douglas Bunn (b. 1928) is most noted—the ground being the All-England Jumping Ground at Hickstead, Sussex. Britain's answer to the continental showgrounds, with their banks and permanent fences, and more variety than was seen at any English show before 1960.

In April, 1960, Hickstead staged its first show. In those days it was very different to the present-day, well-set-out show ground: a roped arena, a barn with a telephone and a few tents to serve as offices. And a lot of antipathy and apathy to overcome. From the beginning there were those who were opposed to the permanent and unusual fences for which Hickstead has become known. Time and again the cry 'this isn't show jumping' would go up from those quite happy to farm around the small county shows jumping interminable posts-and-rails. But those who travelled the international circuit soon found that a few preliminary outings at Hickstead could make a good deal of difference. It is no coincidence that

Frank and Mary Chapot

the United States team make Hickstead their base when in England.

Each year the ground has developed, both in the number of rings, catering for hundreds of novices as well as the top ranking internationals, and in the sophistication of the International Arena, inside and out. Permanent stands have grown, a double-deck clubhouse for spectators. An innovation for 1970 is the lake, replacing the old Table, which is based on the well-known one at Aachen.

Bunn makes no secret of his wish eventually to stage the Royal International Horse Show, and when the London–Brighton Motorway is built, if not before, his dream may well come to pass.

Gonda Butters

South Africa

Gonda Butters (b. 1944) was the 'star' of the only South African team which ever toured to Europe, in 1958, before the horse sickness ban came into being.

The team was in fact a junior (under eighteen) one, and in the European Junior Championship that year, in Hanover, finished runners-up to Britain.

Gonda Butters, from Cape Town, who was awarded her junior Springbok colours in the year she came to Europe and her full colours in 1962, was champion of South Africa in 1961 on Gunga Din, another of the horses she had brought to Europe, again in 1965 on Eldorado and in 1967 with Ratification.

Henrique Callado

Portugal

The most consistently successful Portuguese rider since the war, and responsible for much of the success of the others is Colonel Henrique Callado (b. 1920), who made his Olympic debut in London in 1948, and was still riding at that standard in Tokyo in 1964.

Two of the best horses he has ridden in recent years are Joc de l'Ile, a French-bred son of that great sire Furioso, which he rode in Tokyo, and with which he won one competition in the 1963 European championship, and Konak, winner of many major competitions and his partner in the 1961 European Championships.

Now director of the school at Mafra, which started as a cavalry school and now takes in civilian trainees as well, he still leads the Portuguese teams in Nations Cups.

Sam Campbell

Australia

A member of the Australian team in Mexico, Campbell (b. 1944) and April Love finished equal 26th, and their team ninth. In the following year he had a successful tour of the continental indoor shows: he was leading rider in Hanover, and

Diana Conolly-Carew and Barrymore

was the winner of the Dortmund Championship.

In England for the mandatory quarantine period before returning to Australia April Love lamed herself quite early on, but recovered in time to finish second to Raimondo d'Inzeo and Bellevue for the Irish Trophy, the Grand Prix of the Dublin Horse Show which carries world record prize money, and was worth £1,250 to the Australian for second place.

Frank Chapot

United States

Frank Chapot (b. 1934), a salesman for his family's leather goods firm in New Jersey, has been a stalwart of the United States team since the Stockholm Olympics in 1956.

He joined the show jumping squad in 1955, and in 1956 rode Belair into 27th place individually, with the U.S. team fifth. Three years later he took over Diamant, the horse with which Fritz Thiedemann had finished second in the 1953 World Championship. Though no longer in the first flush of youth Diamant made a useful contribution to the U.S. team's tour of Europe, and then in Chicago helped them win the Pan American Games gold medal, with rounds for eight and then four faults.

In the 1960 Olympics Chapot rode the veteran Trail Guide, who was then twenty and had been in the Stockholm Games, ridden by Hugh Wiley. Chapot did not start for the individual competition, but in the team event he had the best United States total, twenty for the two rounds, to help his team take the silver medal.

It was the following year that Chapot joined up with his best horse, the giant San Lucas. Chapot rode him in the U.S. team which retained the Pan American Games gold medal in Sao Paolo, but he caught an infection at the Games and was out of action for several months. In the Tokyo Games, where the U.S. was sixth, San Lucas had recovered well enough to take the individual seventh place.

Chapot and San Lucas, a fine team combination, helped the U.S. to win the four Nations Cups they contested in Europe in 1968, in London, Dublin, Ostend and Rotterdam.

Major Placings Olympic Games: 1960, team bronze with Trail Guide. Pan American Games: 1959, team gold with Diamant; 1963, team gold with San Lucas; 1967, team silver with San Lucas. European Championship: 1966, second with San Lucas.

Mary Chapot

United States

Mary Chapot (b. 1944), who was Miss Mairs until she married fellow team-member Frank Chapot in 1965, was the first United States rider ever to win a Games gold medal when she triumphed at the Pan American Games in 1963. She has also represented the United States in

Jim Day and Canadian Club

the Olympic Games at Tokyo and in Mexico.

Possibly the most stylish rider in a team famed for its uniform elegance, Miss Mairs made a great impression when she made her European debut in 1964. She had a most successful Royal International, winning the Imperial Cup on her German-bred Anakonda and the most valuable event of the show, the John Player Trophy, on Tomboy.

In 1968 she rode White Lightning to victory in the Queen Elizabeth II Cup at the Royal International, the first American ever to have won this coveted women's competition, and with two good rounds, for four faults and then clear, helped her team take the Prince of Wales Cup.

Major placings Pan American Games: 1963, individual and team gold medals with Tomboy; 1967, team silver with White Lightning.

Oscar Christi

Chile

Oscar Christi, who died in 1965, was one of Chile's finest post-war riders, and led his team to the silver medal, only five faults behind the British gold medallists, in the Helsinki Olympic Games in 1952. In addition Christi himself won the individual silver with Bambi after a five-horse jump-off for all three medals which was won by Pierre Jonqueres d'Oriola with Ali Baba. Three years later Christi and Bambi were in the bronze medal team in the Pan American Games, won by Mexico, and Christi rode Barrano in the team that took the Pan American bronze in 1959.

Major placings Olympic Games: 1952, individual and team silver with Bambi. Pan American Games: 1955, team bronze with Bambi; 1959, team bronze with Barrano.

Diana Conolly-Carew

Republic of Ireland

Diana Conolly-Carew, one of the most dashing riders to come out of Ireland, has had considerable success throughout Europe and in North America, especially with her brilliant grey Barrymore.

Diana and Barrymore had possibly the greatest triumph in their long and rewarding career in 1966, when they alone could jump clear over a big course for the Irish Trophy, the Dublin Grand Prix. The following spring they gave one of their characteristic dashing displays to win in Rome from Raimondo d'Inzeo and his Olympic horse Bellevue.

Alison Dawes (nee Westwood)

Great Britain

Alison Dawes (b. 1944) was brought up on a Cotswold farm, and made her debut at jumping when she was eleven. Successful in junior and

Oscar Christi

Alison Dawes and The Maverick

young riders classes, her first truly international horse was The Maverick, which she bought from Douglas Bunn in 1963.

Their career together started at a high level, the Royal International, but it was not until two years later, 1965, that The Maverick really showed his paces. Then Miss Westwood was the leading rider at four C.H.I.O.s, Aachen, London, Rotterdam and Geneva, as well as the unofficial international at Enschede. They were also third in the World Championship to Marion Coakes's Stroller.

After being placed three times in the Queen Elizabeth Cup they finally won in 1969. In Dublin they finished third in the European Championship to Iris Kellett.

Major placings World Championship: 1965, third on The Maverick. European Championship: 1969, third on The Maverick.

Jim Day

Canada

Jim Day (b. 1946) was the youngest of the Canadian team which surprised so many by winning the gold medal at the Mexico Olympic Games.

Day's best horse so far is Canadian Club, an impressive looking, 16·2 h.h. chestnut, foaled in 1960 on which he won the individual gold medal at the 1967 Pan American Games—the first Games gold medal that any Canadian show jumper had ever won.

In 1969, as well as making two of the three Nations Cup team, in Harrisburg and in Toronto, where the Canadians beat the United States team, Day rode the then six-year-old Steelmaster to victory in the Rothman's Canadian Championship, formerly the North American Championship, beating his compatriot Jimmy Elder with his Mexico horse The Immigrant.

Major placings Olympic Games: 1968, team gold with Canadian Club. Pan American Games: 1967, individual gold and team bronze with Canadian Club.

Jose Alvarez de Bohorquez

Spain

Jose Alvarez de Bohorquez, the lawyer son of the Marquis de los Trujillos, who was a member of the Spanish gold medal team in the 1928 Olympic Games in Amsterdam, is currently one of his country's most successful riders.

He won the 1961 Nice Grand Prix on Descosido, and with the Anglo-Arab Quizas, who won his first international competition in 1961 and was consistently in the prizes thereafter, reached the final of the 1966 World Championship.

Major placing World Championship: 1966, second on Quizas.

J. A. Bohorquez

Raimondo d'Inzeo

Carlos Delia
Argentina

Carlos Delia (b. 1923), has been the mainstay of the Argentine team ever since he and El Linyera took the individual silver medal in the 1951 Pan American Games.

In the 1960 World Championship he rode Huipil, one of the best show jumping horses of the past decade, to finish runner-up to Raimondo d'Inzeo and on the grey mestizo Popin, Delia won both a team and an individual silver medal in the 1963 Pan American Games, behind Mary Mairs and Tomboy.

Major placings Pan American Games: 1951, team and individual silver, with El Linyera; 1963, team and individual silver with Popin. World Championship: 1960, second with Huipil.

Alfonso Queipo de Llano
Spain

Alfonso Queipo de Llano has been one of the Spanish military team's most successful riders in the last ten years. Although he rode Eolo into fourth place in the 1963 European Championship, his best horse has been Infernal, a son of the great French sire of show jumpers Furioso, bred in 1952, with whom he won the Grand Prix in Rome in 1964. In the Tokyo Olympics they finished 26th, with Spain eighth.

Bertalan de Nemethy
United States

Bertalan de Nemethy (b. 1911), who took over the training of the United States Equestrian Team in 1955, has welded one of the most attractive and most effective squads throughout the show jumping world.

Born in Gyor, Hungary, son of a Count and the owner of large estates, he learned to ride on his father's ponies and horses. He entered the Hungarian Military Academy Ludovica when he was seventeen, and stayed there for four years until, in 1932, he went as a Lieutenant to the 3rd Hussars of Count Nadassy in Schopron.

In 1936 de Nemethy was seconded to the *Reit- und Fahrlehrerinstitut* in Orkenny-Tabor, which was a training school specialising in riders of Olympic potential, three-day event and dressage riders as well as show jumpers. Each year four riders, two each from the Cavalry and the Artillery, entered the school for a two-year course, and most of them ended up in an Olympic team.

In 1944 de Nemethy went from Germany to Denmark, where he worked as a riding instructor until 1952, when he went on to the United States. In 1955, two months after the United States team had put up a fairly disastrous performance in the Pan American Games in Mexico City, where they finished last of the four teams, de Nemethy was engaged as the U.S.E.T.'s trainer.

Carlos Delia and Discutido

From 1955 to 1969 the United States team has competed in 75 Nations Cups, of which they have won 41. Twice, in 1966 and 1968 they have won the President's Cup—on the latter occasion winning all the Nations Cups they entered, in London, Dublin, Ostend and Rotterdam in Europe and New York and Toronto on the North American circuit. From 1965 to 1969 they won sixteen out of the twenty Nations Cups they entered.

In the 1956 Olympic Games the American team was placed fifth, but four years later finished second only to the invincible German trio, Winkler, Thiedemann and Schockemohle. The U.S. team was George Morris, Frank Chapot and Bill Steinkraus. In Tokyo, where Steinkraus had to drop out at the last minute when Sinjon was lame, the U.S. team finished sixth, but in Mexico they missed a bronze medal by the narrowest possible margin, just a quarter of a time-fault in a contest of astronomical scores; Germany's third-placed team had $117\frac{1}{4}$ to the U.S.A.'s $117\frac{1}{2}$. And of course Steinkraus and Snowbound won the individual gold medal but had to drop out of the team competition when Snowbound went lame.

Based at the U.S.E.T.'s National Training Centre, at Gladstone, New Jersey, de Nemethy, who took American citizenship in 1958, continues to produce riders of such ability that it must only be a matter of time before they break America's last important 'bogy', the Olympic team gold medal.

Piero d'Inzeo
Italy

The d'Inzeo brothers, Piero (b. 1923) and Raimondo, have over the past two decades been among the world's outstanding show jumpers, winning between them every major honour: gold, silver and bronze Olympic medals, World and European Championships.

Following closely the theories of Caprilli, Piero d'Inzeo developed a most attractive style, and throughout his career has insisted first and foremost on schooling his horses in a classic and thorough manner.

In the 1956 Olympic Games Piero d'Inzeo and Uruguay took the individual bronze and helped their team to the silver. One of five lying equal second with eight faults behind the eventual winner Winkler's Halla, Uruguay added just three faults after the first round, for a refusal.

Rome, 1960, was the d'Inzeos finest hour. In the individual contest they finished first and second, Piero taking the silver medal on The Rock, with just two mistakes in each round, including the water twice. The Rock had a fairly disastrous first round in the team competition, but rallied in the second and their team took the bronze medal.

Piero rode Sunbeam, bought from Frank Kernan in Ireland, in the Tokyo Games to take the team bronze with the best Italian score, finishing ninth individually. On the German-bred

P. J. d'Oriola and P. d'Inzeo

Fidux, Rome Grand Prix winner of 1968, he finished equal seventh in Mexico, with a disappointing 12-fault second round. Their team finished fifth.

Major placings Olympic Games: 1956, team silver and individual bronze with Uruguay; 1960, individual silver and team bronze with The Rock; 1964, team bronze with Sunbeam. World Championships: 1953, fourth on Uruguay. European Championships: 1958, second on The Rock; 1959, won on Uruguay; 1961, second on Pioneer; 1962, third on The Rock.

Raimondo d'Inzeo

Italy

Unlike Piero, Raimondo (b. 1925) had no immediate urge to display his equestrian skill, and for the first ten years or so of his life was scarcely more than a spectator. He rode, but in an off-hand manner that did little to please his father.

It was probably Piero d'Inzeo's early competition successes that fired the enthusiasm of Raimondo. He went to Rome University, but after two years the call of horses in his blood was too strong; he left, and joined the Italian cavalry, transferring in 1950 to the Italian army-police force, the famed Carabinieri.

Raimondo rode with less style than his brother, but with rather more competitiveness. He liked to study his horse well before taking him into the ring, and then would fling his whole heart into winning, where Piero was most concerned with a fluent performance.

It took Winkler and Halla to foil Raimondo in the Stockholm Olympics. D'Inzeo was riding Merano, probably the greatest horse he ever had, bred in Italy at the Morese stud in Ponto Cagnano and sold to d'Inzeo as a four-year-old for a meagre £200 so that the horse would have a rider worthy of him. In the second round of the Olympics only Halla and Merano went clear, but the Italian horse had had eight faults first time to his rival's four.

Raimondo rode Posillipo in the Rome Olympics in 1960, and first time jumped the only clear round in the entire competition—a phenomenal performance over an extremely tricky course, lightly built and with a treble of decidedly difficult distances. Next time round they slipped slightly from their pinnacle, going in the water and hitting two others, but their twelve-fault total was good enough for the gold.

When the World Championship was held in Venice soon after Rome, d'Inzeo rode Gowran Girl, an Irish-bred mare noted for her difficult temperament. None of the other three finalists, Delia of Argentina, Steinkraus or Broome could find the key to her in the time allowed, and d'Inzeo kept his title.

Major placings Olympic Games: 1956, individual and team silver with Merano; 1960, individual

Anneli Drummond-Hay and Peter Robeson

gold and team bronze with Posillipo; 1964, team bronze with Posillipo. World Championships: 1955, second with Nadir; 1956, won with Merano; 1960, won with Gowran Girl; 1966, third with Bowjack.

Jean Francois d'Orgeix

France

In the immediate post-war days Jean Francois 'Paqui' d'Orgeix, now the Marquis, was one of the most successful and popular of European riders.

At the London Olympics he and Sucre de Pomme won the individual bronze medal for France in a jump-off for the silver and bronze with Ruben Uriza of Mexico and Franklin Wing of the U.S.A., who was riding Democrat.

With his dashing style and crowd-pleasing charm, the Chevalier was a particular favourite at the indoor shows in Paris, at the Vel d'Hiv', and at Harringay, where he came over to get the first Horse of the Year Show off to a sparkling start in 1949.

Major placing Olympic Games: 1948, individual bronze with Sucre de Pomme.

Pierre Jonqueres d'Oriola

France

Pierre Jonqueres d'Oriola (b. 1920) is the only man ever to have won two individual gold medals for show jumping as far apart as 1952 and 1964. He has had enormous success on a number of different horses, winning also the 1966 World Championship.

Along with the Chevalier d'Orgeix he was one of the first French to break the military monopoly in show jumping teams, making his international debut in Geneva in 1946. Riding the Anglo-Arab L'Historiette, which his father had given him, he finished second to d'Orgeix in the Geneva Grand Prix, had his first international victory in Berne and then won the Grand Prix in Zurich.

In 1947 on Marquis III, he went to London and won the first post-war King George V Gold Cup. It was also on Marquis that he rode in his first Nations Cup, at Nice.

D'Oriola rode Ali Baba to a gold medal at Helsinki in 1952 and then repeated the performance in 1964 on Lutteur. D'Oriola first noticed Lutteur at Font-Romeu, in July 1963, when ridden by his owner Florence de Chaffaut. She had been riding the then-eight-year-old for two years, but he was obviously not a girl's horse. D'Oriola could see his potential and spent the winter trying to reach a rapport with him. Taken steadily in training, Lutteur finished the first round at Tokyo in fourth place, with eight jumping faults, including going in the water for the first time ever, and one for time; three others had eight faults. In the second round Schridde and Dozent, with twelve and a half faults first

Ted Edgar and Uncle Max

time, had only one and a quarter for time and were leading when Lutteur came in, with one fence in hand. But he did not need it, flying over the final oxer which he had hit earlier, and in time with half a second to spare.

In Mexico d'Oriola rode Nagir, a horse not up to the standard of Ali Baba, Lutteur (who died in 1969) or Pomone, but helped his team to take the silver medal.

Major placings Olympic Games: 1952, individual gold with Ali Baba; 1964, individual gold and team silver with Lutteur; 1968, team silver with Nagir. World Championships: 1953, third on Ali Baba; 1954, second on Arlequin; 1955, fourth; 1966, won on Pomone. European Championships: 1959, second on Virtuoso.

Anneli Drummond-Hay

Great Britain

Anneli Drummond-Hay (b. 1937) is one of the few riders successful in both three-day events and show jumping. Born in Dorset, she moved soon afterwards to Perth, Scotland, where she was brought up with horses right from the start, indulging in every sort of 'horsey' pursuit—gymkhanas, jumping, even 'flapping' races.

Miss Drummond-Hay on Merely-a-Monarch, won the Imperial Cup, one of the oldest trophies of the Royal International; Monarch was such a brilliant horse that one National Hunt trainer stated that he thought he would have been quite capable of winning the Grand National. They looked certain of a Tokyo Olympic place, but 1964 was a disastrous year: Monarch completely lost his form—because of ill-health, it proved—and Miss Drummond-Hay nearly lost Monarch. She had sold the horse to Mr. Robert Hanson with the proviso that she should ride him until the Olympics. When he went off so much Mr. Hanson tried to substitute David Broome, but this was a short-lived effort.

Gradually brought back to health and, with help from Nelson Pessoa, to form, Monarch again returned to his rider's ownership, in partnership with Col. Tom Greenhalgh. In the autumn of 1967 they went to the indoor C.H.I.O. in Geneva, and won the Grand Prix.

In 1968 Miss Drummond-Hay won the European Championship. The foundation of this success was a little, former hunt horse named Xanthos, who scorched round to win the opening speed class, when Merely-a-Monarch, who is always better over big courses, failed to reach his best form.

Major placings Three-day events: Badminton, 1960, second on Perhaps; Burghley, 1961, won with Merely-a-Monarch; Badminton, 1962, won with Merely-a-Monarch. European Championships: 1963, third on Merely-a-Monarch; 1968, won with Xanthos and Merely-a-Monarch; 1969, second on Xanthos.

Anton Ebben and Prinz Ayax

Toni Ebben
Holland

Ebben (b. 1930) did not start show jumping until he was 21, making his international debut three years later in Germany. A businessman in Hilversum, he finds time to get to most of the important continental shows.

A particularly popular visitor to the Horse of the Year show, he won the Harringay Spurs for the most successful rider there in 1964. His best horse, Kairouan, by the French sire Furioso, is especially effective over big fences.

Ted Edgar
Great Britain

An ebullient character whose boisterousness has not always been to his own benefit, Ted Edgar (b. 1933) first came to show jumping fame on the little mare Jane Summers who was rescued from the knackers in her youth. Edgar bought her in 1952 and she was outstandingly successful in National competitions. In 1957 she won the National Championship, and that year Edgar made his international debut in Rotterdam where he and Jane Summers jumped two clear rounds to give Britain a narrow victory.

Never a man to lack courage, Edgar gained wide acclaim when, in 1963, he went round the tough British Jumping Derby course at Hickstead with one arm in a sling. Despite his handicap he had only two fences down on Jacopo, which his wife Elizabeth rode to victory in the 1964 National Championship, and which was ridden by Elizabeth Edgar's brother, David Broome, in the Tokyo Olympics.

Towards the end of 1968 Edgar bought the former rodeo horse Uncle Max from the American Neal Shapiro. Uncle Max, with an extrovert temperament to match Edgar's, won the high-jump competition at the Horse of the Year Show only a few weeks after Edgar bought him.

In 1969, after a disastrous Aachen—in the Nations Cup Edgar and Uncle Max were twice on the floor, and were eliminated in both rounds—they bounced characteristically back to take the King George V Gold Cup at the Royal International, and at the Horse of the Year show won the Leading Show Jumper title.

Jim Elder
Canada

Jim Elder (b. 1934) can reasonably be claimed as the principal architect in the Canadian team's gold medal victory in the Mexico Olympics.

A member of the team which caused a major surprise by taking the 1958 Nations Cup at the New York show, Elder bought O'Malley in 1959 and trained him for two years before winning the *puissance* at the Toronto Winter Fair, and selling the horse for $30,000 to Yorkshireman Robert Hanson.

John Fahey and Bonvale

Elder had intended riding Pieces of Eight, a prolific winner and his Pan American mount, in Mexico, but that horse developed pleurisy soon after the team's arrival there, and he had to rely on The Immigrant, an Irish-bred who had come to Canada via the United States.

The Immigrant had been bought only in April, 1968 as a six-year-old with an obvious 'pop' but still very green. However, he jumped like a hero in Mexico, getting only twelve faults in the two rounds, and finally finishing sixth. In the team competition The Immigrant had the fifth best score of all, $27\frac{1}{4}$ faults, and the best for his team, leaving them nearly two fences clear of the French.

Major placings Olympic Games: 1956, three-day event team bronze with Colleen; 1968, show jumping team gold with The Immigrant. Pan American Games: 1959, three-day event team gold; 1967, show jumping team bronze with Pieces of Eight.

John Fahey

Australia

John Fahey (b. 1943) became the first Australian show jumper to gain international notice when he and the diminutive Bonvale lost the Tokyo bronze medal only after a jump-off with Britain's Peter Robeson and Firecrest.

Fahey, who had won his first jumping competition when he was only eight years old, and his agile little horse had two fences down in each round in Tokyo; in the barrage they again hit two, while Firecrest went clear.

In Mexico Fahey again rode Bonvale, finishing equal 21st in the individual and having the best score in the Australian team which finished ninth. Unfortunately Bonvale broke down at the beginning of their 1969 tour in Britain, which left him out for the season, and Fahey's other horse, Maestro, though useful, was not of the same calibre.

Lucia Faria

Brazil

Lucia Faria (b. 1945), of Rio de Janeiro, Brazil, learned to ride first with her parents, who were, however, only weekend riders, and then at a club with which Nelson Pessoa has been associated for nearly twenty years as a pupil and latterly as adviser.

At the Mexico Olympics Miss Faria and Rush de Camp finished twelfth in the individual placings, above both her more experienced compatriots, Pessoa and Jose Fernandez, while the team finished seventh.

Andrew Fielder

Great Britain

Perhaps the most unmistakable partnership in

Lucia Faria

Andrew Fielder and Vibart

show jumping is that of Andrew Fielder (b. 1947) and Vibart. Famous for his kick-back and whirling tail, Vibart has been described as 'not a horse, but a helicopter'.

A horse of tremendous power, which Fielder is able to give full reign, Vibart won the Leading Show Jumper title at Wembley in 1963; the only combination able to cope with an extremely difficult course. They won it again in 1966 and 1968.

National champions in 1966, when competition at home was at its strongest, because the swamp fever ban prevented horses going abroad, Fielder and Vibart had their greatest season in 1967—and that crowded into one week. In Aachen they became the first Britons ever to take the Grand Prix, which is always jumped over massive fences; then the following Sunday notched another 'first', in the Hamburg Jumping Derby, the prototype of Jumping Derbies the world over.

Tom Gayford

Canada

Tom Gayford (b. 1929), whose father also rode for Canada, joined the team when he was nineteen in 1949 and contested the three-day event at Helsinki in the 1952 Olympics.

Gayford rode Big Dee in the team which won the bronze medal when Canada contested the show jumping in the Pan American Games for the first time in 1957, but the horse had colic just before the individual competition in the Mexico Games, which let in 'Torchy' Miller and the ex-English horse Beefeater. For the team event, however, he had recovered enough to get round for a respectable $39\frac{1}{2}$-fault total.

Major placings Olympic Games: 1968, team gold medal with Big Dee. Pan American Games: 1959, three-day event team gold medal; 1967, show jumping team bronze medal with Big Dee.

Francisco Goyoaga

Spain

To Francisco 'Paco' Goyoaga, probably the best civilian show jumping rider that Spain has produced, went the honour of winning the first show jumping World Championship, in 1953.

When the F.E.I. decided to hold a World Championship in Paris in 1953 the Spanish Federation alotted to Goyoaga an Army horse, Quorum, which had also been in the 1948 team, ridden by Colonel Navarro.

Since that time Quorum had lost interest in show jumping, napping, and with a tendency to lameness which boded ill for his chances. Nor did they look much brighter in the first of the preliminary competitions, when Goyoaga and Quorum qualified only by the skin of their teeth.

In the final they were matched against the Helsinki gold medallists d'Oriola and Ali Baba, Thiedemann with Diamant and Piero d'Inzeo on

Seamus Hayes and Goodbye

George Hobbs and Royal Lord

Uruguay—a formidable trio, but Goyoaga, who collected just eight faults in the final squeezed home by a quarter of a fault from Thiedemann.

In Aachen Goyoaga and Fahnenkonig were runners-up to Raimondo d'Inzeo and Merano for the World title, in a tight finish, with Thiedemann again just behind, on Meteor. At the same meeting they triumphed in the Grand Prix.

With the French-bred Kif Kif Goyoaga won the Spanish Championship in 1960, 1961 and 1964, and the Grand Prix in Geneva. A serious heart operation put Goyoaga out of action for some time but he returned for a successful swan-song to Geneva in 1965, when Spain scored a surprise success in the Nations Cup. He retired soon afterwards, selling Kif Kif to the Spanish Government for a record £20,000.

Major placings World Championships: 1953, won on Quorum; 1954, third; 1956, second on Fahnenkonig.

Bob Grayston

South Africa

Bob Grayston (b. 1912) has been the best-known South African rider in Europe for many years. He emigrated from England to South Africa in the 1930s, started a riding school in Johannesburg, and made his first post-war tour in 1953, after which he regularly spent his summers in England, often raiding the Continental shows.

Among the many useful horses he brought to Britain was the former show hack The Sea Hawk, one of the best speed horses ever. In 1960 Grayston bought Royal Searcher, a horse once thought of Olympic potential, on which he won many competitions, including the Wills Grand Prix at Hickstead. When he retired in 1968, Grayston sold Royal Searcher to the British-based American Warren Wofford, husband of the former Dawn Palethorpe.

Max Hauri

Switzerland

Max Hauri (b. 1941) was Swiss champion in 1962 and third two years later. A horse dealer, he spends much of his time travelling around Europe and to Ireland buying horses.

In 1962 he shared the Belgian Grand Prix, on Preslan, with the great Irish combination of Tommy Wade and Dundrum. In the 1964 Olympic Games in Tokyo he had the best Swiss performance, finishing tenth individually on Millview, who could have been higher but for his time faults in each round. The team took ninth place.

Seamus Hayes

Republic of Ireland

Seamus Hayes (b. 1925), one of the most popular riders ever to come out of Ireland, reached the

Bob Grayston and Royal Searcher

F. Goyoaga and Toscanella

top of his profession when he came to England as a 21-year-old, in 1946.

He was leading rider in Britain in 1949, 1950 and again in 1952. On Tommy Makin's great mare Sheila he won the Grand Prix at the Royal International Horse Show in 1950, and the *puissance* there in 1952.

It was in 1960 that he first rode the then seven-year-old Goodbye, a chestnut gelding by Rennwood, bred in County Kerry, for Lord Harrington. A year later they won the inaugural British Jumping Derby, with the only clear round, and in 1964 they won it for the second time, after a jump-off with Marion Coakes and Stroller. In 1963 Hayes won the historic Imperial Cup at the Royal International Horse Show with Ardmore, who is now with the Irish Army.

Altogether Goodbye jumped 7 ft 2 in six times before he retired at the end of 1967. With his retirement, and the sale of Ardmore and Doneraile, to the Italians, Hayes has lacked a horse of international calibre in the last season or so.

George Hobbs

Great Britain

Sussex farmer George Hobbs (b. 1924) started show jumping at twelve. At school in Ewell, Surrey, with those two great National Hunt riders Fred Winter and Dave Dick, it was not surprising when he also turned his attention to steeplechasing.

After riding as an amateur he was persuaded to turn professional, which was unfortunate since this also classifies him as a professional for show jumping as far as the Olympic Committee is concerned. In 1957 he started riding one of the most consistent of all British show jumpers, Royal Lord, a former Hunt horse who had won the Foxhunter championship in 1955. Royal Lord started Hobbs's aggravating run of near-misses in the King George V Cup when, in 1961, he finished third. In 1962 Hobbs was second on Atilla, and he was again runner-up in 1963 and 1964 on Brandy Soda. Hobbs's victories on Brandy Soda that year included the £2,000 News of the World Championship; he was leading rider in Dublin and would have been in the Tokyo Olympic team but the I.O.C. would not allow it.

Carol Hofmann

United States

Carol Hofmann (b. 1942), daughter of the president of the vast Johnson and Johnson combine, joined the United States Equestrian Team in 1962, when she was nineteen. She made her first trip to Europe two years later, and won in Ostend, and in 1966 scored in Toronto. She came over to Europe again in 1967, and improved rapidly, and the following year notched two victories at the Dublin show and three, including the Grand Prix, in Rotterdam on her very useful grey Out Late, as well as helping in two Nations Cup wins.

Carol Hofmann and Out Late

Kurt Jarasinski and Godewind

Kurt Jarasinski

West Germany

Kurt Jarasinski (b. 1938) inherited the mantle of the great Fritz Thiedemann, of whom he was a pupil, of riding for the Holstein club at Elmshorn. This club was formed by breeders of Holstein horses, and represents a collective effort to maintain the high quality of this breed, which produces horses for many purposes: riding and driving as well as jumping. Jarasinski also edits the Holstein stud book.

After trials between East and West German riders Jarasinski was among those selected to ride in the Tokyo Olympics, with Torro, which he regards as his best horse. With $22\frac{1}{4}$ faults they finished eighth individually, and of course won a team gold medal.

Major placing Olympic Games: 1964, team gold medal with Torro.

Sophie Joncquez

France

Sophie Joncquez (b. 1949) is one of the rising French women riders. The daughter of a civil servant, she learned to ride when she was seven, at Le Touquet, and became French junior champion.

In 1968 Sophie, a language student, won the Women's Championship in Wiesbaden and the National *Criterium de France*. Despite the absence of dual silver medallist Janou Lefebvre, resting herself and her horses after a long and successful season, Sophie was a worthy winner of the French Women's Championship in 1969.

Iris Kellett

Republic of Ireland

Iris Kellett has over the years been one of the most successful of Irish lady riders, culminating in 1969 with a victory in the European Championship. On her great horse, Rusty, she won the first running of the Queen Elizabeth Cup, a victory they repeated in 1951. In those days the Irish team was entirely military, so Miss Kellett had to confine her talents to individual competitions.

The European Championship in 1969 was held at the Dublin Horse Show, and turned out to be a great home victory for Miss Kellett, on Morning Light, when she won over Alison Westwood and Anneli Drummond-Hay.

Major placing European Championship: 1969, won on Morning Light.

Kathy Kusner

United States

Kathy Kusner (b. 1940), one of the mainstays of the United States Olympic team, numbers among

Sophie Joncquez

Iris Kellett and Morning Light

many other distinctions those of being the only non-European to have won the women's European Championship, and the first woman to be a licensed jockey in America.

When she was eighteen she set an American women's high jump record of 7 ft 3 in on a mare named Freckles, and in 1962 joined the United States Equestrian Team. The following year she won the championship in New York. In 1963 also she was in the U.S. team that won the Pan American Games gold medal riding Unusual, a half-brother to the former Olympic horse Miss Budweiser.

On the then 12-year-old Untouchable Kathy won the 1964 Irish Trophy, the Grand Prix, in Dublin. When she repeated this in 1965 she became the first rider ever to win successive Irish Trophies on the same horse. She also won the Olympic Trial in Rotterdam in 1964, and in Tokyo finished thirteenth individually.

Kathy Kusner and Untouchable, along with Mary and Frank Chapot in the Mexico Olympic team, missed a bronze medal by just a quarter of a fault behind Germany—a small enough margin with scores of over 117 per team—and the season ended unhappily for Kathy when the former Irish team horse, Fru, fell with her in New York and broke her leg.

But Kathy Kusner, who lacks neither determination—she had to take the racing authorities to court to get her jockey's licence—nor courage—her second great love is flying aeroplanes—was not to be stopped for long even by a broken leg, and in 1969 made a single-handed raid of several of the continental shows with Fru, who unfortunately was hurt early on and could not jump often, and two novices, including the promising Touch Turtle who won in Biarritz.

Major placings World Championship: 1965, second on Untouchable. European Championship: 1967, first on Untouchable. Pan American Games: 1963, team gold medal on Unusual; 1967, team silver medal on Untouchable.

Janou Lefebvre

France

Janou Lefebvre (b. 1945) was the youngest ever rider in an Olympic Games when she made her debut in Tokyo at nineteen, and both there and in Mexico she won team silver medals.

Janou was in the French junior team which finished fifth in the European Junior Championships at Hickstead in 1961. She was French champion that year, and she made her senior international debut in 1963. At Aachen, by tradition the toughest of the whole season, she and Kenavo finished second in the Grand Prix to no less a combination than the Rome gold medallists Raimondo d'Inzeo and Posillipo.

Olympic year itself was less impressive, and there were doubts about Kenavo, though not about his rider, but they made the team, and

Kathy Kusner and Untouchable

Janou Lefebvre

jumped two sixteen-fault rounds which placed them fourteenth individually and the team second.

Not especially impressive in the individual competition at the Mexico Games, when they finished 32nd, Janou and Rocket had the best score of their team, and the seventh best overall, $29\frac{3}{4}$ faults to help France take the silver medal, less than eight faults behind the gold medal Canadians in this high-scoring event.

1969 was a great year for Janou Lefebvre and Rocket, for at their own international in Nice they won both the Grand Prix and the championship, they took the Grand Prix in London, where they also had the best Nations Cup performance for their team, and won the *Meisterspringen* in Aachen.

Major placings Olympic Games: 1964, team silver with Kenavo; 1968, team silver with Rocket. European Championships: 1966, won on Kenavo; 1968, equal third with Rocket.

Guy Lefrant

France

Guy Lefrant (b. 1923) has been France's leading military rider in recent years. In the Nations Cup teams since 1948, he was show jumping champion of France in 1951 and again in 1955. He was the national three-day event champion in 1958 and 1959.

Lefrant made his Olympic debut at Helsinki in 1952, when he won the three-day event individual silver medal on Verdun. In Rome in 1960 he won a team bronze medal on Nicias.

Not until four years after that did he make the Olympic show jumping team. With M. de Littry, a son of the prolific sire of show jumpers, Furioso, he finished 20th individually, and joined d'Oriola and Janou Lefebvre in taking the team silver.

Major placings Olympic Games: 1952, individual three-day event silver medal with Verdun; 1960, team three-day event bronze with Nicias; 1964, show jumping team silver with Monsieur de Littry.

Colonel Harry Llewellyn

Great Britain

Colonel Harry Llewellyn and Foxhunter are British show jumping's great heroes, carrying all before them in their heyday and, in the manner of the prodigal son, atoning for their poor first round in the Helsinki Olympics by going clear to clinch Britain's gold medal.

Llewellyn provided two of the horses which won Britain the bronze medal in London: Foxhunter, ridden by himself, and Kilgeddin, the mount of Henry Nicoll. The following week at the International Llewellyn and Foxhunter won the King George V Gold Cup. They took this classic event again in 1950, and in 1953 Foxhunter

Col. Harry Llewellyn

Guy Lefrant and M. de Littry

became the first, and so far the only horse to win the King George Cup three times.

Just to recount all of Llewellyn and Foxhunter's victories would fill a whole chapter. Altogether, between 1947 and 1956 they won no fewer than 78 international competitions, and it was fitting that Foxhunter's final appearance, in Dublin, should have been a winning one.

Foxhunter, who was hunted after his retirement in 1956, died three years later of a ruptured artery. Harry Llewellyn continued to ride, and win, for some time after his great partner's retirement, and since his own retirement from the saddle has officiated with the B.S.J.A., as chairman and often chef d'equipe.

Major placings Olympic Games: 1948, team bronze on Foxhunter; 1952, team gold on Foxhunter.

Mickey Louw

South Africa

Mickey Louw (b. 1944), an insurance broker in Johannesburg, was South African champion in 1964 on Jurigo, the year he was awarded his Springbok colours.

Within seven weeks of his arrival in England he partnered Trigger Hill, a bold-jumping but often erratic performer, to victory in the first major competition of the Royal International Horse Show, the Horse and Hound Cup. At Ascot they won the most valuable prize of the British season, the News of the World Championship, worth £600, and were twice successful at the Horse of the Year Show.

Returning to South Africa, Louw has been a regular member of the team at the only C.H.I.O. which, due to the European horse sickness ban, they can contest, at Lourenço Marques, in Portuguese East Africa. In 1968 he again won the South African championship, with Marlon.

Graziano Mancinelli

Italy

Graziano Mancinelli (b. 1937), though not in the classic mould of the brothers d'Inzeo has proved himself a tough third string to the Italian bow, winner of the 1963 European Championship and a member of his country's team at the Olympic Games in 1964 and 1968.

Mancinelli gained his early riding experience in the stables of the brothers Rivolta in Milan, horsedealers on a grand scale for many years. He made his international debut for Italy in the inaugural European Junior Championships in Ostend in 1952, when Italy beat Belgium. He was again in the team the following two years, when they were beaten by France and then won from a German team which included Alwin Schockemohle and Hermann Schridde.

This experience has given Mancinelli an abiding interest in the Italian junior team: in

Mickey Louw and Trigger Hill

Budapest in 1964 he ensured their victory by riding each horse himself up until the moment it was due to enter the ring.

In 1957 Mancinelli produced his first top-class senior international horse, Ussaro, for the Rivolta stable, when they won major events at home and in the following year were chosen for the Lucerne International. On the German-bred Elke, also in the Lucerne team, Mancinelli showed something of his ability by jumping over 7 ft in the *puissance*.

Mancinelli brought out Rockette, allegedly a full-sister to The Rock, in 1959, and she proved his best horse ever. Winner of an international competition in Venice in the year of her debut, Rockette won the Grand Prix in both Madrid and London two years later.

The Italians had long had difficulty in finding a third Olympic rider to the d'Inzeos, but in 1964, despite the Olympic ruling of 'once a professional always a professional,' the I.O.C. decided at the last minute that Mancinelli was eligible to ride in Tokyo. Riding Rockette, who up to that time had competed in no fewer than 25 Nations Cups, Mancinelli helped his compatriots to take the bronze medal, finishing nineteenth individually.

In the Mexico Olympics Mancinelli, now an established member of the Italian Olympic team, rode Doneraile, which he had taken over from Seamus Hayes. The team finished fifth, and Mancinelli equal 21st individually.

Major placings Olympic Games: 1964, team bronze with Rockette. European Championships: 1963, won on Rockette.

General C. Humberto Mariles

Mexico

General C. Humberto Mariles (b. 1913) was the architect of much of the Mexico team's show jumping success, including their Olympic Games gold in 1948, when he also won the individual gold.

Born in Parral, Chihuahua, son of Captain Antonio Mariles, who was in the Mexican Cavalry, he spent his early years on his father's ranch, then joined the Military Academy in Parral at the tender age of 13. He graduated in 1931, and spent the next three years as a riding instructor there. Then he went on to another military equitation school, where he was primarily responsible for training the Mexican team for international competition.

He went to the Olympic Games in Berlin as a spectator, and what he saw there laid the foundation for his triumph twelve years later. Closely observing all the top riders, he extracted from each what he thought would be most useful for himself and his pupils.

In 1938, when the Military Riding Academy was formed, Mariles was put in charge of it, and he was also captain of the Mexican team from that year until 1956. Three years later the formation of the National Riding Association, also

C. Humberto Mariles

G. Mancinelli and Rockette

under Mariles, catered for civilian riders as well as military.

When the Pan American Games were held in Mexico City, in the grounds of the National Riding Association, in 1955, Mariles led his team to victory over Argentina, Chile and the U.S.A., with two of his team taking the gold and bronze individual medals.

Alas, Mariles' distinguished career came to a sad end for, in 1966, during the time that he was training riders for the Olympic Games in his own country, he was involved in a car accident and as a result of the ensuing shooting, he was sent to prison.

Major placings Olympic Games: 1948, individual and team gold medals, on Arete. Pan American Games: 1955, team gold, with Chihucho.

Lutz Merkel

West Germany

Lutz Merkel (b. 1937) is a comparative newcomer to the German team, but rapidly proved himself a talented performer and a reliable one in Nations Cups in 1969, when Germany first won the President's Cup.

In 1969 he rode Sir in the team which took the Aga Khan Trophy in Dublin, after a jump-off with Britain. Also in Dublin he and Sperber won the Players Top-Score competition and the John Higgins Trophy. Finally he partnered Sir in the team which clinched the President's Cup for Germany by beating Italy in the Nations Cup in Geneva.

Ann Moore

Great Britain

Ann Moore (b. 1950), who made her senior international debut in 1969, looks sure to follow in the high British tradition of successful women riders. After a successful junior career she advanced even more triumphantly into Young Riders (under eighteen) classes. She made the British team for the European Championship three times, in 1965, 1967 and 1968—swamp fever kept Britain out in 1966—on three different horses: Kangaroo, Hopalong Cassidy, and Psalm. Hopalong Cassidy, which Pat Pharazyn brought over from New Zealand, helped Ann make the transition out of junior, but the impressive feature of the Warwickshire girl's success is that she had shown the ability to get the best out of several different animals.

Psalm, who was hunted with the Meynell before the Moores bought him, was brought along slowly, and in 1968 Ann Moore won the individual European Junior Championship as well as a team 'first', and all three of the Young Riders Championships, the B.S.J.A. at Stoneleigh, the Young Riders Championship of Great Britain at Hickstead and the Leading Young Rider at the Horse of the Year Show.

George Morris and Sinjon

Ann Moore and Psalm

George Morris

United States

George Morris (b. 1938) started national jumping in 1955, joined the United States Equestrian Team on the autumn circuit of 1957, and came with the team to Europe in the following three years. In 1958 he rode Night Owl to victory in the Irish Trophy, the Dublin Grand Prix; in 1959 he was second in the Aachen Grand Prix on the same horse, and in 1960 won the Grand Prix in Aachen, again with Night Owl.

He rode Sinjon in the Rome Olympic Games, finishing fourth in the individual placings, and winning a team silver medal. After the World Championships which followed the Rome Games he retired from competitive riding.

In 1963 he went back to riding, and became a teacher, first with Jessica Newberry, and then on his own farm in Salem. Now he works as a freelance teacher and numbers among his pupils Brooke Hodgson, Kristine Pfister and Conrad Homfeld, all of them extremely successful juniors.

Major placings Olympic Games: 1960, team silver with Sinjon.

Marion Mould (nee Coakes)

Great Britain

World Champion at eighteen and silver medallist three years later—the first woman to win an individual Olympic show jumping medal—are the highlights of the brilliant career of Marion Mould (b. 1947, Miss Coakes until she married National Hunt jockey David Mould in 1969).

All her major successes have been with Stroller, the Irish-bred pony, standing only 14·2 hands high, foaled in 1953, and brought over to England by Sussex dealer Tommy Grantham.

Marion had a fantastic year in 1965. At the Royal International she became the youngest ever winner of the Queen Elizabeth Cup—on the smallest horse, and by the smallest margin, a tenth of a second, from Alison Westwood and The Maverick.

America's Kathy Kusner, who had had a highly successful season, was fancied for the World Championship at Hickstead, but Marion quickly gained the advantage by taking first and third places, on Stroller and Little Fellow. In the next event these two finished equal first, and although Kathy Kusner beat her for the final competition her early lead carried her through to the title.

As well as her individual triumphs Marion was in three winning Nations Cups that year, helping win the inaugural President's Cup, and was both the Daily Express and Sports Writers' 'Sportswoman of the Year'.

For all Stroller's lack of inches, there was not much doubt that Marion would be riding him in Mexico, and so it proved. But less than a week before the individual event it became all too clear that Stroller was far from well. He turned out to

Marion Mould and Stroller

Lalla Novo and Trésor

have an abscess on a back tooth, and though given a course of antibiotics, was not at his peak. Only the day before the event was he definitely passed fit to jump.

And jump he did, with one of only two clears over the big first-round course, along with Bill Steinkraus's Snowbound. In the second round they hit the huge parallels at No. 5, and then the second part of the final double. Snowbound, too, hit the fifth, but that was his only fault; but still Marion Coakes and Stroller had won the silver medal.

Their triumph turned disastrously sour in the team event, when Stroller found the extremely big, and difficultly-sited treble beyond him in his second round, stopped, then stopped again and slipped, unseating his rider amidst a mound of poles. Altogether they lost so much time that Marion and Britain were eliminated.

Major placings Olympic Games: 1968, individual silver with Stroller. World Championship: 1965, won with Stroller. European Championship: 1968, equal third with Stroller.

Lalla Novo

Italy

Lalla Novo (b. 1938) started riding in Turin and made her debut in the Italian team in Nice in 1963, when she rode Rahin, an Irish-bred gelding which had been in the Italian three-day event team in the Rome Olympics.

Miss Novo and Rahin were in the winning Nations Cup team at that, their first show, the first of many such team victories.

In 1966 she rode another Irish-bred, Oxo Bob, into third place in the European Championship at Gijon, behind Janou Lefebvre and Monica Bachmann, and the following year at Fontainebleau she started off the women's European Championship meeting by winning on her French-bred horse Predestine.

This competition did not count towards the championship, but she went so consistently throughout the three events which did, winning the third of them, that she finished runner-up for the title to Kathy Kusner.

Major placings European Championships: 1966, third on Oxo Bob; 1967, second on Predestine.

Alan Oliver

Great Britain

Born into a Buckinghamshire farming, hunting and show jumping family, Alan Oliver (b. 1932) was riding almost before he could walk and jumping in open classes when no more than a diminutive eleven-year-old.

The best of the early horses that Oliver rode, indeed almost certainly his best ever, was Red Admiral. In 1951 Oliver won the National Championship jointly with Red Admiral and Red

Salvatore Oppes and Pagoro

Alan Oliver and Sweep

Knight and rode the season's leading money winner, Red Star II; two years later Red Admiral won the Leading Show Jumper title at the Horse of the Year Show.

Oliver's extremely acrobatic style of those days, flinging himself forward and apparently, though not in fact, losing all contact with his horses, made him popular with the crowds but did nothing to endear him to the purists.

Both for the 1952 and the 1956 Olympic Games Oliver was a strong contender, but each time he was left out. Although he has, of course, been successful abroad, Oliver has made the major part of his considerable reputation at home. He won the National Championship again on John Gilpin in 1959.

In 1969 Oliver won two competitions in Rome, was in the team, with Sweep, which won the Nations Cup in Barcelona—one of only two British Nations Cup victories in 1969—and had an amazing season at home. From the start he had a great run of triumphs, taking in the National Championship and ending with three competitions at the Horse of the Year Show, including a second Ronson Trophy, which brought his score of first prizes for the season to 98.

Salvatore Oppes

Italy

Salvatore Oppes was just about the most successful Italian 'No. 3' to the d'Inzeo brothers before Mancinelli was declared Olympically eligible. His best horse was Pagoro, on which he finished fourth in the 1954 World Championship, behind Winkler, d'Oriola and Goyoaga. Pagoro had the best performance of all the horses in that final. Two years later Oppes and Pagoro joined the d'Inzeos in the Stockholm silver medal team, finishing 24th individually.

In the first European Championship in 1957 Oppes finished third to Winkler and de Fombelle, with, once again, Pagoro the leading horse, having gone clear for all four riders.

Major placings Olympic Games: 1956, team silver with Pagoro. European Championship: 1957, third with Pagoro.

Nelson Pessoa

Brazil

Nelson Pessoa (b. 1935) has made the greatest impact on European show jumping of any rider from South America, including a European Championship, three Hamburg Derbies, two British Derbies and innumerable Grand Prix among his achievements.

His best horse has been Gran Geste, a little grey, bred in Brazil in 1952 by a thoroughbred from a native mare. With Gran Geste Pessoa started his European sojourn in fine style in 1961 by winning the *puissance* competition for the Lonsdale Trophy at the Royal International, and

Capt. Billy Ringrose

Nelson Pessoa

taking the Grand Prix in Brussels and St. Gall.

The following year on Espartaco, another Brazilian-bred, he won the Hamburg Derby after a three-horse jump-off in which he was opposed by Raimondo d'Inzeo on his Olympic gold medal horse Posillipo and his World Champion Merano. In 1963 Pessoa finished equal first in the Hamburg classic on Gran Geste and Espartaco, who had the only two clear rounds, and at Hickstead took the British Jumping Derby in a jump-off of four.

He won the 1964 Aachen Grand Prix and the Grand Prix d'Europe on Gran Geste, but elected to ride Huipil, another little horse who stands only just over 15 hands high, in the Tokyo Olympics. With three fences down in the first round and two in the second they just missed the jump-off for the bronze medal, finishing equal fifth.

In 1965 he and Gran Geste won an 'All-American' European Championship from the American Frank Chapot on San Lucas and Hugo Arrambide of Argentina on Chimbote. In the Pan American Games in Winnipeg, Pessoa led the Brazilians to their first ever Games gold medal, from the U.S.A. and Canada, and with Gran Geste took the individual silver behind Jimmy Day and Canadian Club.

Although Pessoa tends to 'pace' his horses, giving them only six to eight shows a year, which gives them a longer competitive life, even such 'evergreens' as Gran Geste, who finally retired after finishing third in the 1969 Hamburg Derby, were past their best for the 1968 Olympics, in which Pessoa rode the Russian-bred Pass Opp into 16th place individually, with the team finishing seventh.

Major placings Pan American Games: 1959, team bronze with Copacabana; 1967, team gold and individual silver with Gran Geste. European Championship: 1965, second on Gran Geste; 1966, won on Gran Geste.

Billy Ringrose
Republic of Ireland

Billy Ringrose (b. 1930), now a Commandant, has been the most successful Irish Army rider of recent years. He rode his first international in 1954, and four years later took over the best horse the Irish Army has had since the war, Loch an Easpaig.

Ringrose and Loch an Easpaig won the Rome Grand Prix in 1961, in which year they triumphed also in Nice, London, Washington, New York and Toronto. In 1963 they won the first leg of the European Championship in Rome, and were again successful on the North American tour. They won the Grand Prix in Nice in 1965, and the London Grand Prix, for the Daily Mail Cup, the following year, when Loch an Easpaig was fifteen.

Among their many Nations Cup victories were the Aga Khan Trophies in 1963 and 1967, but only weeks after the latter victory after jumping a

Peter Robeson and Scorchin

Col. Paul Rodzianko

clear round in the Nations Cup in Ostend, Loch an Easpaig collapsed and died during the second circuit.

Peter Robeson

Great Britain

A stalwart of the British team for many years, winner of both individual and team Olympic bronze medals, Peter Robeson (b. 1929) was in 1969 the victim of a *cause celebre* about his training methods.

One of the most stylish riders Britain has ever produced, Robeson was chosen as reserve for the team which won the gold medal in Helsinki in 1952, and four years later made his debut in the Olympic Games in Stockholm. In the latter he rode Scorchin, finishing nineteenth in the individual placings, with the team taking the bronze medal.

With Firecrest, Robeson rolled up a list of successes both at home and abroad that would stretch a long way, including the Grand Prix at the Royal International in 1964, the National Championship the following year and the King George V Gold Cup in 1967.

One of a dozen short-listed at the beginning of 1964 for the Tokyo Olympic Games, Robeson and Firecrest were the only combination of that dozen to compete. They went round twice with two fences down each time, which left them to jump off with Australia's John Fahey and Bonvale for the bronze medal. In the jump-off Firecrest was clear and slightly faster than Bonvale, who had two fences down, so Britain's record of a show jumping medal at every Olympic Games since the war was kept intact.

Chosen as a travelling reserve for Mexico, Robeson turned down the chance to go when told there would be no room for Firecrest's regular groom.

In 1969 a Sunday newspaper, having sent a reporter and photographer on to Robeson's farm in his absence proclaimed that they had 'proof' of his cruel training methods, but a subsequent inquiry by the B.S.J.A. declared that the tack-rail in question did not necessarily constitute cruelty in 'expert' hands and exonerated Robeson.

Major placings Olympic Games: 1956, team bronze with Scorchin; 1964, individual bronze with Firecrest.

Paul Rodzianko

Great Britain

Probably no one man has had a greater influence on the training of show jumpers in Britain and Ireland than Paul Rodzianko, who in his boyhood was a page to Tsar Nicholas of Russia.

At the Italian Cavalry schools, Rodzianko learned the hard way Caprilli's theories, and put them into practice. He was in Italy for some eighteen months, before returning to his

Alwin Schockemohle and Donald Rex

homeland where he started training a team of show jumpers.

So effective was his training that the Russian team, himself, Captain d'Exe, winner at the show in 1911, and Lieut. Ivanenko, won the 1912 King Edward VII Cup—the predecessor of the Prince of Wales Cup—and they came back and were again victorious in 1913 and 1914, when they won the Cup outright.

Returning to Russia just as the first World War started, Rodzianko went first to the Austrian front, then was posted to the Embassy in Rome, where he was when the revolution came.

After the war he went to England, joined the British Army and was sent with an Expeditionary force to Siberia, returning to leave the Army and set up a training establishment at Windsor. This went well until the depression of the early thirties, when he was offered the directorship of the Cavalry School in Dublin. His success there was immediate and resounding. Two weeks after taking up his appointment, the Irish Army team won the Aga Khan Trophy in Dublin.

During the next four years Rodzianko built up one of the strongest teams in the world, certainly the best Ireland has ever had: men like the late Col. Fred Ahern, who went on to command the Army Equitation School in Dublin; Col. Jack Lewis, winner of the 1935 King George Cup on Tramore Bay; Commandant Ged O'Dwyer, who won the King's Cup the following year on Limerick Lace; Commandant Neylon and Colonel Dan Corry, who more than twenty years later was still capable of replacing an injured rider in the Irish team in Rotterdam.

From Ireland he went again to England, where among his pupils was Mike Ansell, who was to have the most revolutionary effect on British show jumping.

Rodzianko again served with the British Army in the second World War, returned to Ireland afterwards, where he again produced a few top-class riders until 1955 when he returned to England.

Marcel Rozier

France

Marcel Rozier (b. 1936), who was the French No. 3 in Mexico, has made rapid progress, for he only started competitive riding some four years earlier.

The secretary of a riding club in the forest of Fontainebleau, he has had a good deal of success with Quo Vadis, a thoroughbred foaled in 1960 by the American racehorse Pot o' Luck, now at stud in France. Nevertheless Rozier's chances of making Mexico looked to have disappeared when, in February 1968, Prince Charmant fell with him and Rozier broke his leg in two places. But at Aachen, the toughest show of all, less than four months later he was back, twice finished second on Quo Vadis, and rode him in the French Nations Cup team.

Giulia Serventi and Killane

In Mexico they were twentieth in the individual competition, and had the second-best score in the team which took the silver medal.

Major placing Olympic Games: 1968, team silver with Quo Vadis.

Alwin Schockemohle

West Germany

Alwin Schockemohle (b. 1937) started riding soon after the war, when given a pony by his father, and when he was 17 went to the German Federation's training school, at Warendorf, where Hans Gunter Winkler teaches the younger riders of international potential.

Schockemohle was training for both eventing and show jumping, and in Stockholm, 1956, was reserve rider for both teams, but it was not until 1957 that he made his first appearance in an international show jumping competition, on Bacchus at Aachen, which they won. They went on to finish second behind the greatest combination of all, Winkler and Halla, in the Grand Prix. Schockemohle's Olympic debut came in Rome, in company with Thiedemann on Meteor and Winkler with Halla. It would be hard to imagine two better partners for a first Olympic attempt, but although Schockemohle and Ferdl had the biggest score, $17\frac{1}{4}$, it was not far behind Halla's $13\frac{1}{4}$ and Meteor's 16.

The following year Schockemohle was the German champion, with Ferdl, which he repeated two years later with Freiherr, who in 1962 had given him his first victory in the Aachen Grand Prix. In Rome in 1963 Schockemohle and Freiherr only narrowly failed to beat Italy's Mancinelli with Rockette for the European title.

He did not make the Tokyo team in 1964, but the following year set a German high jump record of 2·25 metres (7 ft 4 in) which still stands riding the Hanoverian seven-year-old Exakt. That was their first year together, and they also finished third, to the Tokyo silver medallists Herman Schridde and Dozent, for the European title.

In 1968, Schockemohle and Donald Rex shared the Aachen Grand Prix, with Hendrik Snoek on Dorina, and in Mexico, after finishing equal seventh in the individual, had the best score of all in the team jumping and led his team to the bronze medal.

Schockemohle had his most successful season of all in 1969. He and Donald Rex were almost unbeatable in the early part of the season, swept the board at Fontainebleau, took the International Championship at Aachen, where Schockemohle again shared the Grand Prix, on Wimpel, with Winkler and Enigk.

Major placings Olympic Games: 1960, team gold on Ferdl; 1968, team bronze on Donald Rex. European Championships: 1963, second on Frei-

Hermann Schridde

Harvey Smith

herr; 1965, third on Exakt; 1967, third on Donald Rex; 1969, second on Donald Rex.

Hermann Schridde
West Germany

Hermann Schridde (b. 1937) had early training in dressage, as have so many of the top German riders, and was a pupil of Hans Gunter Winkler at the German national training centre in Warendorf.

He won the German International Championship at Aachen in 1963 on the good mare Ilona. With Dozent, who had been previously ridden by Lutz Merkel and Alwin Schockemohle, Schridde won the 1964 Hamburg Jumping Derby before he went to the Olympic Games in Tokyo.

There the Germans won their third consecutive team gold medal and Schridde and Dozent took the individual silver. Well back after the first round, they were one of the only two combinations—d'Oriola and Lutteur being the other—to jump round without fault, and although they collected $1\frac{1}{4}$ time penalties it pulled them up into second place.

In Mexico Schridde and Dozent were left out of the individual competition, and in the team event they were way below form, collecting $70\frac{1}{4}$ faults, despite which their team took the bronze.

Major placings Olympic Games: 1964, team gold and individual silver with Dozent; 1968, team bronze with Dozent. European Championship: 1965, won with Dozent.

Giulia Serventi
Italy

Giulia Serventi has been one of Italy's most successful women riders for several years since she made her international debut back in 1950.

With the French-bred Doly, by Furioso, she finished second to Pat Smythe in the first women's European Championship in 1957, and then took the title the following year in Palermo, at the expense of Germany's Anna Clement.

Miss Serventi lacked a suitable replacement for Doly, a prolific winner in international competitions, until she bought the Irish-bred Gay Monarch, on which she finished second for the 1968 European title in Rome to Anneli Drummond-Hay. In addition Miss Serventi and Gay Monarch have jumped some extremely good rounds for their country in Nations Cups. One of their best performances was at Aachen in 1967, where they went round twice for just four faults, when Italy failed by only half a fault to catch the British team for the Cup.

Major placings European Championships: 1957, second on Doly; 1958, won on Doly; 1959, equal third on Doly; 1968, second on Gay Monarch.

Neal Shapiro and Uncle Max

Neal Shapiro

United States

Neal Shapiro (b. 1945) started riding when he was seven, and rode Jacks or Better to win the National High Points Championship in the Open Junior Division before he joined the United States Equestrian team in 1965.

An improving member of the team for the past five years, with an interest in trotting racing as well as show jumping, Shapiro made his first European tour in 1966, and his first overseas victory, on Jacks or Better, was at no less an event than the Grand Prix in Aachen.

Harvey Smith

Great Britain

Few men have aroused more ire or more enthusiasm than Harvey Smith (b. 1938), the epitome —almost a caricature—of Yorkshire bluntness, with a will-to-win which has made him one of the most successful show jumpers in Britain over the past decade.

In 1954 Smith bought at auction a big Irish four-year-old for £40 who came to be called Farmer's Boy. Unbroken, Farmer's Boy proved a tractable character who went to his first show only a month after Smith bought him, and within a few weeks finished second to the Olympic horse Flanagan in an Open competition.

It was four years later that Smith made the international grade. At the White City he and Farmer's Boy won the Young Riders' International and had the best British placing, sixth, in the King George Cup behind Hugh Wiley's Master William.

At the 1962 Royal International Smith and O'Malley won the richest prize of the show, the John Player Trophy, after a jump-off with Raimondo d'Inzeo and his Olympic gold medallist Posillipo. Rotterdam the following month was Smith's first taste of continental jumping, where he and O'Malley won the Grand Prix, with a jump-off time more than four seconds ahead of the second-placed Mister Softee. In the Nations Cup they jumped the only double-clear in the whole competition, though not quite enough to hold off the Germans.

In Rome 1963 Smith and O'Malley won the Grand Prix, only the second British success of the event, beating Goyoaga and Kif-Kif. In the European Championship Smith finished fourth in the first competition to Ireland's Billy Ringrose, and equal first in the second with Mancinelli and Schockemohle. Mancinelli and Rockette won the final event and with it the title, ahead of Schockemohle, with Smith third.

At home, and again in 1964, Smith and O'Malley headed the list of prizewinners, a feat Smith repeated in 1965 and 1967 on Harvester and in 1968 on Doncella.

In 1967 Smith finished second to David

Pat Koechlin-Smythe

Broome in the European Championship. On the North American tour that autumn Smith won two competitions and was champion rider at Washington, in New York O'Malley won the Grand Prix, and in Toronto took the *puissance*, equalling the North American record of 7 ft 3 in.

Smith, who had been overlooked for the Tokyo Olympics was selected for Mexico with both O'Malley and Madison Time, who had jumped in his first Nations Cup only that spring, in Rome, when jumping the course twice for just one stop. It was decided that he should ride Madison Time, and he finished eleventh in the individual with two eight-fault rounds and a quarter of a time fault.

Major placings European Championships: 1963, third on O'Malley; 1967, second on Harvester.

Pat Smythe
Great Britain

Ask almost any layman for the name of a show jumper and he will reply 'Pat Smythe'. Even though she is now married, with several children, and retired from international jumping several years ago, her legend is still strong.

Pat Smythe (b. 1928) had few of the advantages which have taken other riders to the top; no rich parents to keep her supplied with high-class horses, but she had determination and an undeniable talent which brought her four victories in the Women's European Championship.

In 1948 she became one of the only two women ever to jump in the King George V Cup, and two years later she and Finality won the Leading Show Jumper competition at Harringay. Meanwhile she had been starting to make her mark on the continent: in 1949 she won the Ladies' Championship in Paris, the Grand Prix in Brussels, and in Geneva, where the British team won their first Continental Nations Cup, was the Leading Lady Rider.

While the selectors of the 1956 Olympic team were cogitating, Pat Smythe starting riding Bob Hanson's Flanagan. She won eleven of the first twelve competitions in which she rode Flanagan in 1955, and then went on to win three competitions in Paris. So it was no surprise when the two of them were included in Britain's team for Stockholm, where, along with Wilf White's Nizefela and Peter Robeson on Scorchin, she won a team bronze medal, the first woman to get an Olympic show jumping medal.

In Spa, Belgium, the following year she won the first European title on Flanagan after a jump-off with Italy's Giulia Serventi on Doly. During all this time, despite so many widespread successes, Pat Smythe had failed to win the classic Queen Elizabeth, but in 1958 she remedied this on John King's Mr. Pollard.

In 1960 Pat Smythe and Flanagan finished eleventh in the individual contest at the Rome Olympics, and the next year she began her hat-

117

H. Steenken and Porta Westfalica

trick of European Championships, at Deauville, Madrid and Hickstead.

It was in 1963 that Pat Smythe married Sam Koechlin, a Swiss lawyer and horseman. Family responsibilities, and later ill-health, gradually loosened the grip that Pat Smythe had had on world show jumping since women were first allowed into the hierarchy, but in 1967 she landed another 'first' when, in Aachen, she was the first woman ever to be chef d'equipe of a British team.

Major placings Olympic Games: 1956, team bronze on Flanagan. European Championships: 1957, won on Flanagan; 1959, second on Flanagan; 1961, won on Flanagan; 1962, won on Flanagan; 1963, won on Flanagan.

Hendrik Snoek

West Germany

Hendrik Snoek (b. 1948) is one of the best of the rising generation of German show jumpers. The leading rider at the Swiss C.H.I.O. in Lucerne, he and his Westfalen mare Dorina shared the Aachen Grand Prix with Alwin Schockemohle and his great Donald Rex. Then, while the Olympic squad was in Mexico, Snoek was one of a small group of Germans who went to the Horse of the Year Show in Wembley, where he and his then-eight-year-old Hanoverian Feiner Kerl were very successful, winning the Daily Telegraph Cup, and finished equal second for the Sunday Times Cup.

With so many first-class riders already established it is not easy for a young German rider to make their first team, but Hans Gunter Winkler is among those who rates Snoek's chance of doing so very highly.

Hartwig Steenken

West Germany

Hartwig Steenken (b. 1941) has been on the fringe of the top German team for several years, first with Fairness, and more recently with the two mares, Porta Westfalica, foaled in 1960 by a thoroughbred out of a Hanoverian mare, and Simona, foaled in 1958, a full-bred Hanoverian.

Chosen for the individual competition in the Mexico Olympics, though not the team, he rode Simona to finish equal 26th, with sixteen faults in the first round.

Bill Steinkraus

United States

Bill Steinkraus (b. 1925), one of the prime architects in the United States team's rise to world power, had his just reward when, in Mexico, he became the first from his country to win a show jumping Olympic gold medal.

He joined the U.S. team in 1951 and the following year rode with the first civilian U.S. team in the Stockholm Olympics on that great horse

Fritz Thiedemann and Meteor

Hollandia. The team took the bronze medal, and Steinkraus was tenth in the individual placings.

Steinkraus took over Democrat, a former Army horse, then 19 years old, for the autumn tour of the North American shows in 1952, and the old horse won every competition he jumped in at Harrisburg, New York and Toronto, eight in all. Steinkraus took over the captaincy of the team in 1955, the year that Bertalan de Nemethy became its trainer. Between them they built up an extremely potent squad.

In 1956 Steinkraus won the first of his two King George V Cups with First Boy (the second was in 1964 on Sinjon), and in the Olympic Games finished 16th individually on Night Owl, with the team taking fifth place.

For the Rome Olympics in 1960 Steinkraus rode Riviera Wonder in the individual, finishing equal fifteenth, and Ksar d'Esprit in the team event, in which the U.S.A. took the silver medal.

In 1964, Steinkraus produced the then six-year-old Snowbound, a thoroughbred by Hail Victory-Gay Alvena, who had started his life as a racehorse. In his first season Snowbound went on the tour to Europe, and in 1965 won the Grand Prix in New York. In 1968 Steinkraus and Snowbound had an extremely successful European tour, winning the Grand Prix in London, and jumping double clear rounds in the Nations Cups in London and Dublin, but the horse gave cause for anxiety by finishing the European season slightly unsound.

He was right for Mexico, however, and in the individual competition, having, along with Marion Coakes's Stroller, been the only one to go clear in the first round, hit in the second only the 'unjumpable' fifth, to give Steinkraus his gold medal. Snowbound had lamed himself again in the process—so badly that Steinkraus had to come in for his medal on the Canadian horse, Jim Elder's The Immigrant—and had to miss the team competition.

Major placings Olympic Games: 1952, team bronze with Hollandia; 1960, team silver with Ksar d'Esprit; 1968, individual gold with Snowbound. Pan American Games: 1959, team gold with Riviera Wonder; 1963, team gold with Sinjon; 1967, team silver with Bold Minstrel.

Fritz Thiedemann

West Germany

Fritz Thiedemann (b. 1918), rates second only to Hans Gunter Winkler among German show jumping riders since the war.

Thiedemann's first major success was in the 1950 Hamburg Jumping Derby with Loretto, the first of five victories in this classic event. On Meteor, a 16·3 hh gelding by Diskus, bred in 1942 by Herr Otto Dreesen, Thiedemann took the individual bronze at the Olympic Games in Helsinki, with the team placed fifth.

Thiedemann completed his third Aachen Grand

Wilf White and Nizefela

Prix in 1955 with Meteor; in the 1956 Olympics Germany won the first of three successive team gold medals, with Meteor taking the individual fourth place.

First in the 1958 European Championship on Meteor, and third the next year with Godewind, Thiedemann won his second Olympic team gold medal in Rome on Meteor, finishing sixth in the individual line-up.

Major placings Olympic Games: 1952, individual bronze with Meteor; 1956, team gold with Meteor; 1960, team gold with Meteor. World Championships: 1953, second with Diamant; 1956, third with Meteor. European Championships: 1958, won with Meteor; 1959, third with Godewind.

Ruben Uriza

Mexico

Ruben Uriza won a team gold medal and an individual silver in the 1948 Olympic Games in London, riding Hatvey, a Mexican-bred of the American Morgan-horse breed. In the jump-off for the minor medals they took the silver with the only clear round in the entire competition.

Uriza was the course-builder for the 1968 Olympics in Mexico, one of the most controversial courses ever built for an Olympic event, which may finally move the authorities to establish a definitive Olympic course, instead of leaving it to the whims and theories of individual designers.

Major placings Olympic Games: 1948, team gold and individual silver with Hatvey.

Tommy Wade

Republic of Ireland

Tommy Wade (b. 1938) and Dundrum have been among the most popular Irish performers for something approaching ten years.

In 1957 Wade upgraded Dundrum, who stands only 15 hands 1½ inches, and was bred locally in 1952. With his considerable jumping ability, Dundrum has frequently been seen at his best in indoor shows; he won the 1961 Ronson Trophy, the *victor ludorum*, at the Horse of the Year Show; and the following year won the Grand Prix in both Ostend and Brussels.

In 1963, Wade and Dundrum won the classic King George V Cup, and then jumped the only two clear rounds in the competition to help Ireland win the Aga Khan Trophy in Dublin.

In 1967 he and Dundrum put up one of their finest performances to help Ireland win the Aga Khan Trophy: after a fall in the first round they went clear to score a narrow victory over Britain.

Paul Weier

Switzerland

In the last ten years Paul Weier (b. 1934) has been

Tommy Wade and Dundrum

the Swiss Champion no fewer than six times, in 1959, 1961, 1964, 1967, 1968 and in 1969. At one time the Swiss championship was decided on World Championship lines, with the top four riders changing horses. Now the best eight riders during the season contest a two-round competition to decide the champion.

Weier made his Olympic debut as an individual in Rome on Centurian, being eliminated in the second round. In Tokyo he rode Satan into equal 14th place, his team finishing fifth.

In Mexico he rode Wildfeuer in the individual, placing equal 21st, and Satan in the team, which came in sixth.

Wilf White

Great Britain

Wilf White, one of the few riders to successfully make the transition from the pre-war ultra-precision of British national show jumping, to post-war internationals, became, with his great horse Nizefela, the prop of the British team.

White, a Cheshire farmer, bought Nizefela in 1946, for about £100. Then a four-year-old, the big horse was by a Shire stallion out of a thoroughbred mare. When he was only seven he made his debut for Britain, in the team for the Nice and Rome shows, and on this tour had his first experience of a Nations Cup.

They were assured of their place in the team for the 1952 Olympics, along with Harry Llewellyn on Foxhunter and Douglas Stewart and Aherlow. In his first round he gave the final gate just the merest touch, but it was enough. Still, it kept Britain in the picture, despite Foxhunter's incredible debacle, and the team went on to win the gold medal.

The course for the 1956 Games was a tricky one, lightly-built and on poor going, but Nizefela jumped it perfectly until the treble three fences from home. A pole down at the last part and another at the final fence left Britain second and White individually equal second behind Winkler and Halla.

In the second round Nizefela came into the spread of parallel poles and small walls perhaps a trifle close and slowly, leaped over it, then nudged a pole off with his characteristic kickback. That was his only mistake, but it left them equal fourth with Thiedemann and Meteor, once again missing an individual medal by a hair's-breadth, though good enough to give Britain the team bronze.

Major placings Olympic Games: 1952, team gold with Nizefela; 1956, team bronze with Nizefela.

Hugh Wiley

United States

Hugh Wiley (b. 1927) had a fairly short but extremely successful career with the United States Equestrian Team. He first rode with the

Hugh Wiley and Nautical

team in 1950, and in the 1956 Olympics in Stockholm he finished equal 11th in the individual, with the team placed fifth, on the veteran horse Trail Guide.

One of the greatest horses ever to jump in the U.S. team, Ksar d'Esprit, who also jumped for Canada when named Revlon's White Sable, was bred on the Wiley's Maryland farm. Hugh Wiley himself rode an equally popular one in Nautical, a palomino, with china blue eyes who was a great favourite with the crowds, and able to win all types of competitions, from speed to *puissance*.

Wiley won the King George V Cup at the Royal International in 1958 on Master William, with Nautical third, and the following season won the King's Cup again, this time with Nautical. He also won the 1959 Grand Prix at the Royal International with Nautical.

In the 1960 Games Wiley and Master William placed equal seventh individually, but were left out of the team competition.

Ted Williams

Great Britain

Ted Williams must, in anybody's book, be rated as one of the all-time 'greats' of show jumping, even though the label of 'professional' has prevented him from ever competing in the Olympic Games.

The original producer of Scorchin, which Peter Robeson rode in the bronze medal team in the 1956 Olympics, Ted Williams brought out in 1953 the then four-year-old with which his name will ever be associated, Pegasus. Pegasus, sold on to Mr. Leonard Cawthraw the following year, was the leading money winner in Britain from 1955 to 1958—a record— and again in 1960.

In 1956 and 1957 Williams won the National Championship and having taken the Leading Show Jumper title at the Horse of the Year Show on Sunday Morning in 1955 and Dumbell in 1956, he proceeded to win it with Pegasus in 1957 and 1960. In the autumn of 1957 Williams and Pegasus went with the British team on the North American circuit, and Pegasus won the Grand Prix at all three shows, Harrisburg, New York and Toronto.

When Pegasus came towards the end of his career his rider might have been expected to do likewise, but in 1963 Mr. Frank Smith bought the first two of the string of South American-bred horses he was to build up, Carnaval and Careta, and asked Ted Williams to ride them.

Though they were of a quite different type to such as Pegasus, the Leicestershire veteran immediately established a brilliant rapport with them, especially Carnaval on whom twice he rode clear rounds when Britain desperately needed them to win Nations Cups, at Paris and Aachen.

Although Williams was given his amateur licence in the winter of 1956, which enabled him to ride for his country, his former professionalism bars him from the Olympic Games, despite the 1964 decision to admit Mancinelli.

Ted Williams

Hans Gunter Winkler

Hans Gunter Winkler

West Germany

Hans Gunter Winkler's (b. 1926) rise can reasonably be called meteoric—World Champion only two years after his international debut. But his success was, as is typical of his countrymen and their horses, founded upon a thorough knowledge of the basic principles of horsemastership.

He made his international debut in Bilbao, Spain, in 1952, and had the great fortune that Halla was one of his first international jumpers. In 1954 Winkler took her to Madrid, and there beat d'Oriola and Arlequin for the World Championship with the holder Goyoaga third. That same year she won the championship in Rome, had many other victories in Europe and North America.

Winkler had to go to a jump-off, with Raimondo d'Inzeo, to retain his world title in Aachen the following year, but then Halla did not let him down.

The 1956 Olympics in Stockholm saw one of the greatest, and most courageous, show jumping performances ever. Halla was going beautifully for Winkler until she stood too far off the last but one fence, and not only hit it but severely wrenched Winkler's riding muscle and left him in considerable agony. So bad was the pain that Winkler had to be lifted into the saddle for the second round; every jump was a torment and he could do no more than guide Halla. But she did the rest, leaping nobly clear, to give Winkler the individual gold and Germany the team gold. This accident kept Winkler from defending his World title in Aachen, but he regained it, now renamed the European Championship, in 1957.

In 1958, now fourteen years old, Halla could finish only third in the European Championship to Thiedemann's Meteor, when for the first time, the title was decided on a cumulative basis of several competitions. Nevertheless Halla was Winkler's choice for the 1960 Olympics, where they won a second successive team gold. Halla was retired to stud in 1961.

In Tokyo Winkler won his third consecutive team gold medal on Fidelitas, but for the first time he was not the 'star' of the show, and he continued to search for Halla's true successor.

In 1968 Winkler won his second King's Cup on Enigk, then eight years old, and elected to ride him in Mexico. They got into the four-sided jump-off for the individual bronze, which went to Broome and Mister Softee, and helped their team to take the bronze.

Major placings Olympic Games: 1956, team and individual gold on Halla; 1960, team gold with Halla; 1964, team gold with Fidelitas; 1968, team bronze with Enigk. World Championships: 1954, won on Halla; 1955, won on Halla. European Championships: 1957, won on Sonnenglanz; 1958, third on Halla; 1961, third on Romanus; 1962, second on Romanus; 1969, third on Enigk.

3

Competitions, Rules and Records

The most important shows of the season are those labelled C.H.I.O. (Concours Hippique International Officiel), the official international shows where the Prix des Nations, or Nations Cups are held; these are team events which provide a guide to the overall strength of a country. In Europe each country is allowed only one C.H.I.O. a year, but in other parts of the world there may be two, although not more than one in each town: so in the United States, where New York has long staged the principal show of the season, there is often also a C.H.I.O. in Harrisburg, and in 1969, as well as the well-established Toronto Winter Fair, Canada had an official show in Montreal. Because of the vast distances involved this is obviously the only fair solution, especially since the establishment in 1965 of the President's Cup, awarded to the country which has the six best Nations Cup results. The United States has, naturally, tended to dominate the North American Nations Cups, but Canada, whose Olympic Gold Medal can be expected to increase national support for the sport as well as their team, will surely challenge this supremacy.

Because a minimum of three teams are needed for a Nations Cup, Australia and New Zealand, who as a general rule compete only against each other, cannot stage one; perhaps the growing strength of the Japanese team could be a possible solution to this problem and in the long term, with air travel becoming faster and cheaper, teams from Europe or America may be able to fly there, although their quarantine regulations would then pose problems for all but the British.

South Africa, which has produced many extremely competent show jumping riders, of whom Bob Grayston, Mickey Louw and Gonda Butters are about the best known outside their own country, also has a quarantine problem, but in reverse. The imposition of the horse sickness ban some ten years ago has prevented South African horses being imported into Europe during this period. This is a ban put on independently by each National government and not by an international organisation, and although representations to have it lifted in Britain have been made, they have met with little response from British authorities. Meanwhile the only C.H.I.O. open to the South Africans, and also of course to the Rhodesians, whose interest in show jumping is comparatively recent but nonetheless enthusiastic, is at Lourenco Marques, where the two countries compete with Portuguese riders.

Apart from the C.H.I.O. a country may stage a C.H.I., or indeed several of them, the principal difference being that a C.H.I. does not include a Nations Cup. It is also possible to hold a 'friendly' event, in which some of the competitions may be open to the riders of one other country.

The pattern for Nations Cups is universal, unlike the Individual Grand Prix: each team consists of four riders (or three if only that number is available) who go round the course twice. In each round the best three scores count, and the total from the two rounds added together produces the final score. So it need not be, and often is not, the same three riders in each round who score. The starting order of the teams is drawn; if after the two rounds two teams are level then all four riders from each jump off over a shortened course with again the best three scores counting, but this time, if still indivisible by scores their positions are decided on time. A jump-off in a Nations Cup is rare, but when they happen can make for the most enthralling competitions of all, as in Dublin in 1969 when Britain took Germany to their limit, the balance swaying from one side to the other throughout the jump-off before the Germans finally triumphed.

Today each rider in a Nations Cup can have only one horse—with one horse in reserve in case any of those selected should have a last-minute accident or illness—but it used to be possible for a rider to ride two horses. In 1926 Fred Bontecou brought two horses over to London from America, Ballymacshane, on which he won the King George V Cup, and Little Canada. He asked the U.S. Army to send him another rider, and between the two of them they failed by only half a fault to beat the British for the Prince of Wales Cup. Had such a thing been possible in post-war days the Italians would probably have been even more successful than they have, with the d'Inzeo brothers able to share all the rides between them!

If a rider is eliminated then he is credited, or rather, debited, with the worst score in the round

Bill Steinkraus and Snowbound

Marion Mould and Stroller at Mexico

plus twenty, which is generally a sufficient penalty to dispose of any chance his team may have unless they can discard that score.

In the Olympic Games team event there are only three riders, all of whose scores count, which not only leaves no margin for error, but can sometimes give a false result, as for instance in Mexico when Stroller's sad mishap on the second circuit did not merely give Britain a harder task but removed any chance of a place whatever. In this respect show jumping must be one of the few sports, indeed possibly the only one, whose greatest goal, an Olympic medal, is run under conditions fundamentally different from every other competition. There is a possibility that this may be changed, and the sooner the better.

Apart from the Nations Cup, the international individual competitions may be divided basically into three types; those designed mainly to test jumping, but with time counting in the first or second jump-off; those to test control and 'handiness'; and those to test jumping power alone, over successive barrages of enlarged fences. For some competitions, although not many internationals except *puissance* events, time may not be called in to adjudicate at all; this is far more common with novice horses, to save them being rushed round a course before they are able to jump it properly, and used to be the general rule with all competitions in many countries, including Britain. The competitions were then, by all accounts, often dull in the extreme, jumped over flimsy, unimaginative courses and with riders able to spend as much time as they liked in the ring, or until the judges wanted to go off to tea, circling time and again if they came into a fence on the wrong stride.

The foundation of the F.E.I. in 1921 gradually brought about a fundamental change, and the sophistication of timing equipment now produces results split by a tenth of a second; automatic timing is obligatory at all C.H.I.O.s, backed up with hand timing in case of accidents, and it is strongly desired in C.H.I.s, with a minimum of three hand watches as an alternative.

Times within which the course must be completed are also prescribed: most competitions have a speed of 377 yards per minute, and Nations Cups 433 yards per minute. The time allowed is calculated from the length of the course, with a penalty of a quarter of a fault for each second over the time allowed and elimination for exceeding the time limit, which is double the time allowed. In timed jump-offs the penalty is one fault for each second over the time allowed. This accent on time naturally calls for accuracy in the measurement of the course, which alas is not always observed. A notable deficiency in this respect was the Nations Cup in Geneva in 1965, when only four of the entire field went round with time-faults, and it was later discovered that the course had been mis-measured by no less than 86 yards. There is a fairly general consensus of opinion, too, that the course for the team event in the Mexico Olympics was also measured incorrectly; certainly the amount of time faults was well above average even by Olympic Games' standards.

Individual Competitions

Competitions under F.E.I. Rules come under one of three categories, Tables (or *Barèmes*, see glossary) A, B or C. Table A includes most of the 'normal' competitions, that is those with one or two jump-offs (with or without the clock), *puissance* competitions and competitions against the clock from the start in which the fastest round with the least number of faults wins. Under Tables B and C, which are against the clock from the start, faults are converted into seconds, which are added to the time taken to complete the course and these scores decide the winner; under Table B 10 seconds are added for each fault, under C the penalty can vary from 3 to 17 seconds, according to the length of the course and the number of fences to be jumped.

Most competitions to be decided by a jump-off are run over courses of about a dozen fences, reduced for the barrage, but never to less than half the original course, and never to fewer than six, and some or all of the remaining fences may be made higher or broader. For a *puissance* event the course starts with six to eight fences—it is only in the first round of a *puissance* that there is a time limit—which are reduced in number and increased in height and width until only two are left, one upright, usually a wall, and one spread fence, generally either a triple bar or an oxer. The aim of a *puissance* is to go on until only one horse is able to jump the raised fences, but a jury can, after four or five jump-offs, decide that the first place should be divided among whichever horses are still in the running. In Britain there are few true *puissance* competitions as these are more suited to the big, strong Teutonic type of horse.

Nelson Pessoa and Gran Geste

Ann Backhouse and Bandit

Most of the high-jump events are of *'puissance-type'*, with the regulations stating that the first prize will be divided if more than one horse is still clear after the third jump-off.

Another type of competition designed solely to test a horse's ability to jump over big fences is the Six-Bar, which is rarely seen in Britain, or indeed in Europe, although it is apparently popular in South America. In this, six fences, composed as the name suggests of bars all identical in construction, are placed in line about 34 ft apart. They may be all the same height, perhaps about 4 ft, or they may rise progressively from less than 4 ft to over 5 ft. As in the *puissance* they are raised for each successive barrage until producing a result or until, again after four or five barrages, the jury decide to let those still in divide the prize. As with the *puissance*, the six-bar calls for a strong horse, for it is possible for the last fence to go above six feet. It seems a pity that these events are not run more often in Europe, for a number of shows could to their advantage introduce rather more variety into their programmes.

Speed competitions have several variations. The common form is to have a set course over which the fastest (and clearest) rider triumphs; in others a rider may complete the course and then start to go round again, jumping as many fences as possible in a given time, which may be up to ninety seconds; or he may choose his own line over a given number of fences; or jump fences of different dimensions and values in a set time.

The title fault-and-out is self-explanatory: usually in such an event time separates those who have completed the full course to get maximum points; but others are run over successive barrages of the full course with some fences being enlarged each time.

In addition to the single events there are relays, for two or three riders, or for one rider with two horses, which can give an advantage to the agile horseman. There are also some more specialised events, and competitions run under special formulas which are not included in the general repertoire.

One of these is the Grand Prix in Aachen, which starts off over a normal, big Nations Cup-type of course, with big combinations and a water jump of about 15 ft, and then, after the first round, develops into a *puissance* with, in 1969 for instance, the final wall going up to 6 ft 10 in, when Winkler on Enigk and Schockemohle on Wimpel divided. Such conditions will as a rule result in victory for the best all-round horse, since many of the *'puissance* specialists' will be put out in the first round by the sizeable water jump.

The formula devised for the Mexico Olympic individual competition, which was tried out in the Rome Grand Prix in the spring of 1968, was run in two rounds, the first a Nations Cup-type with approximately the top third of the horses in that round going into a second, over much bigger fences, the scores of both rounds being added together. Two-round competitions are fairly common, usually for the championship of a show; sometimes the second course is bigger and sometimes it is left the same.

The European Championship endeavours to find the best all-round rider and horse by having three or four competitions of different types. The final is usually run in two rounds, the first over eighteen fences of which the first six are of the 'speed' variety, then six *puissance* fences, and finally six Nations Cup obstacles. The second course is over the first and last six fences of that course, with both faults and times for the thirty fences being added together to find the winner. Thus the emphasis is placed on jumping at speed, which is, or should be, the essence of show jumping.

The formula for the Men's World Championship is both unique and extremely controversial. The qualifying rounds are conventional enough, producing four riders and horses. In the final the four riders have to ride not only their own horses, but each of the other three, the total for the four rides being added to find the winner. In theory this should produce the best riders, and usually it does, but it can give a decided advantage to a rider with a horse who combines ability with quirks, to which it may prove difficult for a strange rider to find the answer in the three minutes allowed for this purpose.

No one could deny that Raimondo d'Inzeo was a worthy champion when he retained his title in 1960, but having Gowran Girl to help him was an undeniable asset. Of the other three in the final David Broome, who has described the mare as feeling rather like a little donkey, collected sixteen faults, as did Bill Steinkraus; Carlos Delia, who finished second, had only twelve, but as d'Inzeo's total for his four rounds was only eight one does not need to be a mathematical genius to deduce the foundation stone for his victory.

Now that the European Championship has, quite correctly, been confined to European riders, it is encouraging to see the World Championship for women riders being held again in 1970. So far there has been only one, at Hickstead in 1965, won by Marion Coakes, and that was, in effect, a European Championship, from which non-Europeans were not then barred, with a more exalted name. Might it not also be a good idea to have a European team championship, similar to that held every four years in the Americas, in conjunction with the Pan American Games?

The President's Cup is the World Championship for teams, based on the season's results in Nations Cups. Points gained depend upon the number of teams in the competition: for three, four or five teams the winner receives five points, for six teams six points, for seven or more seven points. The second team gets one point fewer than the winner, the third two points fewer and so on, with each team getting at least one point. To compete for the President's Cup each country must be represented during the season by at least six different riders, which helps to some degree to spread Nations Cup experience, and only the six best results from each country count for the Cup.

With the varying difficulties that some nations experience in travel, especially the American teams and those from Portugal and Eastern Europe, this is the most equitable arrangement; without this the middle European nations, in which I include Britain, would almost inevitably monopolise the competition.

Age Limits

Horsemen are frequently more conventional than their fellows, possibly because they realise from their experience with horses that change is best brought about gradually, and in an age dedicated to the whims of youth the F.E.I. is one of the few international sporting bodies to have age limits which debar the young from competing against, and perhaps beating, their elders. Thus all riders under eighteen years of age are prohibited from competing in Nations Cups, Grand Prix or *puissance* competitions, although with special dispensation those over sixteen may compete against senior riders in other international events. Because of this regulation Andrew Fielder, who with Vibart would almost certainly have made the British team in Tokyo in 1964, was not allowed to go, as he was then only seventeen. The youngest rider to have competed in an Olympic show jumping event was the brilliant French girl Janou Lefebvre, who was nineteen when she won a team silver medal in Tokyo, which she repeated four year later in Mexico.

Even the juniors have a lower age limit in F.E.I. eyes, at 14. Presumably under that age they do not officially exist at all. This particular stipulation caused some red faces among the B.S.J.A. selection committee in 1969 who, all unawares, selected Debbie Johnsey for the team for the European Junior Championships. And Miss Johnsey was but eleven years old. Not until a German journalist pointed out the error of their ways did this come to light. Although there is *something* to be said for debarring under eighteen year olds from competitions in which they might do themselves serious harm—not that a national federation would be likely to select a rider hopelessly out of his depth—there seems little of merit in this lower age limit for juniors. Presumably the reason for its imposition was that, on the Continent, most young riders, of whatever age, ride horses rather than the ponies indigenous to Britain. But as it is on these ponies that the British children usually challenge for the European Junior Championship, with considerable success, it is difficult to see the justice of insisting upon them having reached their fourteenth birthday.

A contributing cause to the general confusion about juniors in Britain is that under B.S.J.A. rules that category ends at sixteen.

Weights

Another regulation that might to advantage be altered is that regarding weights to be carried, for both men and women have to carry the same impost, 11 st 11 lb. Unlike racing, the actual weight carried by a show jumping horse has little effect upon his performance. Someone like, for instance, Harvey Smith would carry at least two stone above the required minimum but this has never had a noticeable effect upon his ability to win all types of competition. Certainly no one would suppose that because a man of slighter build, say Nelson Pessoa, was carrying a stone or two less, that he had an advantage in any way relevant to that weight.

The only time that weight has a deleterious effect upon the way a horse jumps is when it is wrongly distributed, and as most women have to carry a good deal of 'dead' weight, Kathy Kusner, for example, weighs only 7 st 5 lb, it is far more likely to happen with them than with their male competitors. A certain amount of ingenuity can help to obviate this, but since the whole object of the weight ruling is presumably to achieve some sort of parity and not to militate against the women it would seem fairer to drop the regulation completely. In fact it only applies to women riding astride—those riding sidesaddle have no weight restriction!

Juniors riding in senior competition have to carry 11 st, but in junior events, and in attempts on records there is no required weight.

Grading

Although it is one of the most important aspects of show jumping there is complete lack of uni-

Marion Mould and Stroller

formity about the grading of show jumpers. As it is primarily a national matter, since as a rule horses do not compete internationally until they have reached the top grade in their own country, it would be a difficult matter for the F.E.I. to adjudicate on, or to make rules for. It would, in any case, be extremely difficult to frame one set of rules which would work equally in all countries.

In Britain horses tend to be pushed along too fast, too early in their careers. Grading is done according to the prizemoney won: a horse is in Grade C until he has won £150, then in Grade B until his earnings amount to £300. After that he is Grade A for the rest of his life, no matter how much his form may deteriorate with age. The level of prizemoney in Britain is such—in 1969 it exceeded £180,000—that it is easy for a four-year-old of reasonable talent to start a season never having seen a show ring and to finish in Grade A. Indeed, if the horse has luck as well as ability it may take a conscious effort from his rider to prevent this happening. If a rider is bringing along a horse for his own use it is as well to spend a couple of seasons reaching the top grade, but when an owner is looking for a potential buyer for his horse he will obviously hurry it, as the market price for a Grade A horse is higher than that for a Grade C.

Even lower than the Grade C are the Foxhunter competitions, with a £40 maximum, which progress through regional finals to a championship at the Horse of the Year Show. This admirable competition has produced a number of top class winners, among them Douglas Bunn's Beethoven, Top of the Morning, which David Broome rides for Frank Kernan, and Royal Lord, that gallant campaigner who kept on winning for George Hobbs up to the ripe old age of 22.

In France there is an arbitrary grading system which derives solely from a horse's age. The competitions for four-year-olds are jumped over 4 ft courses with no jump-offs or time involved; at five years the fences go up about three inches and there may be barrages, but not against the clock; the next year the horses take another step nearer the finished article, but are still debarred from such punishing competitions as *puissance*. Between seven and twelve years the horses do battle at all levels, but after they have reached twelve years old horses are pensioned off, except for the internationals. This system, though a trifle 'rule-of-thumb' for some tastes, has the virtue of ensuring that a precocious talent is not burnt out too soon, and leaves room for the up-and-coming generation.

In the United States the novices or potential show jumpers often have their early experience in the 'Green Hunter' classes—'Green' being novice. Unlike the British hunter classes the Americans have to show their jumping ability, but of course over less formidable fences than their specialist jumping cousins. The novice jumpers have had to move up to open classes far

Harvey Smith riding O'Malley in the Prince of Wales Cup

too soon, but in 1969 there were moves to bring the United States system into line with the British.

What appears to be a satisfactory grading method is that in vogue in Argentina, where both riders and horses are graded, though the horses, who are apparently expected to be more thoroughly schooled at home than the riders, join in above the lowest grade. There are three gradings for horses, who move up from one to another after three successes in each level. For the top grade horses the competitions are longer than is

Valerie Barker and Atalanta

Caroline Bradley and Ivanovitch

customary in Europe, which may call for more effort initially but is that much more likely to preclude the need to resort to the clock for a solution.

Prizemoney and sponsors

The principal cause of, and reason for, the rapid upgrading of horses, especially in Britain and in some European countries, has been the considerable increase in prizemoney, principally as a result of sponsorship. In 1948 the biggest individual prize to be competed for at the International Horse Show in London was £30: in 1969 this was the lowest first prize, while the John Player Trophy was worth £500 to the winner and even the junior championship carried a first prize of £100.

Not that the John Player is by any means the most valuable competition, even in England, this honour going to the British Jumping Derby at Hickstead which, sponsored as is the whole of Hickstead by W.D. and H.O. Wills, carries a first prize of £1,000. By contrast Australia's top prize is the £250 Forbes Derby, in New South Wales, and that is about twice as much as the next best. In Germany, as might be expected since show jumping there is second only to football as a popular spectator sport, the level of prizemoney is very high. In 1967, when Andrew Fielder and Vibart notched their double of British 'firsts' in the Aachen Grand Prix and, the following Sunday, in the Hamburg Jumping Derby, they collected around £1,500 for their trouble. Some shows give prizes in goods rather than money. The Grand Prix in Amsterdam for instance carries with it a motor-car worth in 1969 about £1,000; and when Alison Westwood had a particularly successful show in Geneva in 1965 she came home bearing, or rather borne in, a car, with a fur coat, two cameras, a watch and a 'treasure-chest' full of lesser prizes.

The most rewarding show of all, however, is now the Dublin Horse Show. Until 1967 Dublin's prizes were, by international standards, on a low level, none of them reaching three figures. Sponsorship was frowned upon by the Royal Dublin Society, the only exceptions being for the Guinness Novice Championship—and Guinness after all is as much a part of Ireland as the R.D.S. itself—and, in 1966, for the Daily Telegraph Junior Match, between teams from the four home countries. With Dublin one of the most difficult and expensive shows for Continental riders to get to it was clear that an inducement, apart from the traditional Irish hospitality, had to be offered, and in 1968 it was—to such effect that every day there was £1,000 to be jumped for, while the Grand Prix, for the Irish Trophy, was sponsored by the Government to the tune of £5,000, with a world record first prize of £1,650.

This general high level of prizemoney is by no means an unmixed blessing. Not only does it persuade some riders to overface their horses, but, especially in Britain, a number of the established riders are reluctant to join the national team abroad for fear of missing out on prizemoney at home. On the whole, however, it is a healthy sign, for commercial enterprises naturally prefer to associate with successful sports from which they can expect to receive kudos and public recognition. In the latter, of course, television has played an appreciable part, for show jumping, with its now simple rules, and having only one 'player' in the ring at a time is an ideal television sport.

Professionalism

The F.E.I. made some fairly sweeping changes to their rules on professionalism at their meeting in Brussels in December 1969. The considerable prizemoney often given has long exacerbated accusations of professionalism in show jumping, and in most countries it is true to say that the top riders, except for the wealthy minority, are not amateurs in the most pure sense. It would be impossible for them to be so, since to stay at the top level of international show jumping entails riding, in competitions and training, almost the whole year round. In Britain a large number of those involved in the sport are farmers, and they are the ones who can most happily combine their job and their sport; but even so, when away for as much as five or six weeks at a time during the peak of the season, they need to leave someone behind to take care of the running of their farms. For most of the others, the jobs with which they are officially credited are often, if not precisely a figment of the imagination, at least a somewhat exaggerated version of reality. This is generally true also of those in the services who represent their countries at the sport. The impossibility of combining effectively a military and a show jumping career was well illustrated by the French during the troubles they had in Indo-China and Algeria: the military side of their team, by tradition a strong one, almost ceased to exist. Mr. Avery Brundage, the President of the International Olympic Committee, has made no secret of the fact that he views show jumping with a jaundiced eye. Eventually, though probably not as long as Mr. Brundage continues in office, the I.O.C. may concede that every sportsman throughout the world is not a millionaire. A realistic appraisal of the situation from the I.O.C.—and by no means only in show jumping—could clear the air and remove the amateur and professional labels, as has been done in cricket.

Until last year under F.E.I. Rules professionals were allowed to apply for an amateur licence, after which they could ride in official international horse shows, as did Ted Williams; but men employed to ride horses or in stables were barred. The new rules were based on the premise that 'it is only necessary to make a distinction between those riders who wish to exploit their success in competition and those who wish to take part purely as a sport'.

A professional is now defined by the F.E.I. as any person who, having reached the age of eighteen:
(a) accepts remuneration for riding Competition horses in show jumping, dressage or three-day event competitions;
(b) sells more than three international competition horses during the current year;
(c) hires out competition horses for the purpose of show jumping, dressage, or three-day event competitions;
(d) receives payment for training competition horses;
(e) allows or has allowed his name or photograph to be used to promote or advertise any product;
(d) is considered, for any other reason, as a professional by the F.E.I. and/or his National Federation.

All riders, amateur or professional, must hold annual licences from their National Federations; and, the most profound change of all, professionals are now able to ride in C.H.I.O.s and Jumping championships. Only from Regional and Olympic Games are they barred. The new rules also require National Federations to publish each year tables showing the prizemoney won by the top ten owner/riders and the top owners other than riders, which should clear up any doubts as to exactly how much riders can make out of show jumping. The Olympic ruling remains 'once a professional always a professional': although a slight breach was made in this archaic dam with the last-minute admission to the Tokyo Games of Italy's Graziano Mancinelli, who started his career in a Milanese stable.

Records

Despite the general competitiveness of show jumping, records as a whole play little part in it. This is primarily due to the difficulty of producing comparable conditions for competitions, which would be a basic essential for comparing results.

For instance, if a runner runs 800 metres and the wind is below a certain strength, and this can be measured, then he may qualify for a record time; similarly with a swimmer, who does not even have wind resistance to bother with. Yet to compare the time of, say, the winner of the Grand Prix in London with the winner of the Grand Prix in Rome would be completely useless, since the courses would be entirely different. Even a comparison of the times of steeplechasers from one course to another avails one of no useful information. Therefore the only records that can be achieved are for single jumps, either high or broad, and as these have to be specially organised —not being a natural consequence of a competition—there is little general enthusiasm to create new ones.

The British high jump record was set up as long ago as 1937, in Olympia, when Don Beard and Mr. Fred Foster's great horse Swank jumped 7 ft 6¼ in, which is not only the British record but appears to be the highest officially jumped at any indoor show in the world. The world record high jump has lasted since 1949 when the Chilean Captain Alberto Larraguibel with the big thoroughbred Huaso jumped 2·47 m (8 ft 1½ in) at Vina del Mar. Huaso was not much of a show jumper apparently, as he took too much of a hold, but he had tremendous strength and courage.

Although *puissance* competitions tend as a rule to end over high walls, for a record jump such as this sloping poles are used, with a brush fence at the base. Huaso a former racehorse by Henry Lee, was carefully prepared for his bid at the high jump record, which had been set at 2·44 metres in 1938 by the Italian Antonio Gutierrez on Ossopo. When the big day came Huaso was joined by another Chilean horse in his record attempt. Each horse was allowed three attempts; at his first Huaso stopped, at his second he nearly fell but at the third the 14-year-old cleared the top bar and the record was his. This was only the fourth time the record had changed hands since Captain Crousse of France jumped 2·35 metres with Conspirateur in 1900.

Two more Frenchmen, Mm. Ricard and Montespieu, set a new height, 2·36 m, in 1912, and in 1933 Lieut. Count Christian de Castries with Vol au Vent, an Anglo-Normand, raised it to 2·38 m in Paris. The high jump record stayed there, until Gutierrez topped it in Rome, but two years after he set the high jump record de Castries took the long jump record. In Spa, Belgium, he and Tenace cleared 7·60 metres (24 ft 11 in). This was beaten several times, in 1946, 1948, 1949 and 1950 before Lieut. Col. Lopez de Hierro on Amado Mio established the record that stands today. In 1951 at Barcelona they jumped 8·30 metres (27 ft 3 in). Although this is the show jumping long jump record it must have been surpassed on the racecourse by steeplechasers going at a flat-out gallop.

So much for the official records; there is no shortage of unofficial claimants. For instance, the Russians claim that in 1953 V. Trapeznikov on Kuniza also jumped 8·30 metres, which would make them joint record holders in the long jump. Obviously there has to be careful and official supervision for a record attempt, or else there would be the wildest of claims, but well substantiated claims in Australia could give them both records. For instance a five-year-old called Thumbs Up is alleged to have jumped no less than 30 ft 7 in in the water-jump competition at the Sydney Royal show—in 1916.

The showground at Cairns, in Queensland, has undoubtedly been the site of some astounding displays of high jumping. In 1936 two horses, Lookout and Euchre, were apparently only a quarter of an inch short of the present world record height of 8 ft 1½ in, and the same year, though not at Cairns, Lookout went up to 8 ft 3 in. The best jump at Cairns appears to have come ten years later, in 1946, when Jack Martin and Gold Medal went over at 8 ft 4 in.

As this is one sphere in which the Australians can show the superiority of their horses without being involved in the long, expensive trek to the Northern Hemisphere perhaps one day they will set an official world record. The significant thing about the record breaking horses appears to be that, as an almost universal rule, their talents lay only in the direction in which they achieved their records. And this is carrying specialisation to a degree where it rapidly severs connection with show jumping proper.

P. J. d'Oriola and Pomone

4 Courses and Training

Courses and fences

The most important man at any jumping show is the course-builder. No matter how good the horses taking part he can make or mar a competition, either by making the course so easy that a score or so horses get through to the timed jump-off, which develops into a 'steeplechase', or, much worse, by resorting to tricks to stop the horses going clear. A competent course-builder aims at building a course of a difficulty relevant to the horses taking part, be they novices or internationals; a course which asks questions that a horse in that particular state of training ought to be able to answer, but with sufficient difficulties to ensure that only those horses, and riders, who deserve to go clear do so.

In the early days of show jumping course building was hardly thought of as in any way a science. The average British country show might have six or eight fences going up one side of the ring and back down the other, with a 'grand finale' over a water jump or triple bar. Little thought would be given to the siting of the fences, and even the jumping of them was often less important than the style with which this was accomplished. Time was of not the slightest import; if a rider wanted to have a circle or two to get right for a fence, well let him do just that. Rules were complex and adjudication on them difficult; at the 1912 Olympics in Stockholm, for instance, slats (thin laths of wood) were used on the fences, penalties were awarded for touches and for knock-downs, or for landing on or within the demarcation lines of spread fences. And in each case penalties for these offences perpetrated by the forelegs cost twice as much as if they were done by the hindlegs.

The disadvantages of such systems of marking are all too obvious: quite apart from the abuse which they were open to, at least at minor shows, there was too much chance of a human error. Gradually changes were made, although the slats were slow to go, and did not finally bow out in Britain until after the last war. In the United States even now the National classes still penalise for 'touches' as opposed to knock-downs, so that rapping is often necessary, and mostly legal, to persuade a horse to jump clean. Under the aegis of the F.E.I. however the sport became more organised, more of a public spectacle, and with more emphasis on time. Combined with an advance in training methods, of both riders and horses, this has brought about a considerable change in the courses, not only on the international circuit but also at most domestic shows. If the prime object of a course is to test the rider's ability and the horse's training then it is equally important in the early days not to ask too much. Many a good horse has been spoiled by being over-faced. Solid fences and 'true' strides must be the prerequisite of any novice course.

Basically a course builder has but four types of fence at his disposal: uprights, parallels, staircases and pyramids. But with these and their variations, a basic knowledge of the abilities of a horse and a dash of imagination he can concoct an excellent variety of absorbing courses. Knowing the general capabilities of a horse is the most essential feature of a course builder, and although, to have it, one need not necessarily have ridden in show jumping a number of the top exponents of the art were also at one time in the highest flight of international competition.

In Britain an obvious example was the late Col. Jack Talbot-Ponsonby. Three times winner of the King George V Gold Cup, and experienced on the continent and in North America, he designed the courses for the Royal International Horse Show and the Horse of the Year Show, which were built by John Gross, the B.S.J.A.'s senior course builder. Arthur McCashin, the resident course-builder at the New York show in Madison Square Garden, was a top-rate rider, both in show jumping and racing, before the war, and afterwards was in the team which won the bronze medal at Stockholm in 1952.

A particularly important figure in this sphere in the next few seasons will be Hans Brinckmann. In the 1930s he was a regular member of the victorious German team, and several times winner of the Grand Prix at Aachen, where he now builds courses acknowledged to be among the toughest in the world. He will be responsible for the Olympic courses at Munich in 1972. Competitive experience at this level is obviously not essential

—if it were there would be precious few eligible for the job—though some experience is a help. Mrs. Pam Carruthers, who show jumped in a rather more modest way, is the resident course builder at Hickstead's permanent ground, and has built the courses at Harrisburg and Washington, and in South Africa.

Talbot-Ponsonby also built courses in South Africa, and Gross did so at the indoor show in 1969. The use of such designers as these, well versed in international requirements, must have played a big part in South African riders' maintenance of high standards during the years of the horse sickness ban. John Gross, incidentally, who joined the B.S.J.A. in 1957, and has been senior course builder since 1960, is an example of a course builder who learned his job 'on the ground', mainly from Jack Talbot-Ponsonby. Now, as well as travelling some 14,000 miles a year officiating at around 30 major shows, he is in charge of the B.S.J.A.'s central jump stores in Aldershot, where the fences are made for distribution all over the country, while course-drawings and advice on fence construction go all over the world.

The first consideration of any course builder must be the standard of horses for which he is building. One of the most difficult jobs is to produce a fair result from a big field of novices without resorting to trickery. On the international level the job is even more complex, but he can then ask more searching questions of both horse and rider. Still, it must be said, without traps, since it might reasonably be assumed that a man who needs to resort to them is not competent.

He will, as a general rule, want to make it a course which can be ridden smoothly, that is to say without constant abrupt checks being necessary, for these are bad for the horse and ugly from the viewpoint of the spectators—an important consideration. The components of the problems that the course-builder may pose are the size of the fences, the distances between one fence and another and their siting. The length of a horse's strides varies considerably, of course, but on average at a strong canter it will be about 10 ft. Fences more than 80 ft apart are considered unrelated, as after the first has been jumped there is room to make fundamental changes of pace and stride before the next. If the fences are within 39 ft 4 in of each other then they are accounted to be part of the same combination fence. Normally a combination fence will have two or three component parts, but there can be more. In Geneva in 1965 Harvey Smith and the brilliant South African-bred The Sea Hawk won a take-your-own-line competition by jumping the whole course as a 'combination', never taking more than two strides between the fences.

Whether the distance between two elements of a combination is easy or difficult depends not only on the measured distance from base to base but also upon the shape of each element, since there should obviously be more space between uprights than between spread fences. Easy distances between two uprights would be 26 ft for one stride and 35 ft for two strides; between two sets of parallels they would be 23 ft and 34 ft: and somewhere between these distances for alternative combinations. So if a distance of, say, 29 ft is set then the rider has to decide whether to try and jump in two very short strides or one very long one. The answer to such a problem as this would depend both upon one's horse—whether he had a naturally long or short stride, whether he was bold enough to try it in one or cautious—and also upon the fences before and after it.

Steinkraus gives as an example of a difficult treble the one built for the 1956 Olympics by Count Casimir Lewenhaupt, who had been in the winning team in 1912. The first element was an oxer with a seven-foot spread which was met on exactly a half-stride from the previous fence; the second element, two short strides away, was a white gate at the maximum of 5 ft 3 in, followed by another oxer, with a 6 ft 6 in spread, at 28 ft. If the rider left out the half-stride to meet the first

Lt. Col. Jack Talbot-Ponsonby and Willie Hendry

Douglas Bunn

oxer boldly the two short strides which followed were extremely difficult; but if he jumped the first oxer off a short stride he risked a knockdown there, with danger of more faults at the two subsequent fences, or of refusals. Apparently most of the successful horses met the combination on a short stride, but Winkler's great mare Halla jumped off a long stride in the first round, and in the second, when she was virtually 'carrying' her rider to victory, went in off a short stride, and both times clear. But Hallas are hard to find! Olympic courses, however, are a law unto themselves, so more of them a little later.

To make a fence higher obviously increases its difficulty, but except in *puissance* competitions, and kindred events such as the six-bar and the fault-and-out over raised fences, height alone is rarely the criterion. A five-foot fence solidly built, especially if it is of the triple-bar variety, will invariably be jumped more cleanly than an upright of skimpy poles several inches lower.

A horse measures the fence he is going to jump from the base, so that if there is no ground-line to guide him his problem is intensified. Which is why, in international competitions, many of the post and rail type of fences have the lowest rail well above the ground. The ultimate of this is the single rail, but this is not often used except in 'speed' competitions. An even more difficult problem is posed if, instead of having no ground line, there is a false one. So if a bush is put in the middle of a set of parallel poles, converting it into an oxer, the horse will see on the ground the base of the bush, which is obviously not in the same vertical plane as the first poles. He may then be inclined to get in too close to the fence.

'Parallel poles', incidentally, is a label often misused for the sake of convenience, for on many occasions they are not exactly parallel, the rear pole being slightly higher than the one in front. This makes it very much easier to jump, as the horse can then plainly see that he is to jump a spread fence and not an upright.

The most commonly used upright fences apart from poles and planks are gates, all three of which will be supported from wings by means of 'cups' —which can vary from being deep and firmly-supporting to flat and easily displaced—and palisades, which may be 'self-supporting'. Walls, and viaducts, are built of individual bricks and usually jumped well until they reach *puissance* heights.

The normal '*puissance*' type of horse will often 'roll' over the top of the wall on his stomach, for, although a horse may stand back at a fence up to about 5 ft 6 in, after that he is more likely to succeed if he comes in on a short stride, with considerable impulsion, and 'climbs' over.

Oxers and the fences which give the type its name are obvious examples of the 'parallel' variety of fence; the staircase is usually a triple-bar, with three poles on separate supports closely aligned and in ascending order. These may be bare poles, or well-packed with bushes, which make them more inviting. Incidentally, McCashin in New York suffers a considerable handicap in being unable to use bushes, for fire prevention reasons. An elegant variation on the triple bar is the 'fan' fence, or spiral staircase, in which the supports on one side are spread out on a radius.

The great advantage of all these fences is their mobility. The most commonly found permanent obstacle is the water-jump, and it is also the fence most likely to cause trouble. It is odd to reflect that horses were jumping ditches long before the Enclosure Act brought other types of fencing into common usage, and yet it is an obstacle so many horses, or their riders, find hard to negotiate. Most water jumps have a bush in front of them, as a take-off guide to the horse; it becomes easier if a pole is put over the water, which makes a horse aim for height as well as length; the most difficult water to jump is the 'naked' variety, which leaves horse and rider completely to their own devices. It is particularly noticeable of water jumps, but is equally true of all others, that the wider they are the better they jump. A gate 4 ft 6 in high and only 5 ft wide will be more often knocked down, or stop a horse, than one of the same height but ten or twelve feet wide. Apart from water, permanent obstacles are rare in Britain, with the exception of Hickstead, which was started by Douglas Bunn with the principal intention of giving British riders and horses experience of the type of fence they would be likely to encounter at European shows.

Aachen, which like Hickstead is used solely for

horse shows, is known for its variety, including the Aachener, similar to Hickstead's Devil's Dyke, its table and lake; Hamburg's Derby Bank is the prototype of such obstacles, which look more fearsome than they are; Lucerne is noted for its banks; Rotterdam adds a 'gated' bank to the trees and unique shape which make it one of the most attractive of all. Most of the showgrounds on the Continent have their special features.

It is not only the distance of one fence from another that can be used to set a problem, but their placing in relation to the perimeter of the arena. A double of oxers, which might be of no more than average difficulty with a clear approach, can become almost unjumpable if set only four or five strides from the ringside. Changes of direction are an integral part of any course design, but though they can legitimately test both obedience and impulsion they should not necessitate violent checking.

The heights of fences will be governed by the type of competition, so that those in a *parcours de chasse*, aimed to test the handiness of a horse, will obviously be smaller than in a Grand Prix. The precise heights are obviously left to the course-builder, but the F.E.I. issues certain guide-lines. Thus the length of the course cannot exceed the number of fences to be jumped multiplied by sixty—in metres. The starting line must be between six and a half and twenty-seven yards from the first fence, and the finish between sixteen yards nine inches and twenty-seven yards from the last, although indoor shows may vary this.

Instructions are more definite for Nations Cups, which is fair, for there should be some uniformity, though most course-builders are still able to cater for the 'home team's' strongest qualities. With the exception of indoor shows the course must be about 867 yards long, with thirteen or fourteen fences, between 4 ft 3 in and 5 ft 3 in, and including at least one double or one treble, but not more than one of each or three doubles. A water jump of a minimum of 13 ft is obligatory, again indoor shows excepted—an exception was also made in London in 1968 when the Royal International went to Wembley Stadium and the authorities there were opposed to having their world-famous turf dug up.

The natural contours of a ring can be used to increase or decrease difficulties, since a fence jumped uphill will need more effort than coming down. The course may also be affected by natural phenomena. Heavy rain which makes the ground soft will obviously increase the difficulty of the fences—the jury may then lower them—while bright sunlight, causing deep shadows which may confuse the horse, as sometimes happens for instance in the cypress-bounded Piazza di Sienna in Rome, is a hazard difficult to allow for. A truly expert course builder can usually tell roughly how many clear rounds he will produce over a particular course—though occasionally an unforeseen circumstance or miscalculation can throw him well out—and this is important in such a tightly-timed show as the Horse of the Year Show, when it is necessary to produce a 'finish' within the time alloted by television.

Olympic Courses

Olympic courses are intended to provide a searching test of the best riders and horses in the world. Few have passed without criticism, but probably none quite so widespread or so outspoken as that for the team event in Mexico, built by the 1948 gold and silver medal winner Ruben Uriza.

Since the Mexicans won in London, with a total of $34\frac{1}{4}$ faults, the winning scores have progressively mounted, save that the British team's $40\frac{3}{4}$ in 1952 was slightly more than the Germans' 40 four years later. When they won in Rome and Tokyo the German team's scores were $46\frac{1}{2}$ and $68\frac{1}{2}$. The Canadian gold medal team in Mexico had an aggregate of no fewer than $102\frac{3}{4}$ faults. The reasons for this astronomical leap were primarily the placing of the combination fences, both of which followed too closely on the preceding fences, and the time, which was so short that in the whole competition only four rounds did not collect time faults—both of David Broome and Mister Softee's, Raimondo d'Inzeo's Bellevue first time and Marcel Rozier's Quo Vadis in the second round.

The heights of Olympic courses have, obviously, increased over the years: in 1912 the maximum was 4 ft 6 in, and most were about 3 ft 7 in. In Mexico the maximum was 5 ft 3 in; the lowest was the first, at 4 ft 7 in, and that was an oxer with a 4 ft 11 in spread. Moreover the ground was holding. But it was not the dimensions of the fences that caused the trouble so much as their placing.

Invariably in Olympic courses it is the combination fences which cause the most faults. In Mexico the treble came only five strides after a triple bar 4 ft 11 in high with a 6 ft 6 in spread. A big treble should be able to be 'attacked', but this started with a 4 ft 11 in wall, which, if taken in a reasonable way, could leave a horse short of impulsion for the parallels that followed, the first 4 ft 11 in by 5 ft 7 in, the second 4 ft 11 in by 5 ft 11 in. No fewer than 108 times was one or other of the three elements knocked down—mostly the final parallel—apart from the many refusals there. It was this fence which knocked

OLYMPIC TRIAL 1969
Designed by J. B. Gross

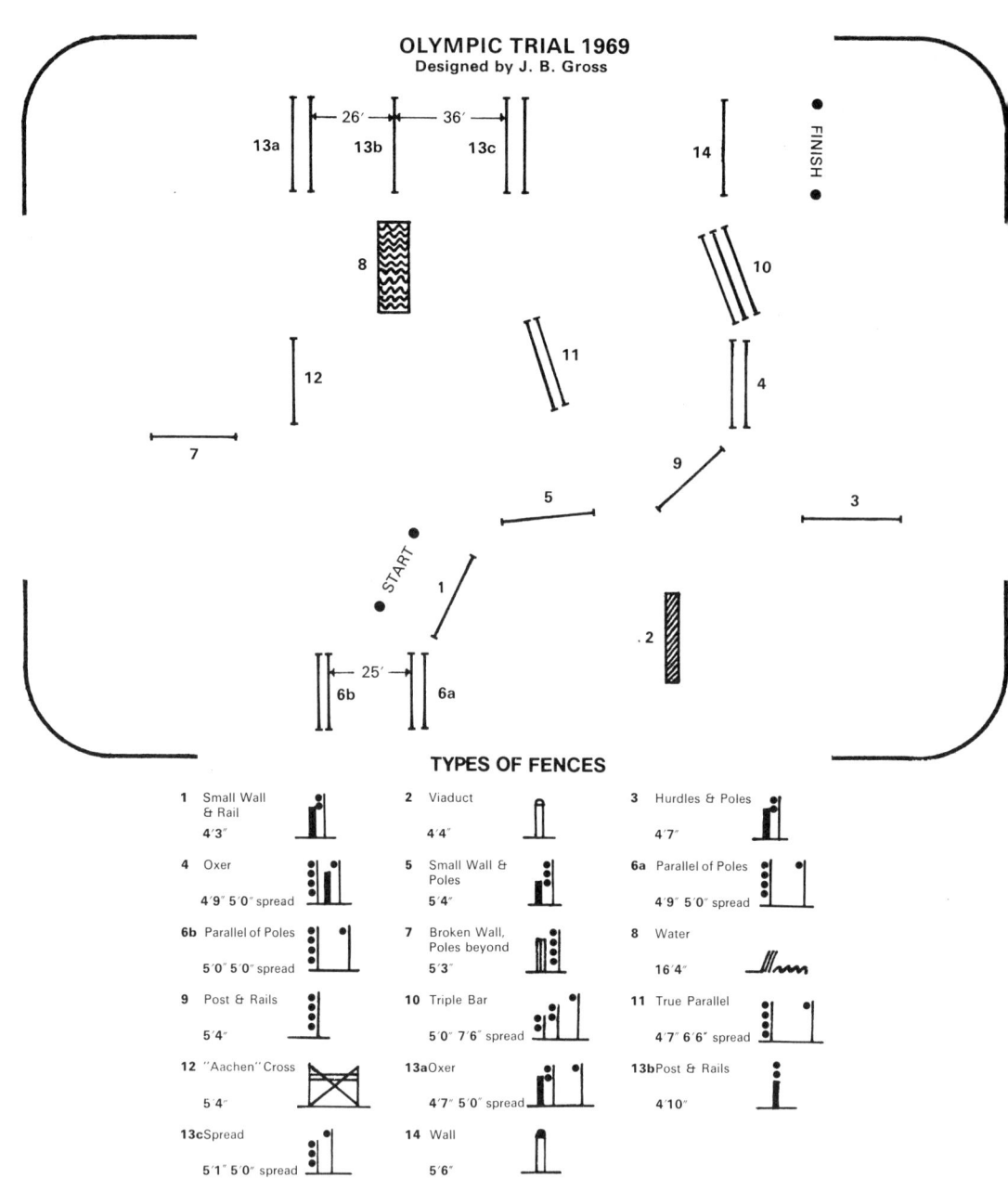

TYPES OF FENCES

#	Name	Dimensions
1	Small Wall & Rail	4'3"
2	Viaduct	4'4"
3	Hurdles & Poles	4'7"
4	Oxer	4'9" 5'0" spread
5	Small Wall & Poles	5'4"
6a	Parallel of Poles	4'9" 5'0" spread
6b	Parallel of Poles	5'0" 5'0" spread
7	Broken Wall, Poles beyond	5'3"
8	Water	16'4"
9	Post & Rails	5'4"
10	Triple Bar	5'0" 7'6" spread
11	True Parallel	4'7" 6'6" spread
12	"Aachen" Cross	5'4"
13a	Oxer	4'7" 5'0" spread
13b	Post & Rails	4'10"
13c	Spread	5'1" 5'0" spread
14	Wall	5'6"

out Britain's hopes, when Stroller came to grief there on his second circuit. Harvey Smith, with Madison Time, in both his rounds, and d'Oriola, on Nagir, and Winkler with Enigk, on their second, decided the best way to deal with the treble was deliberately to knock a brick out of the wall so as to be correctly placed for the parallels.

The water, at No. 11, claimed no fewer than 51 victims, although it was the same size as in the individual, when only ten horses faulted there. The reason was possibly psychological, for only six strides after it came a double of wide, true parallels, the first 4 ft 9 in by 5 ft 7 in, the second 4 ft 9 in by 5 ft 11 in. In the two rounds a total of 79 horses hit the first parallel, and throughout only three horses jumped the water and the double of parallels clear: Enigk and Schockemohle's Donald Rex first time, and Piero d'Inzeo's Fidux on the second round. Raimondo d'Inzeo had a particularly unpleasant experience there when Bellevue, surprised by the distance, put in a wild leap at the double, hit his rider in the face and loosened three of d'Inzeo's teeth.

Time played a particularly significant part in the destination of the bronze medal, for which Germany beat the United States by just a quarter of a fault. Germany had a total of $13\frac{1}{4}$ time faults, while U.S.A. had $17\frac{1}{2}$. Canada had $10\frac{3}{4}$ time faults in their $102\frac{3}{4}$ total, and France $6\frac{1}{2}$. None of these in the first four teams were caused by refusals.

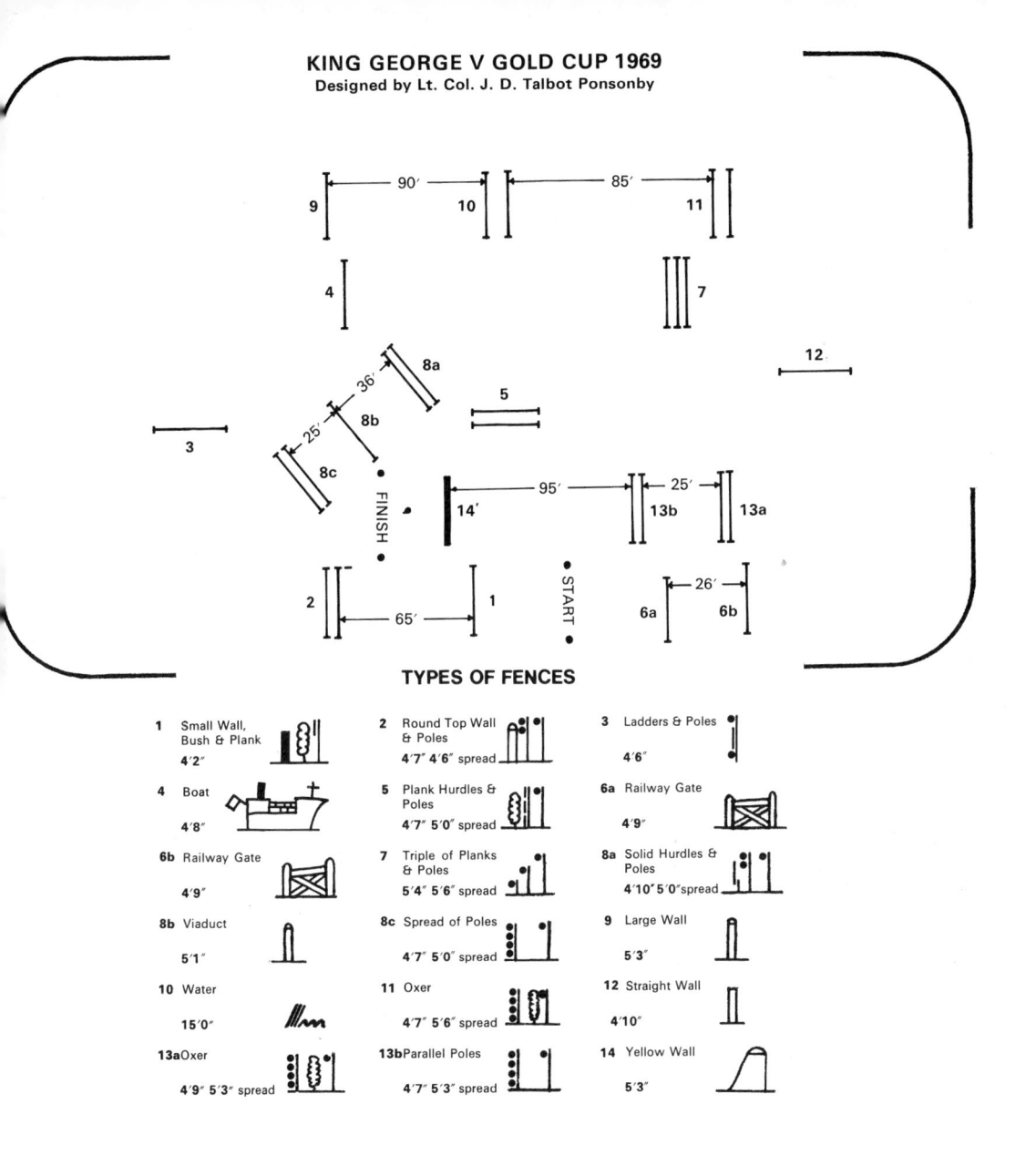

KING GEORGE V GOLD CUP 1969
Designed by Lt. Col. J. D. Talbot Ponsonby

TYPES OF FENCES

1 Small Wall, Bush & Plank — 4'2"	**2** Round Top Wall & Poles — 4'7" 4'6" spread	**3** Ladders & Poles — 4'6"
4 Boat — 4'8"	**5** Plank Hurdles & Poles — 4'7" 5'0" spread	**6a** Railway Gate — 4'9"
6b Railway Gate — 4'9"	**7** Triple of Planks & Poles — 5'4" 5'6" spread	**8a** Solid Hurdles & Poles — 4'10" 5'0" spread
8b Viaduct — 5'1"	**8c** Spread of Poles — 4'7" 5'0" spread	**9** Large Wall — 5'3"
10 Water — 15'0"	**11** Oxer — 4'7" 5'6" spread	**12** Straight Wall — 4'10"
13a Oxer — 4'9" 5'3" spread	**13b** Parallel Poles — 4'7" 5'3" spread	**14** Yellow Wall — 5'3"

The Mexico course produced the closest result since the war, with less than fifteen faults covering the first four teams. In Tokyo the comparable margin had been nearly twice as much—Germany's winning 68½ to the fourth-placed British team's 97¼—while at Rome the United Arab Republic's 135½ was 89 faults behind Germany's total. It is of little more than mathematical interest that Canada's 102¾ would not have got them in the medals in any other post-war Olympic Games, because, as has been said before, it is impossible to compare performances over entirely different courses.

It has been suggested that there should be one prescribed course for all Olympic Games, to be decided by a technical committee appointed by the F.E.I. This would certainly remove any accusations of unfairness although the opponents of this idea suggest that to have the same course each time would make for dullness. This theory is not borne out by the various Jumping Derbies, which generally stick to precisely the same course each year and still manage to produce supremely exciting competitions. And is the Grand National not run over the same fences—or very nearly—each year, with no depreciation in thrills? The Olympic Games are the pinnacle of every country's sporting ambitions, and the one essential is that the course they jump should be worthy of the occasion.

Training and Breeding

This section is not intended as a thorough treatise on the training of show jumpers, which would in any case take far more space than is available here, but rather contains observations on the basic principles and development of jumping.

As has been said, jumping is a comparatively recent development in riding horses, and there are those, some experienced horsemen, who assert that jumping is not only unnatural to a horse but positively contrary to its inclinations. For instance, Count Toptani, in his *Modern Show Jumping* refers to jumping as 'a definitely unpleasant movement for the horse and executed only under compulsion'. This is a premise difficult to accept, but there is no doubt that a horse's attitude to jumping will be coloured by his initial training, which, if in the hands of an inept, ignorant or impatient person may well result in a horse considering jumping to be an 'unpleasant movement,' to be done only under compulsion. If, on the other hand, patience and imagination are used, a horse can, up to the limit of his ability, be taught to enjoy his jumping. Undoubtedly many of them experience the same exhilaration as their riders.

A name which is soon mentioned when methods of training show jumpers are discussed is that of Federico Caprilli, who has been called the 'Father of show jumping' and whose writings on the subject have had a fundamental effect on the approach to riding over fences in all parts of the world. The 'Forward Seat', which is credited to Caprilli, was diametrically opposed to the customary British hunting seat, which relied for stability on sitting firmly in the saddle, leaning forward at take-off and right back when landing, the feet thrust firmly forward in long leathers. The forward seat is based on balance, in short on getting a rider's weight off a horse's quarters, since it is the rear end of a horse which it uses for propelling itself both forwards and upwards, and spread evenly on the forehand.

Before going in any more detail into Caprilli's theories, mention must be made of the jockey who revolutionised Flat racing, James Todhunter 'Tod' Sloan, an American who, in the late 1890s, proceeded to win race after race in Britain, often beating superior horses, by the simple expedient of using leathers much shorter than any of his English contemporaries would have dreamed of, crouching over the withers and allowing the horse full freedom to propel himself along unimpeded. As the only object of racing is to get past the post first, unlike hunting, or even show jumping in the early days when style counted for a good deal, Sloan's fellow jockeys soon fell in with his ideas, and they spread throughout Europe. It is, therefore, not unlikely that the young Caprilli saw in action on the racecourse what must be accepted as at least the precursor of his system. However, riding and training horses is an art rather than a science; changes come gradually, through development of an idea rather than through a blinding discovery of a hitherto concealed reality.

Caprilli, born in 1868, the son of a wealthy shipbuilder, went through the cavalry school at

French Officer taking a jump with his hands tied behind his back.

Modena, and spent a good deal of his time working on theories concerning the mechanics of a horse's body, both on the flat and over fences. Attempting to put his half-evolved theories into practice Caprilli suffered a great number of falls, but persevered with his ideas, which, briefly were to the effect that a rider should sit forward, rising slightly out of the saddle during the jump, always maintaining firm contact with the mouth but allowing the horse to round his back and use his neck and head as balancers, as when jumping free, without a rider. In 1904 Caprilli was given a squad of recruits at the cavalry school at Pinerolo, and within four months his methods of training had brought a marked improvement; within a few years the cavalry schools of most countries in Europe had accepted, at least in part, the principles he expounded. Caprilli himself died, falling from a horse, aged only 39.

Col. Joe Hume Dudgeon in the 1920s was probably most responsible for propagating the theory of the forward seat in Britain, but not without a good deal of opposition from those who felt, however it might suffice for a 'continental circus', it was out of place in the English hunting field. Most countries have now adopted, or adapted, the system; the saddle is no longer regarded, at least among the more knowledgeable and athletic horsemen, as a mobile armchair. The sympathy of, say Raimondo d'Inzeo with Merano, of Winkler with Halla, of David Broome and of several of the Americans speak eloquently of the merits of the forward seat. But in the present standard of international jumping, which calls for speed as well as fluency of jumping there is rather more domination than Caprilli advocated.

Shape and Breeding

Before one can even think about training a horse, the first essential is to find the right one. Jumpers, it has been said often enough, come in all shapes and sizes. True enough, against such as Foxhunter or Merely-a-Monarch one can set, say, Pegasus, no beauty but one of the greatest show jumpers of all, or Vibart, who would hardly win a *concours d'elegance* but has beaten many a better looking horse when it comes to jumping fences. Nor is size a criterion, as Stroller, Dundrum, Bonvale and many others have proved. Nevertheless, if the effort that must go into producing a top-class show jumper is to bear fruit it is sensible to look for the sort of horse most likely to succeed.

To cope with the big courses likely to be encountered, and often to be jumped at speed, a horse will need athleticism and power: so the 'motor' should be well constructed, with a short back, strong quarters, a hind leg none too straight; plenty of heart room; sloping shoulders so that the forelegs can be tucked well under over the jump; a good, strong neck; a straight foreleg, not back at the knee or it will be more likely to have trouble landing time and again, often on firm or hard ground; and an honest head and eye. More knee action than would be considered ideal in, for instance, a show hunter is not a drawback, for the more a horse folds up his legs the less high does he need to jump to clear a fence, while another may leap eighteen inches over the top rail and drop just one leg on it. Thus it is that some horses with hackney blood in them have made successful jumpers.

Though they come in all sizes, from Stroller's 14 hands 2 inches to San Lucas's 17·3 h.h., the ideal height is about 16·1 or 16·2 hands high. There is a general preference for geldings rather than mares—few entire horses make the very top grade—mainly because mares are less likely to have the right temperament, and may come into season at the wrong time. Yet one of the greatest of all, Halla, was a mare. Winkler, who won two World Championships and three Olympic gold medals on her, had an intuitive understanding of the mare; though she was a nervous animal and could be difficult, he found the key to her nature, and was well rewarded in Stockholm for his patience.

Breeding of show jumpers is a haphazard business. The racehorse breeder will spend much time poring over stud records, racecourse performances, sire and dam lines before deciding to which stallion he will send his mare, but the majority of show jumpers happen, as it were, by accident. One of the reasons for this is the long time that a show jumper needs to reach the peak of his powers, often not until he is nine or ten years old, or even more: so that his sire may by then have died, or passed into obscurity, perhaps been gelded. That is if the sire was even known, for some of those, especially out of Ireland, have fairly anonymous parentage—hence the apocryphal story of the buyer seeing a horse he liked the look of, asking what it was by and being asked in return 'What would you like him to be by?'

Water Serpent, sire of The Rock and Rockette, has been a prolific sire of jumpers, but with little doubt the record in this respect must go to the French-based Furioso, by the 1937 Ascot Gold Cup winner Precipitation-Maureen, whose progeny includes d'Oriola's Tokyo gold medallist Lutteur, his world champion Pomone, Virtuoso, three times champion of France, Curioso, Kairouan and Joc de l'Ile, who were, or are outstanding in Austria, Holland and Portugal respectively.

The United States team has come down heavily in favour of thoroughbreds, Snowbound, Sinjon, San Lucas and Untouchable among others having started their competitive careers on the racecourse. The outstanding sire of American show jumpers is Bonne Nuit, who numbers among his progeny such outstanding performers as Night Owl, Hollandia, Miss Budweiser and Riviera Wonder. Generally speaking, however, three-quarter bred horses tend to be more amenable to the discipline which must go into their training. The Irish light draught mare who used to produce the ideal type of hunter is now a rare bird, though efforts have lately been made to encourage breeders with classes at the Dublin Horse Show. Successful thoroughbred crosses in Britain have been Vibart, by the hurdler Hyross out of a Clydesdale mare, and North Flight, one of the best mares of recent years, by the Cleveland Bay stallion Lord Fairfax from a thoroughbred mare. In France the Anglo-Arab and Anglo-Normand crosses have been especially successful, and in recent years the Government has offered financial incentive to breeders of show jumpers.

The Germans, whose horses have been so successful at the sport, approach the matter scientifically. The Holstein breeders have a club at Elmshorn, with their own stud book, and a recognised 'type' at which to aim. Fritz Thiedemann used to ride for them, as Kurt Jarasinski does now, and without doubt the Holstein breed's best advertisement in the field of show jumping was Thiedemann's Meteor, European Champion of 1958, twice in the gold medal team and, in his day the most prolific winner of major competitions in Europe. Apart from the Holsteins, the Hanoverians are the most popular for show jumping in Germany, but Winkler tends to favour a 'lighter' type than either of them; both Halla and Sonnenglanz, his 1957 European Champion, who were bred by Gustav Vierling, were by trotting stallions out of the half-bred mare Hélène. Halla, incidentally, returned to Herr Vierling when she retired from show jumping and has bred seven foals, though none of them has, as yet, shown ability to compare with that of their fabulous dam.

In view of the current vogue in favour of South American-bred horses, especially those from Argentina and Brazil, which is largely due to the efforts of Nelson Pessoa, who has both created a demand by his considerable success and then supplied the horses, Count Toptani's remarks on horses from that continent make interesting reading:

'I want right away to refute the common belief that South American success in recent horse shows is mainly due to the fine quality of their horses. This is far from being true; in fact it is to the contrary. In Argentina, horses are very inferior—at least as far as show horses are concerned. When I say inferior I mean inferior to the wonderful horses bred in France; the Anglo-Arabs, the Anglo-Normands, or the splendid Irish hunters and their English cousins, and naturally far inferior to the great German horses, the Trakeneres, Hanoveraners and Holsteiners.'

Toptani's over-all argument is that it is superior horsemanship rather than superior horses that has been triumphant, but the success of South American horses in European hands does not exactly substantiate that argument.

Into Training

One fundamental upon which all great trainers of horses agree, whatever 'system' or nuance thereof they may favour, is that each horse must be treated as an individual. It is worse than useless to say that there is a 'right way' to do a thing, and determine that it shall be done exactly according to the preconceived pattern by each and every horse.

From the very beginning it is essential to win a horse's confidence, and this can only be done gradually, so that in the moment of supreme trial, when the rider asks his horse for a particular effort he will get an instant response, which may make the difference not only between success and failure in the competition, but also between jumping a fence or landing short, perhaps with disastrous results. Before one can even think about asking a horse to learn to jump he must be taught to use himself on the flat, for it has been rightly said that it is the approach which makes the jump.

Bill Steinkraus, an erudite writer as well as a great rider, in his book *Riding and Jumping* defines the essentials for the jumper, who obviously does not need, indeed would not benefit from, being trained as is an Haute Ecole dressage horse.

Bill Steinkraus says that, primarily, 'the rider must be able to control his horse's forward movement and impulsion in a smooth and evenly gaited way; he must be able to turn accurately and correctly; and it will be a great convenience if he can make a correct single flying change of lead. The turn on the haunches and on the forehand, the shoulder-in, and correct halts and half-halts are indispensable foundations for the achievement of these aims.'

'We must require from the jumper a high standard of excellence, relatively speaking, of the ordinary trot and the ordinary canter; but, on average, I think we should place more emphasis on extension than on collection'.

The advantages of thorough schooling on the ground cannot be over-emphasised. The United States team, who since 1955 have been trained by Bertalan de Nemethy, and who have now as elegant and effective a team as any country in the world, and the Germans, who run them very close, are fervent adherents to this belief. Hans Gunter Winkler, with little doubt the most successful German show jump rider of all, was taught dressage by his father, who kept a riding stable, but was never taught to jump: with the fundamental principles of riding that he learned from his father he studied the top-class show jumpers, extracted from their styles what he

Diana Conolly-Carew and Barrymore take a short-cut

needed for himself, and two years after his international debut was World Champion.

D'Oriola, whose father was himself a fine show jumper and apparently a great stylist, won both his Tokyo gold medal and his World Championship two years later on horses, Lutteur and Pomone, who had had comparatively little experience of international jumping but who were well schooled at home.

There were those who thought, perhaps still do, that the foundation of the National Equestrian Centre, with its well-equipped indoor school, at Stoneleigh, Warwickshire, would produce a British 'school' similar to those at Warendorf in Germany and Gladstone in the U.S.A. but the British approach tends to differ from either of those countries, more suitable to the independent nature of the riders concerned. Whereas both Germany and America have squads who, with occasional additions or subtractions, tend to supply their countries' Nations Cup teams time after time, in Britain selection is usually done on a last-minute basis, according to which riders and horses are in the best form. Although this haphazard method had produced much success in ordinary international competitions, for the Olympic Games it may well be that the long-term selection of a small group of riders and horses, perhaps six to eight riders, well in advance—at least two seasons beforehand—would enable Britain to regain the premier Olympic honours.

The training of horses and riders in Britain is mostly in the hands of private individuals who run their own schools or take a few pupils, men like Edy Goldman, Lars Sederholm and Dick Stillwell. Some riders, David Broome and Alan Oliver for instance, owe almost their entire training to their fathers, and George Hobbs, along with many other riders, benefited greatly from the advice of his brother Wally who, unhappily, died in 1969.

The pace of life generally is so fast that there is a tendency to look for short cuts in everything, but for training horses patience is everything. A horse learning to jump literally starts at the bottom, stepping over a pole on the ground. For the early stages, and indeed as constant refresher courses for horses even of the highest standard of training, *cavalletti* are used.

These (Italian for 'little horses') are poles set in wooden crosses, preferably with legs of unequal length, so that the poles can be varied in height, from perhaps twelve to eighteen inches. The learner-horse will be trotted, first over one of these, then over a series placed at intervals of about two yards. The pace is kept even, and this exercise will bring the horse into the right position for learning to jump as well as hardening the muscles he will need for jumping. By natural progression a small fence, no more than three feet high, will be placed to follow the *cavalletti*; its distance will be varied, for even at this early

Winkler and Halla, 1959

stage the horse should learn the rudiments of regulation of stride, which will be invaluable in competitions when he meets fences built to 'difficult' distances: that is to say distances which may be greater or less than his normal stride. Even the most advanced of horses will benefit from 'tune-ups' over *cavalletti* and small fences, and many international riders, especially the Italians, use them frequently.

There follows training over a series of small fences, preferably built with variety to stop the horse from getting bored, including spread fences as well as uprights, with the distances also varied. The novice will also be introduced to 'related' fences. These are fences near enough to each other for the first to effect the jumping of the second: an in-and-out will measure about 12 ft; fences with one stride between will be from 22 to 26 feet apart; with two strides from 31 to 39 feet. If a fence is within six strides of another it can be considered related, if more than 80 ft away, there is room to adjust the approach.

The use of spread fences, such as parallel poles, is important so that a horse will learn to use his neck and arch his back, for a horse which does not do this will always have to put far more effort into his jumping than one who does, will not be able to reach such heights nor have as long a jumping life.

The three basic essentials for jumping fences are impulsion, pace and balance. The whole object of the forward seat is to place the weight of the rider where it will least impede the horse. To jump successfully, the horse too must be taught to distribute his weight in the most advantageous manner, and for him there is the additional disadvantage of a rider on his back, for which he was not designed. If taken slowly, with freedom of the head and neck, the horse will learn to use them as his natural balancing equipment. This is the object of the *cavalletti*, while Colonel Talbot-Ponsonby, in *Harmony in Horsemanship* also suggested the use of undulating ground, as a lot of work across ridge-and-furrow will inevitably make a horse use his hind-quarters, bringing them under him, and stretch out his head and neck, or he will sprawl and stumble.

Impulsion has been likened to the winding of a clockwork spring, and should not be confused with pace. A horse may come into a fence quite slowly, but as long as it has impulsion it may negotiate the obstacle safely. Impulsion, for which balance is vital, implies that the horse's muscles are tensed but controllably so, and ready for immediate action.

When a horse is experienced at jumping small fences, and if his education has been so gauged that he is enjoying it, he may, if he is bold, or 'hot', start to rush at his fences. This needs to be countered, the method advocated by Steinkraus being to circle before a fence, and to continue to circle for as long as may be necessary, before jumping it. This exercise can also be useful to the rider, in ensuring that he does not start making last-minute adjustments before take-off, which will almost invariably have unpleasant consequences.

The use of 'loose schools' in the training of jumpers is a matter of debate. Toptani is against it, believing that they teach a horse bad habits, including wilfulness, and that there is little point in teaching a horse to do something that it will not do again, jump without a rider on its back. Talbot-Ponsonby, on the other hand, advocated this type of training, because 'it improves balance, freedom and liberty; it encourages the horse to make use of his head and neck, round his back and fold his legs.'

Perhaps the greatest advantage of training a jumper in a loose school is that it does make him to a certain extent self-reliant, and for those moments when the rider may have erred in his approach to a fence to have a horse who knows from experience what is required of him can make all the difference in the world.

In Britain, of course, more than in any other country, a horse may receive a lot of his early education in the hunting field, and there is nothing better than this for teaching both horse and rider to make snap decisions. Following hounds one continually encounters unaccustomed fences and if one is not to be hopelessly left behind he must soon learn how to get to the other side with the minimum of delay. It is no coincidence that Ted Williams, a hunting man for many years, has proved himself so adaptable —at the top in the old days of precise, national jumping and just as effective in recent years in top-class international competitions.

With the horse ready for more advanced work, it is as well to be sure that the rider is equally prepared. Major Piero Santini, pupil and translator of Caprilli, suggested that the verb 'to sit' should be eliminated from the vocabulary of the riding man. Obviously, to achieve anything like the right effect a rider will not 'plonk' himself into the saddle like a sack of potatoes, but will sit in the centre of the saddle, balanced, and relaxed, maintaining contact with the mouth but interfering with the horse as little as possible.

To this end it is no disgrace to have a neck strap, and to use it: for what is often considered an undignified practise is very much better than endeavouring to retain one's balance by hauling on a horse's mouth. The reins are purely a means of communicating with a horse, not a 'safety strap'; schooling in a jumping lane without reins is a useful exercise in ensuring a rider's independence of them.

Not only will the horse be jumping slightly bigger fences by now, but, in order to maintain that fluency between fences which must be a prime objective, this is the moment to ensure that the horse does not waste time once he has landed. If the approach and balance have been all that they should have been the horse may, of his own accord, stride off immediately on landing; if not then he must be urged to do so. To do this, of course, it is imperative that contact with the horse should have been maintained throughout the jump. This may seem obvious, but it is not an uncommon sight to see a rider, in the mistaken idea that he must do so to give a horse his freedom, lose contact completely.

As a show jumping horse will be faced with not just one fence to jump but a series, probably about a dozen or so, and two or three of these combination fences, doubles and trebles, he must be accustomed to the problems this will entail. This, like all else, must be built up slowly, in small groups of fences, with variety as the keynote. More is written of fences in another chapter, but, basically, there are only four types: upright, parallel, staircase and pyramid. The problems that can be posed, by their correlation to each other, by their placing in relation to the perimeter of the arena, by the construction and the materials used, are numerous.

Since boldness in a horse, and his confidence in the rider, are among the most potent weapons in any show jumping combination's armoury, great care must be taken not to impair them. Inevitably during his competitive career a horse will encounter badly built fences, flimsy, uninviting affairs, and at difficult distances, but in these early stages tricks must be discarded. Solid fences, well within his compass; doubles, and, when he can deal capably with these, trebles, that he will meet on the right stride. When the horse is ready to jump a course there is a great advantage in having a small paddock or enclosed area to simulate the ring in which he will eventually perform.

A type of obstacle which perhaps causes more bother than any other is the water jump. Sometimes even 12 feet of water will cause a horse to stop, or he will land in it, even though he may frequently cover more than that distance in a jump over an ordinary 'dry' fence. More often than not the cause of this is not the horse's inability, or even unwillingness, to jump water so much as the rider's approach, both mental and physical, to the matter. The thing to remember is that a horse jumping properly is jumping in a bascule, an arch, and if one wishes him to cover a distance he must also attain a certain height. Thus, he must go into the water jump with impulsion; not at a flat-out gallop commenced at the far end of the arena, and frequently losing momentum at the very moment when it should be increasing, but rhythmically, with gathering crescendo.

Except at Hickstead banks are not a common feature of the British show ring, but they are frequently met on the Continent, varying from the comparatively small 'Irish single bank' to banks of the 10 ft variety met during the Hamburg and Hickstead Derbies. There is no intrinsic difficulty in jumping a small bank, the main objection to them being that a horse unaccustomed to banking a fence may try to fly it, while, if a horse does take kindly to banking it may mistake a thick bush fence for a bank: either error could cause serious damage.

Once a horse has shown himself capable of coping with the four basic types of fences, and of straightforward combinations of fences, he is ready to begin his competitive career. This is by no means the end of his education, on the contrary, all he has done so far is to pass his entrance examination; the need to take things slowly, not to over-face the horse must still be ever present.

Punishment and Cruelty

Nothing is more calculated to arouse fierce argument, both in equestrian circles and often even more heated, outside, all too often by people who know little of what they are talking, than discussions on the respective merits of 'the carrot' and 'the big stick' in the training of horses.

There is nothing new in this controversy. The ancient Greeks, cultured race that they were, were wholly in favour of kindness and patience. Xenophon, whose writings 400 years B.C. still have a remarkable relevance, wrote: 'Young horses should be trained in such a way that they not only love their riders, but look forward to the time they are with them.' The riding masters in the early days of classical horsemanship which coincided with the Renaissance, in the 16th and early 17th centuries, were concerned solely with the subjection of the horse. He was a chattel to do their bidding, and the bits which were used to achieve their required aims leave no doubt that it was not 'all done by kindness'. Pluvinel, who became riding master to Louis XIII, was the first major figure of the period to favour humane ideas, in his book *Manege du Roi*, printed in 1623.

Until fairly recently riding horses was solely a matter of personal pleasure: one hunted, or learned dressage, or simply rode, for no other reason than that one enjoyed it. Today, of course, competition is everything and in show jumping, national pride and prestige and, in many countries, profit have become important motives for success. Not only is there prize money to be won, and in fairly substantial quantities thanks to the ever-growing number of sponsors aware of the publicity which this increasingly popular sport commands, but also the possibility of selling jumpers at a good price has increased.

It is necessary to differentiate between punishment and cruelty. It is impossible to train a horse or any other animal, or a child, correctly without occasional punishment. The sharp slap when high spirits develop into wilful naughtiness is a necessity, or one is most likely to end up with a 'spoiled brat'.

A sharp, slap, and administered *at once*, that surely is the criterion. It is worse than useless to wait until one has taken the horse out of the ring and then punish it, for how is the bewildered creature to know why it is being beaten? But before a horse is punished at all one must be sure that whatever he has done deserves it. If he has done something wrong because he failed to understand what was wanted of him then surely the rider is every bit as deserving of punishment.

If, therefore, one is truly merely trying to correct a fault and not to give vent to one's own anger—if for instance the horse has stopped suddenly and deposited his rider inelegantly in the midst of a flurry of poles—then it is better not to punish at all than to punish unfairly and risk spoiling that carefully built up rapport.

The whip, of course, is but one source of punishment; the spurs can be effective in persuading a recalcitrant horse to move in the required direction, and are equally possible to abuse; while one of the most unpleasant sights is to see a rider sawing away at a horse's mouth with the bit. If punishment must be administered it is essential to remember Xenophon's advice: 'Punishment should never be given in anger because action committed in anger will later be regretted'. And horses have long memories.

So much for punishment of a trained horse. An entirely different matter is the use of artificial methods either as a short cut in training, or to persuade a horse which no longer wants to jump to the best of its ability to do so. Much publicity has been given to this matter in recent years, and it reached a head in Britain in 1969 when Peter Robeson was accused in a national Sunday newspaper of using 'cruel methods' to train his horses.

The methods referred to were the use of tack rails, which are poles with a large number of small nails knocked into them, and poles wrapped around with hedgehog skins. After an official inquiry the B.S.J.A. stated that they did not consider such poles, which weighed only about half as much as a normal pole, were cruel when 'used by an expert'. This alas was a statement bound to be open to misinterpretation, for what might be a 'short, sharp sensation' in the hands of such an experienced horseman as Robeson could certainly be much less remedial in the hands of other riders who might also consider themselves as 'experts'. Bill Steinkraus in *Riding and Jumping* considers them as good a way as most to remind a habitually careless horse to pick his feet up, in that they do not punish the horse which does jump clear.

Rapping, on the other hand, or poling as it is known in the United States, is openly permitted in some American shows. A light bamboo pole is used for this purpose, and Steinkraus writes that it can 'in the hands of a skilful and experienced horseman, accomplish results that are beneficial and almost indispensable.' Certainly this is preferable to the fixed fences which were in vogue with Mariles' Mexican team, which might teach a horse to pick his feet up but could do considerable damage in the process.

The prime argument in favour of either raping or tack rails is that, by administering that 'short, sharp sensation', it does less damage to a horse's legs than if he constantly batters them against a series of heavy poles. As with so many other things appertaining to the training of horses, spurs, whips, even reins, it is all a matter of degree: what can be a sensible remedy in the hands of one man may cause unnecessary and useless pain in the hands of another. If such practices are necessary, and it is generally agreed that to a greater or lesser extent they are, then it may well be desirable that the American practice of allowing rapping at shows and under supervision should be universally extended. Then those who believe themselves to come under the B.S.J.A's heading of 'experts' might be disabused, while the riders who feel it necessary to inflict upon their horses rather more severe 'treatment' at home in the hope that the memory of it will suffice throughout the show will no longer need to do so.

In a different category again come those riders who, with young and inexperienced horses, have neither the time nor patience, nor in some cases the knowledge, to school the animal properly and so will resort to artificial means. It is sad to see young horses brought along too fast, being asked difficult questions before they know the answers to the easy ones, for even if they do have sufficient precocious talent to be able to 'shine' for a short while, their brilliance will inevitably be short-lived: Raimondo d'Inzeo spent two years working on Merano, his greatest horse, before he ever brought him into the show ring, and like all the d'Inzeo horses Merano went on winning for years. Cruelty can be mental as well as physical, and asking a horse to do something which is beyond him is as unfair as putting a non-driver into a car and telling him to drive it, on pain of being beaten if he refuses.

The more highly-bred a horse is, the more he will be liable to mental suffering: some years ago a continental dressage rider bought several English thoroughbred stallions, endeavoured to train them in the same harshly-disciplined way that she had used, successfully, on her Hanoverians, and finished with a collection of nervous wrecks which were good for nothing. There is no substitute for patience and understanding. Given this, and reasonably good luck, a show jumper may go on for many years.

To give the last word on the subject to Xenophon, or rather to Simon of Athens quoted by Xenophon: 'What a horse does under compulsion he does blindly, and his performance is no more beautiful than would be that of a ballet-dancer taught by whip or goad. The performances of horse or man so treated would seem to be clumsy displays of clumsy gestures rather than of grace or beauty. What we need is that the horse should of his own accord exhibit his finest airs and paces at set signals.'

Alberto Larraguibel and Huaso jumping 8 ft 1½ in

5 Appendix

OLYMPIC GAMES

Paris 1900

PRIZE JUMPING   1st HAEGEMAN (Belgium)
2nd Van der Poele (Belgium)
3rd De Champeavin (France)

HIGH JUMP   1st GARDERE (France) 6 ft $1\frac{3}{16}$ in
2nd G. Trissino (Italy)

LONG JUMP   1st VAN LANGENDONCK (Belgium) 20 ft $\frac{3}{16}$ in
2nd G. Trissino (Italy)

Stockholm 1912

TEAM   1st SWEDEN (Count Casimir Lewenhaupt on Medusa; Count Hans von Rosen on Lord Iron; Lt. Frederick Rosencrantz on Drabant; Lt. Gustaf Kilman on Gatan)
2nd France (Lt. D'Astaford on Amazone; Capt. J. Cariou on Mignon; Comdt. F. Meyer on Allons V; Lt. Seigneur on Cocotte)
3rd Germany (Capt. Sigismund Freyer on Ultimus; Graf von Hohenau on Pretty Girl; Lt. Deloch on Hubertus; Prinz Karl von Preussen on Gibson Boy)

INDIVIDUAL   1st CAPT. J. CARIOU (France) on Mignon
2nd Lt. von Krocher (Germany) on Dohna
3rd Baron E. Blommaert de Soye (Belgium) on Clonmore

Antwerp 1920

TEAM   1st SWEDEN (Count Hans von Rosen; C. Konig; Daniel Norling)
2nd Belgium (Capt. Count de Oultremont; Lt. Coumans; Baron de Gaiffier)
3rd Italy (Magg. Ettore Caffaratti; Giulio Cacciandra; Magg. Allessandro Alvisi)

INDIVIDUAL   1st LT. TOMASSO LEQUIO (Italy) on Trebecco
2nd Magg. Allesandro Valerio (Italy) on Cento
3rd Capt. Gustaf Lewenhaupt (Sweden) on Mon Coeur

Paris 1924

TEAM   1st SWEDEN (Ake Thelning on Loke; Axel Stahle on Cecil; Age Lundstrom)
2nd Switzerland (Lt. Alphons Gemuseus on Lucette; Werner Stuber; Hans Buhler)
3rd Portugal (Borges d'Almeida on Reginald; Martins de Souza; Mouzinho d'Albuquerque)

INDIVIDUAL   1st LT. ALPHONS GEMUSEUS (Switzerland) on Lucette
2nd Lt. Tomasso Lequio (Italy) on Trebecco
3rd Lt. Adam Krolikiewicz (Poland) on Picador

Amsterdam 1928

TEAM   1st SPAIN (Marquis de los Trujillos on Zalamero; J. Navarro Morenes on Zapatazo; J. Garcia Fernandez on Revistade)
2nd Poland (C. Gzowki on Mylord; K. Szoszland on Alli; M. Antoniewicz on Readglet)
3rd Sweden (K. Hansen on Gerold; C. Bjornstjerna on Kornett; Ernst Hallberg on Loke)

INDIVIDUAL   1st CAPT. F. VENTURA (Czechoslovakia) on Eliot
2nd Capt. M. L. M. Bertran de Balanda (France) on Papillon
3rd Maj. Chasimir Kuhn (Switzerland) on Pepita

Los Angeles 1932

TEAM   Not awarded: no team of three completed the course

INDIVIDUAL   1st LT. BARON TAKEICHI NISHI (Japan) on Uranus
2nd Major Harry Chamberlin

(U.S.A.) on Show Girl
3rd Lt. Clarence von Rosen (Sweden) on Empire

Berlin 1936

TEAM 1st GERMANY 44 flts (Lt. Kurt Hasse on Tora; Capt. Martin von Barnekow on Nordland; Capt. Heinz Brandt on Alchimist)
2nd Holland 51½ flts (Lt. Johan Greter on Ernica; Lt. Jan de Bruine on Trixie; Lt. Henri van Schaik on Santa Bell)
3rd Portugal 56 flts (Lt. Jose Beltrano on Biscuit; Capt. Marquez de Funchal on Merle Blanc; Lt. Manae e Silva on Fossette)

INDIVIDUAL 1st LT. KURT HASSE (Germany) on Tora 4 flts (4 flts in 59·5 sec in jump-off)
2nd Lt. Henri Rang (Rumania) on Delphis 4 flts (4 flts, 72·8 sec)
3rd Capt. Jozsef Platthy (Hungary) on Selloe 8 flts

London 1948

TEAM 1st MEXICO 34¼ flts (Humberto Mariles on Arete; Ruben Uriza on Hatvey; Alberto Valdes on Chihuchuc)
2nd Spain 56½ flts (Jaime Garcia Cruz on Bizarro; Navarro Morenes on Quorum; M. G. Y. Ponce de Leon on Foratido)
3rd Gt. Britain 67 flts (Lt.-Col. Harry Llewellyn on Foxhunter; Lt.-Col. Henry Nicoll on Kilgeddin; Major Arthur Carr on Monty)

INDIVIDUAL 1st HUMBERTO MARILES (Mexico) on Arete, 6¼ flts
2nd Ruben Uriza (Mexico) on Hatvey, 8 flts (0 in jump-off)
3rd Chev. F. M. d'Orgeix (France) on Sucre de Pomme, 8 flts/(4 flts)

Helsinki 1952

TEAM 1st BRITAIN 40¾ flts (Harry Llewellyn on Foxhunter; Wilf White on Nizefela; Douglas Stewart on Aherlow)
2nd Chile 45¾ flts (Oscar Christi on Bambi; C. Mendoza on Pillan; Ricardo Echeverria on Lindo Pearl)
3rd U.S.A. 52¼ flts (Bill Steinkraus on Hollandia; John Russell on Democrat; Arthur McCashin on Miss Budweiser)

INDIVIDUAL 1st PIERRE JONQUERES D'ORIOLA (France) on Ali Baba, 8 flts (0, 40 sec in jump-off)
2nd Oscar Christi (Chile) on Bambi, 8 (4, 44 sec)
3rd Fritz Thiedemann (Germany) on Meteor, 8 (8, 38·5 sec)

Stockholm 1956

TEAM 1st GERMANY 40 flts (Hans Gunter Winkler on Halla, Fritz Thiedemann on Meteor, Alf. Lutke-Westhues on Ala)
2nd Italy 66 flts (Raimondo d'Inzeo on Merano, Piero d'Inzeo on Uruguay, Salvatore Oppes on Pagoro)
3rd Gt. Britain 69 flts (Wilf White on Nizefela, Peter Robeson on Scorchin, Pat Smythe on Flanagan)

INDIVIDUAL 1st HANS GUNTER WINKLER (Germany) on Halla, 4 flts
2nd Raimondo d'Inzeo (Italy) on Merano, 8
3rd Piero d'Inzeo (Italy) on Uruguay, 11

Rome 1960

TEAM 1st GERMANY, 46½ flts (Alwin Schockemohle, on Ferdl, Hans Gunter Winkler on Halla, Fritz Thiedemann on Meteor)
2nd U.S.A. 66 flts (George Morris on Sinjon, Frank Chapot on Trail Guide, Bill Steinkraus on Ksar d'Esprit)
3rd Italy 80½ flts (Antonio Oppes on The Scholar, Raimondo d'Inzeo on Posillipo, Piero d'Inzeo on The Rock)

INDIVIDUAL 1st RAIMONDO D'INZEO (Italy) on Posillipo, 12 flts
2nd Piero d'Inzeo (Italy) on The Rock, 16
3rd David Broome (G.B.) on Sunsalve, 23

Tokyo 1964

TEAM 1st GERMANY 68½ flts (Hermann Schridde on Dozent, Kurt Jarasinki on Torro, Hans Gunter Winkler on Fidelitas)

2nd France 77¾ flts (P. Jonqueres d'Oriola on Lutteur, Guy Lefrant on M. de Littry, Janou Lefebvre on Kenavo)
3rd Italy 88½ flts (Piero d'Inzeo on Sunbeam, Raimondo d'Inzeo on Posillipo, Graziano Mancinelli on Rockette)

INDIVIDUAL 1st PIERRE JONQUERES D'ORIOLA (France) on Lutteur, 9 flts
2nd Hermann Schridde (Germany) on Dozent, 13¾
3rd Peter Robeson (G.B.) on Firecrest, 16

Mexico 1968

TEAM 1st CANADA 102¾ flts (Jim Day on Canadian Club; Jimmy Elder on The Immigrant, Tommy Gayford on Big Dee)
2nd France 110½ flts (Janou Lefebvre on Rocket, P. Jonqueres d'Oriola on Nagir, Marcel Rozier on Quo Vadis)
3rd Germany 117¼ flts (Herman Shridde on Dozent, Hans Gunter Winkler on Enigk and Alwin Schockemohle on Donald Rex)

INDIVIDUAL 1st BILL STEINKRAUS (U.S.A.) on Snowbound, 4 flts
2nd Marion Coakes (G.B.) on Stroller, 8
3rd David Broome (G.B.) on Mister Softee 12

PAN AMERICAN GAMES

Buenos Aires 1951

TEAM 1st CHILE 64 flts (Alberto Larraguibel on Julepe, Joaquin Larrain on Pillan, Ricardo Eccheverria on Bambi, C. Mendoza on Van Dick)
2nd Argentina 100¼ flts (Carlos Delia on El Linyera, Campos Molinuevo on Ramito, Ruchti on Mineral)
3rd Mexico 109 flts (Roberto Vinals on Alteno, Rodriguez on Mexico, d'Harcourt on Malisco, Alberto Valdes on Arete)

INDIVIDUAL 1st CAPT. ALBERTO LARRAGUIBEL (Chile) on Julepe, 16 flts
2nd Lt. Carlos Delia (Argentina) on El Linyera, 24 flts, 1 m 58·0 s
3rd Lt. Joaquin Larrain (Chile) on Pillan, 24 flts, 2 m 2·8 s

3rd Capt. Ricardo Eccheverria (Chile) on Bambi, 24 flts, 2 m 2·8 s

Mexico City 1955

TEAM 1st MEXICO 71¼ flts (Roberto Vinals on Acapulco, de la Garzia on 14 de Agosto, d'Harcourt on Petrolero, Humberto Mariles on Chihucho II)
2nd Argentina 89¾ flts (Lucardi on Banturro, Molinuevo on Ramito, Ruchti on Discutido, Mayorga on Desengano)
3rd Chile 122½ flts (Leuenberg, Rojas on Baranco, Arrenda on Maiten, Oscar Christi on Bambi)

INDIVIDUAL 1st LT. ROBERTO VINALS (Mexico) on Acapulco, 10¾ flts
2nd Jorge Lucardi (Argentina) on Banturro, 18
3rd Lt. Jaime de la Garzia (Mexico) 14 de Agosto, 27¼

Chicago 1959

TEAM 1st U.S.A. 32 flts (Frank Chapot on Diamant, Hugh Wiley on Nautical, Bill Steinkraus on Riviera Wonder, George Morris on Night Owl)
2nd Brazil 59 flts (Francisco Rabelo on Castigo, Carvalho on Ouro Negro, R. P. Guimares Ferreira on Marengo, Nelson Pessoa on Copacabana)
3rd Chile 80¾ flts (Zuniga on Pillar, Joaquin Larrain on Sinbad, Simonetti on Charanal, Oscar Christi on Barrano)

No individual classification

Sao Paolo 1963

TEAM 1st U.S.A. 44¼ flts (Mary Mairs on Tomboy, Frank Chapot on San Lucas, Kathy Kusner on Unusual, Bill Steinkraus on Sinjon)
2nd Argentina 52½ flts (Carlos Delia on Popin, Amaya on Escipion, Damm on Swing, Osacar on Santiago)
3rd Chile 69 flts (Simonetti on El Gitano, Perez on Trago Amargo, Zuniga on Maiten, Arrendondo on Choir Boy)

INDIVIDUAL 1st MARY MAIRS (U.S.A. on Tomboy, 9¾ flts

2nd Lt.-Col. Carlos Delia
(Argentina) on Popin, 12½
3rd Americo Simonetti (Chile)
on El Gitano, 13½

Winnipeg 1967

TEAM 1st BRAZIL 8 flts (Nelson
Pessoa on Gran Geste, Antonio
Alegria-Simoes on Samurai,
Jose Fernandez on Chantal,
R. P. Guimares Ferreira on
Shannon Shamrock)
2nd U.S.A. 16 flts (Kathy
Kusner on Untouchable, Mary
Chapot on White Lightning,
Frank Chapot on San Lucas, Bill
Steinkraus on Bold Minstrel)
3rd Canada 24 flts (Jimmy Day
on Canadian Club, Tommy
Gayford on Big Dee, Moffatt
Dunlop on Argyll, Jimmy Elder
on Pieces of Eight)
4th Mexico; 5th Chile; 6th
Argentina.

INDIVIDUAL 1st JIMMY DAY (Canada) on
Canadian Club, 0 flt, (8 flts in
38·7 sec in jump-off)
2nd Nelson Pessoa (Brazil)
Gran Geste, 0, (8 in 39·8 sec)
3rd Manuel Mendevil Yocupicio
(Mexico) on Veracruz, 4

WORLD CHAMPIONSHIP

Paris

1953 1st F. GOYOAGA (Spain)
Quorum 8 pts in final
2nd F. Thiedemann (Germany)
Diamant 8¼ pts
3rd P. J. d'Oriola (France) *Ali
Baba* 16 pts
4th P. d'Inzeo (Italy) *Uruguay*
24 pts

Madrid

1954 1st H. G. WINKLER (Germany)
Halla 4 pts in final
2nd P. J. d'Oriola (France)
Arlequin 8 pts
3rd F. Goyoaga (Spain) To final
as holder 12 pts
4th S. Oppes (Italy) *Pagoro* 16 pts
5th J. Garcia Cruz (Spain)
Quoniam 30 pts

Aachen

1955 1st H. G. WINKLER (Germany)
Halla 4 pts in barrage
2nd R. d'Inzeo (Italy) *Nadir*
8 pts
3rd Major R. Dallas (G.B.) *Bones*
4th P. J. d'Oriola (France)
retired

Aachen

1956 1st R. D'INZEO (Italy) *Merano*
1¾ pts in final
2nd F. Goyoaga (Spain)
Fahnenkonig 3 pts
3rd F. Thiedemann (Germany)
Meteor 4 pts
4th C. Delia (Argentina)
Discutido 25 pts

Venice

1960 1st R. D'INZEO (Italy) *Gowran
Girl* 8 pts in final
2nd C. Delia (Argentina) *Huipil*
24 pts
3rd D. Broome (G.B.) *Sunsalve*
28 pts
4th W. Steinkraus (U.S.A.) *Ksar
d'Esprit* 56 pts

Buenos Aires

1966 1st P. J. D'ORIOLA (France)
Pomone 16 pts in final
2nd A. de Bohorques (Spain)
Quizas 19 pts
3rd R. d'Inzeo (Italy) *Bowjak*
30 pts
4th N. Pessoa (Brazil) *Huipil*
35¼ pts

MEN'S EUROPEAN CHAMPIONSHIP

Rotterdam

1957 1st H. G. WINKLER (Germany)
Sonnenglanz 8 pts in final
2nd Capt. de Fombelle (France)
Bucephale 11 pts
3rd S. Oppes (Italy) *Pagoro*
24 pts

Aachen

1958 1st F. THIEDEMANN (Germany)
Meteor 106 pts
2nd P. d'Inzeo (Italy) *The Rock*
98·3 pts
3rd H. G. Winkler (Germany)
Halla 98 pts

Paris

1959　1st P. D'INZEO (Italy) *Uruguay* 8 pts in final
2nd P. J. d'Oriola (France) *Virtuoso* 16½ pts
3rd F. Thiedemann (Germany) *Godewind* 24 pts

1960　No championship

Aachen

1961　1st D. BROOME (G.B.) *Sunsalve*
2nd P. d'Inzeo (Italy) *Pioneer*
3rd H. G. Winkler (Germany) *Romanus*

London

1962　1st C. D. BARKER (G.B.) *Mister Softee* 4 pts
2nd H. G. Winkler (Germany) *Romanus* and P. d'Inzeo (Italy) *The Rock* 8 pts each

Rome

1963　1st G. MANCINELLI (Italy) *Rockette*) 6 pts
2nd A. Schockemohle (Germany) *Freiherr* 8 pts
3rd H. Smith (G.B.) *O'Malley* 16 pts

1964　No championship

Aachen

1965　1st H. SCHRIDDE (Germany) *Dozent* 11 pts
2nd N. Pessoa (Brazil) *Gran Geste* 14 pts
3rd A. Schockemohle (Germany) *Exakt* 15·5 pts

Lucerne

1966　1st N. PESSOA (Brazil) *Gran Geste* 6 pts
2nd F. Chapot (U.S.A.) *San Lucas* 9½ pts
3rd H. Arrambide (Argentina) *Chimbote* 11 pts

Rotterdam

1967　1st D. BROOME (G.B.) *Mister Softee* 15½ pts
2nd H. Smith (G.B.) *Harvester* 20½ pts
3rd A. Schockemohle (Germany) *Donald Rex* 22 pts

1968　No Championship

Hickstead

1969　1st D. BROOME (G.B.) *Mister Softee* 6 pts
2nd A. Schockemohle (Germany) *Donald Rex* 6 pts
(Mister Softee clear in last round in 2 m 53·8 s; Donald Rex, 8 faults in 2 m 54·9 s)
3rd H. G. Winkler (Germany) *Enigk* 8 pts

WOMEN'S EUROPEAN CHAMPIONSHIP

Spa

1957　1st MISS PAT SMYTHE (G.B.) *Flanagan* 16 flts in j.o.
2nd Miss Giulia Serventi (Italy) *Doly* 22¾ flts in j.o.
3rd Mme. M. d'Orgeix (France) *Ocean*

Palermo

1958　1st MISS GIULIA SERVENTI (Italy) *Doly*
2nd Miss Anna Clement (Germany) *Nico*
3rd Miss Irene Jansen (Holland) *Adelbloom*

Rotterdam

1959　1st MISS ANN TOWNSEND (G.B.) *Bandit* 30 pts
2nd Miss Pat Smythe (G.B.) *Flanagan* 29·33 pts
3rd Miss Anna Clement (Germany) *Nico* and Miss Giulia Serventi (Italy) *Doly* 23·83 pts each

Copenhagen

1960　1st MISS SUE COHEN (G.B.) *Clare Castle* 41¾ pts
2nd Mrs. Dawn Wofford (G.B.) *Hollandia* 39⅛ pts
3rd Miss Anna Clement (Germany) *Nico* 38⅛ pts

Deauville

1961   1st MISS PAT SMYTHE (G.B.)
Flanagan 45·95 pts
2nd Miss Irene Jansen (Holland)
Icare 35·845 pts
3rd Miss M. Cancre (France)
Ocean 35·25 pts

Madrid

1962   1st MISS PAT SMYTHE (G.B.)
Flanagan 26·33 pts
2nd Mrs. Helga Kohler
(Germany) *Cremona* 25·50 pts
3rd Mrs. Paula de Goyoaga
(Spain) *Kif Kif* 24·33 pts

Hickstead

1963   1st MISS PAT SMYTHE (G.B.)
Flanagan 5·5 pts
2nd Mrs. Arline Givaudan
(Brazil) *Huipil* 7·5 pts
3rd Miss Anneli Drummond-Hay
(G.B.) *Merely-a-Monarch* 8·5 pts

1964   No championship

Hickstead

1965   1st MISS MARION COAKES
(G.B.) *Stroller* 4 pts
2nd Miss Kathy Kusner (U.S.A.)
Untouchable 6 pts
3rd Miss Alison Westwood
(G.B.) *The Maverick* 8 pts

Gijon

1966   1st MISS JANOU LEFEBVRE
(France) *Kenavo* 3 pts
2nd Miss Monica Bachmann
(Switzerland) *Sandro* 9 pts
3rd Miss Lalla Novo (Italy)
Oxo Bob 10½ pts

Fontainebleau

1967   1st MISS KATHY KUSNER
(U.S.A.) *Untouchable* 5 pts
2nd Miss Lalla Novo (Italy)
Predestine 11·5 pts
3rd Miss Monica Bachmann
(Switzerland) *Erbach* 13·5 pts

Rome

1968   1st MISS ANNELI
DRUMMOND-HAY (G.B.)
Merely-a-Monarch 6½ pts
2nd Miss Giulia Serventi (Italy)
Gay Monarch 11½ pts
3rd Miss Marion Coakes (G.B.)
Stroller and
Miss Janou Lefebvre (France)
Rocket 12 pts each

Dublin

1969   1st MISS IRIS KELLETT
(Ireland) *Morning Light* 4 pts
2nd Miss Anneli Drummond-Hay (G.B.) *Xanthos* 6 pts
3rd Miss Alison Westwood
(G.B.) *The Maverick* 8 pts

PRESIDENT'S CUP

1965   1st GT. BRITAIN, 35 pts
2nd Germany, 31 pts
3rd Italy, 30 pts

1966   1st U.S.A., 27 pts
2nd Spain, 26 pts
3rd France, 20 pts

1967   1st GT. BRITAIN, 37 pts
2nd Germany, 26 pts
3rd Italy, 21 pts

1968   1st U.S.A., 34 pts
2nd Gt. Britain, 26 pts
3rd Italy and Germany 25 pts

1969   1st GERMANY, 39 pts
2nd Gt. Britain, 35 pts
3rd Italy, 29 pts

Based on results in Nations Cups: each country may count only its six best results.

EUROPEAN JUNIOR TEAM CHAMPIONSHIP

Ostend

1952   1st ITALY
2nd Belgium

Rome

1953   1st FRANCE
2nd Italy
3rd Belgium

Rotterdam

1954 1st ITALY
     2nd Germany
     3rd Holland

Bilbao

1955 1st GERMANY
     2nd Holland
     3rd Spain

Spa

1956 1st GT. BRITAIN
     2nd France
     3rd Germany

London

1957 1st GT. BRITAIN
     2nd Italy
     3rd France

Hannover

1958 1st GT. BRITAIN
     2nd South Africa
     3rd Italy

London

1959 1st GT. BRITAIN
     2nd Germany
     3rd France

Venice

1960 1st GT. BRITAIN
     2nd Poland
     3rd Italy

Hickstead

1961 1st GERMANY
     2nd Holland
     3rd Gt. Britain

Berlin

1962 1st GT. BRITAIN
     2nd Germany
     3rd France

Rotterdam

1963 1st GT. BRITAIN
     2nd Germany
     3rd France

Budapest

1964 1st ITALY
     2nd Gt. Britain
     3rd Belgium

Salice Terme, Milan

1965 1st GT. BRITAIN
     2nd Italy
     3rd Germany

Copenhagen

1966 1st ITALY
     2nd Belgium
     3rd Switzerland

Jesolo

1967 1st GT. BRITAIN
     2nd France
     3rd Germany

Stoneleigh

1968 1st GT. BRITAIN
     2nd France
     3rd equal Ireland, Germany and Denmark

Dinard

1969 1st SWITZERLAND
     2nd France
     3rd Germany

Glossary

BARÈME All international competitions are run under one of three *Barèmes*, or Tables: 'A', in which the accent is on jumping ability; 'B' and 'C', are designed to test a horse's speed and manoeuvrability as well as his jumping.

BARRAGE An alternative term for jump-off.

BASCULE From the French *'basculer'*, to swing; in this context the action of a horse in rounding himself over a jump.

B.H.S. British Horse Society, the parent body of equestrian sport in Britain, affiliated to the F.E.I.

B.S.J.A. British Show Jumping Association, the controlling body of show jumping in Britain.

CAVALLETTI From the Italian, means literally 'little horse'; poles, usually set on cross-pieces, used in the training of horses.

C.H.I.O. *Concours Hippique International Officiel*, official international horse show, which includes a Nations Cup; in Europe each country is allowed to stage only one a year, but outside Europe it is possible to have more than one (e.g. in U.S.A. the annual New York C.H.I.O. is often complemented by another in Harrisburg). A C.H.I. is an international show at which a Nations Cup is not permitted; a country may stage several C.H.I.s each season.

COMBINATION A fence comprising two or more separate elements at a distance not more than 39 ft 4 in from each other; the usual combination fences are doubles or trebles.

CUP The support in, or on which a pole, or other supported part of a fence rests; the depth, or shallowness of a cup has considerable bearing upon how difficult or easy it may be to knock a fence down.

DERBY A type of competition which incorporates usually a number of permanent fences, such as banks, and is run over a longer course than the normal competition; often approximates an enclosed cross-country course; the prototype is in Hamburg.

F.E.I. *Federation Equestre Internationale* (International Equestrian Federation), the world ruling body of equestrian sport, founded in 1921, with its headquarters in Brussels.

F.N. *Federation National* (National Federation), affiliated to the F.E.I.

FORWARD SEAT The method of sitting a horse now commonly used in most equestrian sport, and generally attributed to Federico Caprilli (see chapter on training).

FOXHUNTER COMPETITION An annual competition for novice horses, named after Lt. Col. Harry Llewellyn's great horse, which progresses through preliminary rounds and regional finals to a championship held each year at the Horse of the Year Show.

GRADE The standard which a horse has reached, calculated in Britain by the amount of prizemoney won: a horse is Grade 'C' until he has won £150, Grade 'B' up to £300, and then Grade 'A'.

GROUNDLINE The line at the base of a fence by which a horse calculates his jump; the absence of a groundline obviously makes a fence more difficult to jump, while a 'false' groundline, for instance one set in the middle of a spread fence, increases the difficulty still further.

HAND The height of a horse is measured in 'hands'; equal to four inches.

IMPULSION Controlled power of a horse

159

JUMP-OFF sometimes likened to the spring of a clock.
This is needed when two or more horses have had equality of faults and/or time in a previous round; under F.E.I. rules most competitions, other than those based on time in the first round, have one or more jump-offs, usually culminating in a jump-off in which, in the equality of faults, time is the deciding factor. The principal exception to this is the *puissance*.

NAPPING Refusal of a horse to do what is wanted of him; e.g. an unwillingness to enter a ring, or a bad-tempered display of wilful disobedience.

NATIONS CUP A competition between teams of four riders and horses from each country, of which three count towards the final total, run in two rounds. (See chapter on competitions.) Only held at a C.H.I.O.

OVER-FACE To ask a horse to do too much, to jump a fence or course beyond its capability or experience.

OXER A brush fence with a pole on the take-off side. A double oxer has a pole on each side.

PARALLELS Usually poles, but may be planks or even walls; often this term is used when the pole on the take-off side is slightly lower than the further pole. When they are at exactly the same height, which makes the fence much more difficult to jump, the description 'true parallels' may be used as a distinguishing label.

POLING An American term for *rapping*.

PUISSANCE A type of competition designed purely to test a horse's jumping power, with jump-offs over successively enlarged fences.

RAPPING A method of making a horse jump higher or more cleanly; as the horse jumps a practice fence a pole is raised to rap him. (See chapter on training.)

REFUSAL When a horse refuses to jump a fence; the third refusal in any competition under F.E.I. Rules automatically disqualifies a horse.

SLATS Narrow laths of wood or metal which used to be placed on top of a fence; horses were penalised for knocking them off, which necessitated extremely careful jumping.

SPREAD FENCE A fence which incorporates width as well as height.

TABLE A translation of *Barème*.

TRACK In some competitions an exact track may be marked on a course-plan, in addition of course to the fences; failure to keep to such a specified track results in elimination.

TRIPLE BAR A fence of the 'staircase' variety, with three poles on separate supports, each higher than the one in front; frequently interspersed with bushes; the easiest of all types of fence to jump.

UPRIGHT A fence in one vertical plane, usually poles or planks, which requires only an upward effort from the horses.